TURNOUT

A Firefighter's Story

by Bill Hall

Greenberg Publishing Company, Inc.
Sykesville, Maryland

Copyright © 1991
by Greenberg Publishing Company, Inc.

Greenberg Publishing Company, Inc.
7566 Main Street
Sykesville, MD 21784
(301) 795-7447

First Edition
First Printing

Manufactured in the United States of America

Greenberg Publishing Company, Inc. offers the world's largest selection of Lionel, American Flyer, LGB, Marx, Ives, and other toy train publications as well as a selection of books on model and prototype railroading, dollhouse building, and collectible toys. For a complete listing of Greenberg publications, please call or write at the above address and request a current catalogue.

Greenberg Shows, Inc. sponsors *Greenberg's Great Train, Dollhouse and Toy Shows*, the world's largest of its kind. The shows feature extravagant operating train layouts, and a display of magnificent dollhouses. The shows also present a huge marketplace of model and toy trains, for HO, N, and Z Scales; Lionel O and Standard Gauges; and S and 1 Gauges; plus layout accessories and railroadiana. It also offers a large selection of dollhouse miniatures and building materials, and collectible toys. Shows are scheduled along the East Coast each year from Massachusetts to Florida. For a list of our current shows please call or write at the above address and request our current "show schedule."

Greenberg Auctions, a division of Greenberg Shows, Inc., offers nationally advertised auctions of toy trains and toys. Please contact our auction manager at (301) 795-7447 for further information.

ISBN 0-89778-235-6

Library of Congress Cataloging-in-Publication Data

Hall, Bill, 1948-
    Turnout / by Bill Hall. -- 1st ed.
        p.   cm.
    ISBN 0-89778-235-6
    1. Hall, Bill, 1948-   . 2. Fire fighters--Maryland--Baltimore-
-Biography.   I. Title
TH9118.h34a3 1991
363.37'092--DC20
[B]   91-20393
                                                               CIP

Cover photograph of Bill Hall was photographed by Howard Meile.

This book is dedicated
to God
who has continued to protect me as a firefighter;
to the thousands of firefighters
throughout the world
whose fortitude and commitment
protect their communities
and loved ones;
and to those firefighters
who gave their lives
in the line of duty while on their final
turnout.

Contents

Acknowledgments

Any book of this magnitude depends on the cooperation and assistance of countless people, many who gave encouragement and aid in remembering the stories told herein. With a grateful heart I acknowledge the many firefighters who assisted me and allowed their stories or names to appear in *TURNOUT*:

Paramedic Wilbur B. Belt, Sr., Lt. James Boyer, Capt. Joseph V. Brocato, F.F. Arthur F. Cate, F.F. James P. Catterton, Capt. Martin Catterton, Capt. Joseph R. Clawson, F.F. Charles D. Davis, F.F. Fred Ehrlich, Lt. Mitchell M. Fisher, Paramedic Wayne Geldmacher, Lt. Stephen G. Gibson, B.C. William J. Goodwin, F.F. Charles Grantland, B.C. Donald N. Heinbuch, E.V.D. Charles E. Huber, Sr., Paramedic Mark S. Hofmann, Capt. Philip Janson, F.F. Frank J. Kelly, Lt. Brian LaHatte, Paramedic Robert A. McCurdy, F.F. Paul Merkler, Capt. Frank Rainey, F.F. Richard (Juicy) Reed, F.F. Timothy J. Reilly, Lt. Robert F. Scarpati, F.F. Walter F. Schultheis, F.F. August T. Stern, F.F. Douglas M. Wagerman, F.F. Robert H. Wagner, E.V.D. Adam Watkowski, and F.F. Dennis E. Williams.

The photographs used to correspond with the stories in this book were carefully chosen from the collection presented to me. I extend my warmest thanks to the following photographers for providing the dramatic photos for *TURNOUT*:

James B. Atkinson, Bill Britcher, Steven Hirsch Eisen, Howard Meile, David P. Schmitt, Carl L. Vaughn, and Douglas M. Wagerman.

Many people at Greenberg Publishing Company, Inc. contributed to the completion of this book. First and foremost, I express my tremendous thanks to Bruce and Linda Greenberg for believing in me enough to publish my book. It is a dream come true for me, thanks in part to their efforts. I wish to thank Carole A. Norbeck, Dee Wright, Donna Dove and Linda Greenberg for refining my work with their meticulous editing skills. My appreciation also goes to Samuel Baum, who oversaw production; Donna Dove, once again, who was responsible for the design and final layout, editorial direction and book compilation; Maureen Crum, who designed the cover and arranged the photos inside the book; Patti Hare, who typed many corrections; Andrea Kraszewski, who assisted with last minute details and corrections; and Donna Price, who proofread the entire manuscript. I offer a special thanks to Pat Shipley, who has worked with enthusiasm to promote this book.

I'm also grateful to Charles Briggs, a manuscript reader, for his suggestions.

I would be remiss if I did not thank the Baltimore City Fire Department for hiring me nearly 20 years ago, without which there would be no *TURNOUT*.

And finally, my deepest "thanks" goes to Carol and our children for putting up with me during this project. I couldn't have realized this dream without their love and support.

Bill Hall
July 1991

Introduction

Fire kills with excruciating pain! Flame causes a person's skin to peel like the layers of an onion, damaging nerves and inflicting torturous pain. Intense heat in the air surrounding a blaze can cause the body to swell like a water balloon and turn as red as a cooked lobster. In severe heat exposure, the body will explode. Fire produces smoke and toxic fumes which can kill, stealing oxygen, searing raw the lining of the lungs and tearing apart the bronchioles with sandy granules of dust like small pieces of broken glass. Death from fire may take seconds, minutes, hours, days, or months.

So, what kind of madness makes someone run into a burning building when everyone else is running out?

As a Baltimore City firefighter, my job is to save people and property from being destroyed by fire or fire-provoking conditions. My home base is a "super firehouse" known as Steadman Station, sometimes known as the busiest firehouse in the nation. It is here that I have been privileged to work with the heroes of modern firefighting. I've responded to over 15,000 emergency calls since my first "turnout" nearly twenty years ago.

"Turnout!" is fire talk for "Let's go!" The term describes how a firefighter *turns* over to roll *out* of bed and into his boots to respond to a call.

Through a mixture of curiosity, luck and persistence, I've experienced many facets of firefighting. I've been a Fireman, a Paramedic and a Rescue Technician. Rarely does a firefighter have the opportunity to serve as all three. It is an experience I would not have traded for any other. Like a long-distance runner, I believe I was "designed" to be a firefighter.

Baltimore was where I grew up, mostly on the South Side, in the Locust Point area near historic Fort McHenry. This is where the red glare of rockets and fiery bomb blasts inspired Francis Scott Key to compose the national anthem.

As a boy, I often visited the fire station, one block from my home, that housed "17" Engine and "19" Truck. My dad or John Gould, a family friend, would accompany me and lift me up to sit at the wheel of the mighty red truck and ring its proud bell. Sometimes they found me standing alone in the station house, gazing up at the long brass pole that disappeared into the darkness above. Whenever a fire call came in, I raced over to watch the men slide the poles, slip effortlessly into their giant suits, and leap onto the noisy fire trucks which seemed to bound like powerful lions out into the tranquil streets.

I waited patiently until the fire trucks silently returned to the station and rolled unnoticed into their berths, like sleepy old dogs. I marveled at the hook and ladder truck, which seemed to be going in two directions, and stood captivated watching the tillerman and driver work in tandem to glide the apparatus backwards into the station.

As a young man, I remember when my dad, sisters and I piled into the family car one rainy night to see what neighbors said was a serious accident at Fort Avenue and Light Street. We pushed through the crowd to discover that a fire truck had careened into the corner drug store, killing a firefighter and the store owner. I grieved for the fireman who never made it to his call, and envied the courage of men who went to work not knowing if they would return home at the end of their shift. These were men who cared enough about their communities to defend them, men who risked their lives for those of total strangers.

Little did I realize then the impact of these experiences. One incident that served to propel me to a career as a firefighter happened in 1971. I was 23, living in the heart of "the Port City" and serving my last six months in the U.S. Coast Guard, while assigned to a tug boat at the end of Pratt Street.

As friends and I walked to the movies one night, we heard fire engines approaching. We turned a corner to see flames blowing from the windows of a rowhouse. The engine company shot past us, and almost as soon as they pulled to a stop attached the hoseline to a hydrant and aimed a torrent of water at the front of the house. Then incredibly, with only the hoseline as a shield, they walked into the flaming building! They seemed to step fearlessly into the mouth of a fire-breathing dragon with nothing but water for a weapon! Other companies arrived to back them up, and soon the inferno was quelled. The effect of that fire was overwhelming. It rekindled my childhood dreams, and I walked away knowing that I wanted to be a firefighter. On April 3, 1972, I entered the Baltimore Fire Academy.

Why am I writing this book?

To many people, firefighters are a bunch of "backyard bums" who deal cards, tell bad jokes and play pool both day and night, that is, when they are not watching television or sitting in front of the station making comments at passers-by. Not true.

I want people to know what a firefighter feels and experiences; what it is like to work with 70 pounds of protective equipment on your back; to breathe through a mask while straining to lift people and objects heavier than yourself; and to do your best to control your adrenaline and pulse while carrying tools, ladders and people through hell-like conditions when you cannot see, hear, smell, talk or breathe and, where your only exit may flash-over in flames instantly, trapping you in a fiery torrent.

Imagine being responsible for keeping someone alive as his vital signs weaken, or smoke or water has filled his lungs, or compression has stopped his heart.

As a medic you hope you are administering CPR effectively or giving the correct dosage of drugs, and wonder whether you should challenge a doctor's advice on the radiophone.

As a rescue technician, you know that when freeing a trapped person in a mangled vehicle, one wrong move may paralyze him for life or even kill him.

Everyone in the Fire Service encounters trauma regularly, and certain incidents make you want to leave your job.

It takes a special kind of person to *want* to do this job. It is a job of life-saving, property-saving and life-loving. It is a job of total satisfaction and incomparable frustration.

These stories are based on actual incidents. The firefighters portrayed in this book are actual firefighters in Baltimore City. However, the names of the victims, as well as some of the firefighters, have been changed to protect their privacy.

I would be remiss if I did not mention the unsung heroes of this profession . . . the spouses and children who know that when their husband or dad goes to work, he is not going to a neat, clean office or desk job. He may never come home again.

Your understanding and support are a firefighter's strength. As you read this book, place yourself in the front seat and ride with us. Charge into burning buildings and homes and help us rescue victims. Lean next to us as we splint the broken leg of a fall victim or give CPR to a badly burned child. Climb into a wrecked car and see what we see, feel what we feel. Let the euphoria of saving someone overwhelm you, as it does us. Experience the same despair we feel when a patient dies.

"Turnout!" for the next emergency call.

Bill Hall
July 1991

1 Alarm!

The concrete monolith stood in the heart of the city, a testimonial to the innovative design of America's fire-resistant office structures. It embodied the latest fire prevention technology regulated by law. Its one flaw was that most floors lacked sprinklers. Sprinklers were not yet required in new building construction, although lobbyists were actively pursuing a change in state law.

Nearby, at the city's largest fire house, the firefighter on watch duty lazily turned off the television set after listening to the Star Spangled Banner announce the end of the broadcast day. He yawned and stretched as he scanned the apparatus floor, eyeing the red and white steel guardians in their bays.

Tuning the AM-FM radio to a popular station, he sat back in his chair and began the predawn ritual of watchmen in firehouses the world over: he picked up the newspaper, reached for his coffee cup and began routinely checking the clock on the wall above him. Several calls had come in throughout the night for single engines or trucks, but none had been for his station. His watch duty progressed slowly. After what seemed like hours, the clock showed only 3:00 a.m.

Just four blocks away, on the sixteenth floor of the monolith, sparks crackled from a computer terminal. Curls of smoke began to rise. In the console beneath the terminal an orange flame appeared and grew, rapidly filling the small work station. Soon the flame lapped at the carpeting and the cloth-covered desk chair. Within moments, the chair burst into flames, igniting boxes of paper nearby. Heavy, black smoke engulfed the room.

Back at the station, the firefighter on duty came out of the bathroom rubbing his eyes, wishing he was asleep like his comrades. He checked the clock again . . . 3:49 a.m. What an unusually uneventful evening, he thought.

At the sixteenth floor of the high rise, a smoke detector screeched its alarm. It triggered an automatic signal which alerted the security guards on the first floor to the danger above, while simultaneously transmitting an alarm to Fire Department headquarters downtown.

The heat in the computer room rose dramatically as the fire charged forward like a roaring army with no one to stop its advance. Flames rolled out and greedily consumed the fragile contents of the room, causing the burning furniture to expel toxic fumes. Suddenly, the tempered glass in the room exploded from the heat and smoke allowing the superheated gases to escape and envelope the sixteenth floor.

At the droning tone-signal of the incoming call, the firefighter's sleepy eyes widened. He jumped to his feet, nearly knocking over his chair. As the dispatcher called out the responding units, the fighter quickly wrote them down on his watch sheet. Without hesitation, his adrenalin pumping, the watchman turned out his companies: "TURNOUT! Engine 23, 38, 15, 27, Truck 1 . . ." Instantly, lights came on, speakers coughed out unit numbers and street address, and large metal doors rolled open from their sleeping positions. Blankets and sheets were tossed aside as human legs found boots standing at attention next to each bunk. Buttons clicked and suspenders snapped as turnout clothing was donned.

In less than 60 seconds, ordinary men were transformed into soldiers of superhuman courage and compassion as we slid down gleaming poles of brass to our waiting chariots. Diesel exhaust filled the bays of the huge station as engines revved. Slowly at first, then faster, the giant rigs slipped from the station, each carrying four men. Air horns blared, sirens wailed, rotating beacon lights threw eerie patterns on nearby buildings, while headlights stabbed into the darkness of the nearly-deserted streets.

Hours later as I drove home, the fire now out, my mind replayed the events of early morning. I remembered turning the corner in the fire truck and seeing in horror the flames in the bulging windows of the building I had pointed to frequently as the architectural pride of the city. I thought of the tactical fire command center set up on the fifteenth floor of the burning building, and how methodically everyone worked together to do his job in the middle of the blinding chaos. I saw George White and me pulling the 2-1/2-inch hoseline down the smoke-filled hallway to bring it upstairs. I remembered the lump in my throat when I heard someone yell, "We've got a man down!" I recalled the valiant efforts of the truck company men as they tried in vain to revive their fallen friend. I reflected on the confusion that followed while officers attempted to get an accurate head-count of the firefighters.

Much later, a formal investigation revealed that the fire service key to the elevators had been turned off but that Firefighter Sam Karnicki was aboard. The heat-sensing elevator call-buttons, activated by the temperature of the sixteenth floor, called the doomed elevator to that level. When the doors opened, Sam was greeted by heat estimated at 2000 degrees — enough to turn heavy steel building girders into twists of ribbon. The doors were, in turn, frozen open by the smoke blocking the light sensors. Sam didn't suffer long.

When I arrived home, my wife Carol was busy hustling the children off to school. We exchanged hugs and kisses without saying anything. I watched the turmoil and listened to the predictable excuses of kids resisting the start of another school day. Quietly, I drank a cup of coffee. How strange it seemed that some lives come to a crashing halt while others go on and on, caught up in an endless routine.

After the kids left, Carol came over and sat next to me.

"What's bothering you?" she asked. I put my cup down and forced back the tears, "We lost Sam Karnicki this morning."

Carol looked dumbfounded. We both knew Sam. In his forties, a family man and an experienced firefighter assigned to Ladder Truck 2, his Southern drawl seemed to belie his quick and easy humor. I had come to enjoy his friendship in the two years we had worked together.

Carol got up, propelled by some inner remote control that takes over in moments of intense shock, put her arms around my neck and stood silently hugging me. As a firefighter's wife she knew that was as much as she could do. That day, one of our worst fears had become a reality. We cried for his family.

At Sam's funeral, the long row of firefighters in blue snapped to attention at the command of the senior officer. An engine bearing Sam's flag-draped casket in its hosebed slowly moved down the street from the funeral home on its way to the cemetery near the city line. In the midst of their pain and grief, Sam's family in the black limousine felt the consolation of pride that Sam was so nobly honored in his death. But as the engines approached the gate to the cemetery, tears flooded their faces and their voices quivered.

At the entrance to the burial grounds, two companies had fully extended their aerial ladders to touch each other and form an arch. As the casket was born through, a firefighter clanged an engine bell for his comrade.

An honor guard made up of several hundred men lined the field at the tent where Sam's family awaited his eulogy.

Every firefighter seemed transfixed. Only those in the Fire Service can truly comprehend a moment like this. We pay tribute not to the way our fallen comrade died but to the way he lived — to serve the public and the people. Sam paid the ultimate price for that honor.

It is for love of fellow man and the honor of the profession that we answer each call, no matter how dangerous. We know that, at any time, it could be our last alarm. We and our families live with that possibility daily. It may sound strange but at times like these, when the reality of our mortality is strongest, we are proudest to be firefighters.

The nearness of death makes a man look at himself in a new perspective. We realize that we are not immortal. We can die in a second. Things that are trivial take on new importance — like a simple kiss from your wife as you leave for the station, or making time after a grueling shift to help your kid with homework.

Life in the Fire Service is many things. Above all, it is unpredictable. Some calls actually leave you with a smile on your face.

On a bright, sunny day Engine 38 responded to a call for a water leak in a low-income high rise. As the engine arrived, the firefighters spotted a woman on the tenth floor, waving her arms frantically and screaming for them to hurry because her baby was being drowned. The captain, suspecting foul play, grabbed his radio and called for police assistance. Because the elevators weren't working, the crew anxiously ran up the long stretch of stairs to the hysterical woman.

Finally, they reached the tenth floor, their legs rubbery from the long ascent. The mother, clad only in a wrinkled housecoat, pushed them into the apartment and toward the bathroom. As the crew cautiously approached, the sound of rushing water became deafening. Disregarding their own safety, they barged into the bathroom, followed by the weeping mother. They stopped cold.

In the bathtub stood an 11-year-old "baby" trying to quell the flooding waters from the broken faucet. The tub was overflowing and the "baby," roughly 250 pounds of him, clad only in undershorts, turned to the firefighters and said, "Will somebody please help me?"

At the sight of the samurai wrestler-sized boy, the entire crew shook with suppressed laughter, barely able to contain themselves.

The apartment manager said the water couldn't be cut off without shutting off all water to the 110 units. So the firefighters ended the crisis by coaxing the baby out of the tub and reattaching the faucet with equipment from their toolbox (much to the pleasure of the mother).

Have you every wondered what happens when a hearse catches fire? Engine 23 responded to an automobile fire at one of the West Side's biggest intersections.

13

It was a sweltering summer day. As they approached the scene, they observed a hearse spouting flames and smoke from under its hood. The crew immediately pulled off their booster hose and pried open the superheated hood. The driver stood by as they turned their hoses on the engine, silently watching with a resigned look on his face. Through the thick black smoke it was apparent that the engine was demolished.

When the fire was extinguished, the acting lieutenant questioned the driver. But the driver seemed more concerned about getting the body out of the hot car and to the City Morgue, two blocks away. As the firefighters put up their equipment, the driver of the still-steaming hearse promptly turned, opened the back doors and pulled the body bag out onto a wheeled stretcher. While the firefighters watched flabbergasted, and stunned pedestrians and motorists looked on, the driver wheeled the body through the traffic and down the street to the morgue.

As a paramedic, one of the most unnecessary calls I ever responded to was during my detail to Medic Unit 4. The Baltimore City Fire Department runs an emergency ambulance service. At present there are 18 units assigned for first-line service to a city of approximately 800,000 people. Needless to say, the emergency ambulance service receives a great many calls which are clearly *not* emergencies. Whether out of ignorance, loneliness, laziness or hypochondria, some people clearly "abuse" the service. They dial 911 for everything from toothaches to taxi rides.

At 4 o'clock, early one morning, we were dispatched to a dilapidated high rise building to aid a person suffering from a seizure. Surprisingly, the elevator worked. Most of the time, elevators in unkempt buildings are broken and we have to carry people and equipment up or down several flights of poorly lighted stairs — often in rough areas. In the elevator, the stench of urine was overpowering. But at this hour of the night, it was worth taking the elevator, especially for a call on the seventh floor.

When we arrived at the door, I knocked and was greeted by a hulking, black man in a torn T-shirt who led us inside the darkened apartment. "He's over there," the man pointed. Sitting in the corner in a tall-backed chair, with a glass of red wine on the floor next to him, was a 15-year-old boy.

"How do you feel?" I asked. "I heard you had a seizure?"

"I'm okay. I feel fine now," the boy replied.

I took his vital signs and asked, "Do you want us to take you to the hospital? It's 4:00 a.m. We're already here."

The large man interrupted, "I'm his guardian." Turning to the boy, he urged, "Go ahead. Let'em take you!"

The boy shook his head sheepishly. "Nah, I don't want to go now. But if you come back in the morning, I'll go with you!" he smiled.

"Okay," I agreed, careful to contain my irritation, "you do that." Sure enough, the boy's guardian called back at 9:00 a.m. for the free ride to the hospital.

Fred Ehrlich, a feisty kind of firefighter, served as my driver on ambulance duty one wintry day when we received a call for a "sick case" on the southwest side of town. We entered the house and raced up a long steep, narrow staircase.

This was particularly difficult for Fred, as he is rather short and round. He resembles Danny DeVito in the TV series *Taxi* and has about the same cynical sense of humor.

At the top of the stairs, he brushed the sweat from his balding head and looked inside the doorway. Then he put his hands on his hips and frowned at me. Before us stretched a scene reminiscent of the *Sound of Music*. A woman in her forties lay propped up in a large bed, surrounded by nine children ranging from four to 18 years old, standing in order of age.

"What's wrong?" I asked her.

The woman, her face twisted in anguish, began:

"Well, I've only got one good leg and the other one hurts. I've got a heart condition and high blood pressure. I'm also a diabetic. My kidneys are bad and I've got stones in my gallbladder. My left lung has cancer and my right lung has emphysema. I've got glaucoma in my right eye. My good leg's got phlebitis and might have to be amputated. My stomach makes too much acid, and it makes me feel terrible." Fred shifted his feet.

"How long has all this been going on?" I inquired.

"Oh, my, I'd say about 10 or 15 years!" she replied.

I struggled to keep my composure. Fred bit his tongue. "What made you decide to call an emergency ambulance today?" I asked.

She looked at me stone-faced and said, "I feel sick."

The room was filled with bottles of medication. A bell sat at her side that when rung would bring at least four children running to her bedside. I looked at Fred, who quickly turned his eyes to the floor. Calmly, I took the woman's vital signs. They were normal.

"Ma'am, you don't need an emergency ambulance," I said. She looked frustrated. Fred mumbled all the way down the steps about his back and his feet and the cold air. We could hear her bell ringing angrily in the background as we headed for the next call.

––––––––––––––

Ted Belt, a no-nonsense paramedic, received a call for a seizure patient at a busy downtown intersection. As the sirens wailed through the crowded downtown traffic, the dispatcher advised Ted and his partner that police were on the scene.

When the ambulance arrived, the men found a group of passers-by crowded together in football huddle formation. Ted grabbed his kit and pushed through the crowd. A police officer knelt over a white man in his forties.

The patient lay prostrate on the cool concrete with his eyes closed, seemingly unconscious. Ted took his vitals and found they were normal, so he asked the crowd, "Did you see this man have a seizure?" No one answered.

The man's eyes began to flutter. Ted tried to open them with his fingers, but the man seemed to be holding them shut. Ted realized that the man was only pretending to have had a seizure. The patient closely resembled a street person that frequented the area, one who had been known to call for ambulances for non-emergency situations. Medics refer to such people as "regulars." They fake seizures hoping to be admitted to a hospital to get food, a clean bed and maid service, or simply to draw attention from passers-by who might offer them help.

"Regular" calls are especially frustrating to medics who rarely have enough time to handle real emergencies. Some street people pull this stunt several times a week, despite repeated failures.

When the man continued to fight Ted's attempts to open his eyes, Ted decided to have some fun with him. He reached down and opened his medical box.

Paramedics in Baltimore have a nickname for ammonia capsules, or smelling salts. They call them "silver bullets."

Ted pulled two silver bullets out of the box, cracked them, and inserted them into each of the man's nostrils. He saw the man's eyes suddenly open wide, welling up with tears.

Quickly, Ted stood up over the man, held out his hands, and yelled, "HEAL!" Instantly, the patient jumped to his feet, snorting the two silver bullets out of his nose and gasping for breath. The crowd erupted in laughter as the sniffling man stomped his feet and wiped away the tears that were streaming down his face.

The medic and his partner called to the dispatcher as they drove away, "Medic one, place us back in service. This call will be handled by police."

———————

A firefighter never knows when he'll end up leaving a chunk of himself back at the scene.

One of the most heart-wrenching and helpless situations I have ever experienced in the Fire Service occurred during a high rise apartment fire in an affluent area of Baltimore.

A young police officer on foot patrol was making his usual rounds on a quiet street, twirling his nightstick with precision. He turned the corner and gasped. Directly in front of him, a 10-story apartment building stood aflame. Fire leaped out of the eighth, ninth and tenth floor windows. Smoke the color of asphalt rose from the fifth floor and up. People hung out of the windows screaming for help. Luckier residents scurried out of every lower access onto the sidewalk.

"419 to dispatch — URGENT!" yelled the young officer.

"Come in 419," dispatch replied, "all units standing by."

"Send fire units to the Bach Apartments," his voice quivered. "The building's on fire! People are hanging out the windows. I'll try to assist. HURRY!"

"Roger, 419", the dispatcher said coolly.

Officer 419 barged through the main doors as more panicked occupants streamed out around him. He saw one body bounce on the hard concrete outside the doors, and he was determined not to see another.

His adrenalin pumped madly as he raced up the stairs to the fifth floor and ran down the halls yelling and banging on doors. Some occupants heard him and made their escape. He found a woman overcome with smoke, and dragged her to safety outside. In the distance he heard the telltale wail of fire department sirens. Finally! To 419, it seemed he had struggled alone in the inferno for an eternity. He rushed back into the burning building and vaulted up the steps.

At the end of the fifth floor hallway, a blast of intense heat and heavy smoke suddenly forced him back. The fire, it seemed, was winning the battle.

As he backtracked to the opposite end of the hallway the stairwell collapsed, sending sparks and waves of smoke rolling toward him. Choking and flushed, he realized he was trapped. There was only one thing to do . . . the one thing he had been drilled not to do. He punched the elevator button and waited.

The smoke and heat were nearly incapacitating. Finally the elevator opened. In desperation, 419 stepped inside, praying to make it to the fresh, night air. The doors closed and he began to descend. As he passed the fourth floor, he realized something was wrong. The elevator began jerking erratically. Suddenly, it dropped three floors — to the basement. He hammered at the "door open" button, but the doors remained steadfastly shut. He reached for his portable radio.

"Dispatch, this is 419. I'm in the north elevator at the fire. It's disabled in the basement and I can't get the doors open." He began to cough as smoke entered the cracks of the door.

"Easy, 419. We'll get the fire units to you quickly," the dispatcher crackled.

"Roger," 419 replied.

The heat in the elevator was getting worse. Without any warning it was jolted by a large thud, followed by several smaller ones, as floors collapsed onto the elevator. Tears flowed from his eyes as he realized he might not make it out. His thoughts turned to his wife and little girl.

At the fire command post, the police colonel was talking with the deputy fire chief. They listened with helplessness as 419's voice pleaded over the radio, "Somebody, please help me! It's getting so hot! I can't stand it! Help me out of here!" Concerned police officers in the area, alerted to 419's cries over the radio, began to gather near the fire scene. Suddenly a woman rushed toward the building, crying hysterically. A police officer restrained her, as she screamed that she was Officer 419's wife. She had heard his impassioned pleas over their home radio scanner. I have never seen such raw fear as I did watching her eyes as she gazed into the flames hoping, praying, pleading.

With all the occupants accounted for, the fire units concentrated their efforts on the basement. The city-wide channel broadcast 419's last words: "Help me, please. I can't take it anymore!" Another rush of falling floors covered the north elevator shaft, and the radio went silent.

When we finally cleared the rubble and reached the elevator shaft, our sense of failure was overwhelming. We pried open what had become a tomb for 419.

His body had swollen from the searing heat. Gently, it was covered and placed on an ambulance stretcher. When the firefighters carried him past the police command post, Officer 419's emotionally drained wife collapsed in the arms of the police colonel. Each officer saluted the body as it passed by. A firefighter closed the doors of the ambulance and raised a final salute to the heroic young officer. We turned away to begin the arduous task of overhauling the fire — checking for hot spots, clearing out the debris, and somehow getting on with life.

———————

Big cities grow slowly and die slowly. Sometimes the dead sections are around for years before new growth emerges. Large city blocks of vacant buildings and abandoned houses bring their own special kind of firefighting horror. One case in particular gave me the shivers. It was the closest thing I've seen to premeditated murder — of firefighters!

It was a clear, crisp fall day. At mid-day an arsonist peered down the trash-strewn streets, looking for possible witnesses. He knew he would be less obvious by blending in with the daytime crowd. He turned quickly and entered the open doorway of a decaying, empty building. He ran up the stairway to the top floor, clutching his tools tightly. There he set up shop and began his perverse work.

Meanwhile, at the Steadman Firehouse the firemen sat in the kitchen talking and drinking coffee. As they laughed, joked, cursed and poked fun at one another, the room took on the air of a high school cafeteria.

Suddenly, the station intercom double-beeped an alert, and the kitchen fell instantly silent. The dispatcher reported a building fire just down the street from the station. Racing to their poles, they slid to their units and burst into the heavy morning traffic. They could smell the smoke, but when they turned the corner they could see nothing but a light eerie haze.

The arsonist shot out the open door and mingled with the growing crowd in front of the building. He flushed with excitement as he saw the fire apparatus career around the corner.

Unit by unit the firefighters jumped from their apparatus and entered the building. Following the smoke, they ascended the stairs six stories to the top floor. There, several tables, abandoned by the former tenant, stretched from one end to the other. Shreds of cloth, trash and paper were scattered about the room. The men began their search. Although the scent of petroleum was in the air, the fire load was small, so the men scattered to find the source.

The firebug watched intently as more firefighters entered the building. He rubbed his sweaty hands and wiped them up and down his thighs. His mouth went dry as he unconsciously began to pant. "Soon," he thought. "Soon!"

Without warning the room erupted with balls of fire, followed by heavy, black smoke. Panic struck the firefighters as they scattered, desperately searching for an exit through the flames and tar-like bellows of smoke. A few of the 25 men were fortunate enough to make it down the stairwell, but most were forced to scramble to any opening, even windows.

The arsonist watched with glee as smoke poured from the windows. "What a show," he thought, wiping his oily hands. "What a wonderful show!" He licked his parched lips and smiled as the firefighters began swarming out of the blaze like ants.

Firefighters Augie Stern and Captain Frank Rainey leaped out of a window to a fire escape. They shouted for help as the smoke snaked around them. They could not descend because of the blinding smoke and intense heat.

Lieutenant Carrabean wasn't as fortunate. He, too, dove out of a window, but was only able to grasp the bottom rung of the fire escape. Flames shot out of the window at his hands and face. The lieutenant's hands clung desperately to the rung, as he dangled six stories above the asphalt and summoned strength he never knew he had.

Both Stern's and Rainey's faces burned from the heat. Their hair had been singed and their faces were blackened from the smoke and soot. But the sight of the lieutenant, suspended in mid-air, propelled them into action.

Rainey held onto Stern as he descended the fire escape ladder. Stretching out as far as he could, his hand grasped the lieutenant's wrist. After nearly 15 minutes, Rainey and Stern together were able to pull Carrabean to the relative safety of the fire escape, which seemed to appear and disappear in the smoke.

By now, the fire engulfed several floors. The fire command officer directed all of his efforts to the three men trapped on the fire escape. Ever so slowly, an aerial ladder was raised to the fire escape. The men, exhausted and burned by the intense heat, painfully pulled themselves onto the truck ladder and made their descent down its long frame.

First and second degree burns covered Lieutenant Carrabean's face and hands. Augie Stern and Frank Rainey suffered first degree burns on their faces and necks.

The arsonist stood proudly surveying the leaping flames when a strong hand clamped his shoulder. Within seconds he was handcuffed. The arson investigator, well-trained in his art, had witnesses, evidence and telltale signs of the firebug that showed this man to be responsible for the blaze.

Arson costs untold billions of dollars in damages to homes, property and businesses each year. Countless lives are lost. It is a hideous crime. The arsonist, like a premeditating murderer, is a professional criminal. He knows exactly how to achieve the desired result. Here, the arsonist had not only destroyed a building but had almost killed an entire first alarm assignment of 25 men.

The arsonist laughed as the door of the police cruiser closed. Would he ever have to pay the price for his actions? Was it an obsession? Was he planning the delayed fireball eruptions to trap firefighters? Or was he working for someone else with a vendetta or a motive who would get him off without punishment? We would never know the answer. All we knew was that it had been a very close call for many firefighters. Too close!

their systems, and then to qualify and quantify their severity. However, the information warfare warrior is continually seeking and finding weaknesses in the technology that can be exploited with newer technology.

At present the normal software defenses for information systems are not only simple but obvious—the use of firewalls, encryption, frequently changed passwords, multiple layers of software to identify and nullify unauthorized access or operations, files which document and develop profiles of unusual activities, and programs that attempt to identify intrusions or, at least, document and record them. Even the relatively unsophisticated hacker can access poorly protected information systems and has access to programs that can damage or steal data in milliseconds.

Most defenses in information technology require user cooperation, and many users are not prepared, educated, or even sensitive to the nature and scope of the problem. Precisely because most people do not understand the technology they rely upon, they do not know how to adequately protect their information systems against unauthorized intrusion. The need is for approaches that obviate user involvement.

Serious information warfare adversaries will likely develop and test their weapons carefully and then attack first against poorly prepared targets—private sector and/or defense contractors having few rudimentary defenses and no history of informing government organizations of their experience with information warfare attacks. The adversary's goals would not be, necessarily, any serious disruption of such vendors. Their goal would be to merely test their attack mechanisms. Once success was assured, they would move on to more seriously defended targets employing more serious attacks. This escalation of targets would continue as they refined their information warfare methods. But they would always avoid their ultimate target until they were assured of the efficacy of their attack strategy.

Once the adversary was certain that his attack strategy was effective, once he had defeated the lesser foes, he would employ his proven strategy against his ultimate target. Such an approach could be disastrous when unleashed against even the most prepared current defender. It would be carefully orchestrated, tested at every level, and proven against, ultimately, the most capable defenses short of, or possibly even superior to, the DOD equipment and systems. The information warfare adversary does not factor deterrence into his equation; demonstrations of his prowess are counterproductive if they encourage defensive efforts. The information warfare warrior works in shadows and hides his very existence.

One possible solution would be to have these potential targets connected to a central processing activity that is then connected to the WWW. Such a connection could be transparent to the user with information on software attacks updated on a daily basis. Any attack against any user could be catalogued and ultimately sorted and collated to develop modus operandi (MOs), threat assessments, adversary psychological profiles, and threat projections. Essay 14, Emergency Response Management at the National Operations Centers, and Essay 15, Information Integration and Process Applications for Emergency Management Operations Centers, in this series outline the concept for an emergency management operations center (EMOC) that could provide these functions and processes on a routine basis. The threat to the information technology infrastructure surely necessitates coordinating this effort at the national level so that effective responses to this and other NTW threats can be undertaken.

It should be noted that high priority targets (national infrastructure, DOD) would need to be factored into this response scenario as well. Additionally, special consideration would have to be given to those government contractors who are under contract for "black" programs and companies with highly proprietary commercial material. Assuring the security of classified, proprietary, and privileged data would be critical to participation. While unable to share raw data, the participants would still be able to share details on attacks such as method used, detection tool, time of attack, and other information that would alert other participants to the attack and provide valuable clues on how to prevent future attacks.

Such a program would not need to be all encompassing to begin with. There is no "critical mass" for the success of such a concept. Certainly the more participants in the system, the more information would be gained on all varieties of software threats. With such information, the EMOC could develop threat projections and countermeasures and offer them to approved subscribers free of charge. As the value of this concept becomes more widely known, legitimate subscribers would participate.

Hardware Defenses

Countermeasures for the EMP threat are well understood but can be expensive to implement. Hardware can be shielded with metal enclosures to prevent EMP pulses from penetrating from the ambient levels produced by both nuclear and conventional threats and damaging hardware and software. Necessary connections to users and information sources can be protected from EMP pulses generated exterior to the hardware. External connections are actually a more serious threat since the currents generated by EMP are generally proportional to the length of the conductor subjected to the EMP environ-

2 Firehouse Life

What is it like to live half of your life in a cement-block building with a group of men who think a good day is charging up and down the stairways of hell in 70 pounds of gear carrying, dragging or pulling people weighing up to 200 pounds in temperatures well above 90 degrees?

In a word: Fantastic!

While some aspects of station life are best left unmentioned, I'll do my best to provide an accurate picture of what goes on inside the "home" of this tightly knit brotherhood.

There are three essential areas in every firehouse: the bunk room, the kitchen, and the coffee pot! Like anywhere else a group of men congregate, you'll find swearing, raw humor and prank-playing that would make television's *MASH* unit look like *Mr. Roger's Neighborhood.*

At the beginning of a shift, firefighters hang around the kitchen drinking coffee. Story-telling and joking occupy most of the time and help take the edge off between calls. Occasionally, towards the end of a long shift, an argument about the showers or a missing candy bar breaks out.

The transformation from juvenile jokester to seasoned rescue worker still impresses me after almost 20 years. Firefighters may laugh and argue at the top of their lungs while the Fire Department radio chatters in the background. But as soon as their unit numbers are called out for a response, their mouths shut and their ears perk up. In less than a heartbeat, they shoot like darts from the kitchen, bunk rooms and offices to their apparatus.

Civilians find it hard to understand the apparent nonchalant attitude of firefighters in the face of a tragedy. Witnessing a fireman extinguish a fatal blaze or drag a body from a gruesome accident, and then watching him laugh and chatter moments later as if nothing had happened, seems callous and insensitive. What most people don't understand, however, is that a firefighter cannot dwell on a tragedy. If he does, he might hold back in the next situation. And any hesitation, no matter how slight, could mean the difference between the victim's life or death, or his own.

If we internalized our emotions, we'd succumb to battle fatigue within weeks; or worse, we'd bring the tension home where it could sabotage our marriages and destroy our families.

Instead, we find ways to release the tension quickly and harmlessly. Immediately after returning from a call, firefighters gather in the station kitchen to "talk out" their incidents. The kitchen provides a safe environment to express our pain at the loss of a life, or our mental and physical exhaustion after fighting a major building fire, or our button-bursting pride at assisting in the birth of another baby, or our gratitude and joy when a person walks away from an accident that should have killed him.

In the kitchen we can release the anger we struggled to control at the sight of a man or woman who has long-abused a child. We can boast in the friendly company of our rivals at being the "first in" on a major fire call. We can release the anxiety already building up inside — the fear of the next call . . . the one that is already out there . . . waiting.

We are human, and emotions can paralyze our ability to respond effectively. Humor helps us rebound from our feelings. It's not surprising that most firefighters are "World Class Black Belts" in the art of the practical joke. A water pistol fired from under the table unleashes a pandemonium of water warfare. It's funny to see grown men walking around soaking wet, right down to their underwear, especially in an "environmentally controlled atmosphere."

For example, one such diversion occurred on a grueling winter night shift composed of four, 14-hour evenings. In the middle of a call, the battalion chief, who had been particularly harsh during the shift, leaped into his turnout boots only to find they had been filled to the knees with water. He squooshed his way to the apparatus and to the site of the emergency, muttering a few choice remarks on the way.

Immediately after returning to the station, we were ordered into a "line-up." Whenever a shift starts, we line up to hear orders for the day. A line-up is also called to pass on information and, on occasion, to chew men out, or, in this case, to make ground beef of us.

Another instance occurred when a firefighter dispensing fuel was surprised by cold water poured with remarkable accuracy on his head and down his neck from the second story window. Again, we were told to "line up."

One snowy night, we were directed to clear the snow from the front of the station. Suddenly our exhaustion was replaced by an adolescent urge to pack the snow into tight little balls and hurl them at each other. The fire captain just happened to be walking by his pumper when a case-hardened missile exploded on his nose. "You.. . . Line up!"

Firehouse antics aside, the finest part of station life is the people. I've worked with some of the best firefighters in the profession.

Augie Stern, for example, was a ranger in the invasion of the Philippines. He was a giant of a man in every way. Until his retirement, Augie served on rescue squad, a duty he performed with remarkable wisdom, strength and courage. He proved to me and many other people that the mandatory retirement age of 55 for firefighters could mean discarding the best skilled men. Thanks to him, the rules have changed. Augie often served as first acting lieutenant when the lieutenant was off duty or away. He was rather like General Schwarzkopf, with a good sense of humor. Everyone respected him. He knew how to talk to people, and how to get a troubled firefighter to discuss his feelings. I always found comfort in sitting with Augie over coffee.

Wayne Geldmacher, my best friend, is about 5'10" and a bit stocky, with white hair that dusts the sides of his head. A good natured, well-organized and deeply religious man, Wayne loves his job and his family. We met serving on Engine 23 six months after I entered the Fire Department. Later, when we were both assigned to ambo (ambulance) duty, we spent almost 11 years as partners. In a way, Wayne and I matured together as firefighters, husbands and fathers. We're pretty consistent in most things. The only major difference between us was that he had three sons and I had four daughters. Some would say, that's still pretty consistent.

Over our years together on ambo, Wayne and I came to know and depend on each other's reactions so much so that the usual stress was all but eliminated. There is no firefighter with whom I'd rather work. Through the years, many people have said that if they ever needed an ambo, they wanted ours to respond. Wayne is like a brother to me.

If I had two brothers in this business, the other would be Bob Wagner. Depending on how he wears his hair, which is salt and pepper colored, he looks a little like George Peppard. A controlled workaholic, Bob's engine is always revved. His energy is infectious. The captain jokingly has said that if he were Ben Hur, Bob and I would be his horses. No sooner would a call come in than Bob would be out the door, with me at his coattails. In his free time, Bob makes things with his hands — earring and pin sets, paintings and even a beautiful cradle for his granddaughter. Bob is also a creative prankster who loves a good laugh.

You'll come to know several other heroes in the following stories.

———————

One of the funniest men I've ever known is Walt (Schultz) Schultheis. Schultz is assigned to Aerial Tower 102. To most of us, Schultz is the "Prince of Prank." If he weren't a firefighter he'd make a great dentist, cracking jokes while instruments dangled from your lips. Fortunately, he is as skillful at taking a joke as delivering one. One night he met his Waterloo.

Steadman Station does not have a classic gong to turn companies out for a response. Rather, turnout is signaled by a tone-alert system which is hooked up to the speakers and doors. When a call comes in, it is broadcast either simultaneously to all quarters throughout the firehouse or only to the individual units needed for a single response. The lights go on, speakers spout out locations and companies, and doors magically open. However, when the system is in the night mode, the responses can bleed through the speakers well before the man on watch turns out the units. The extra few seconds of advance warning affords a rare opportunity for trickery.

On this evening, Schultz had pulled a few too many stunts on a pair of firefighters. After he went to sleep, they crept into the bunk room of Truck 2 and up to Schultz's berth. Moments later the duo surfaced in the station kitchen with Schultz's eyeglasses. One found black crepe paper and gave it to the other who took out scissors and cut two pieces the shape of the eyeglasses and taped them to the glass areas. Finally, they slipped back to the snoring Schultz and placed the spectacles back on the chair exactly the way they had found them.

Sometime during the night a call was transmitted to Steadman Station units. Schultz heard the bleedover before the lights came on. He jumped from his bed and grabbed his glasses. Placing them on his face, he began yelling "Let's Go!" Then in the dim light, panic struck. Schultz began screaming in terror, "I can't see! I can't see! I'm blind. Help me! I can't see!"

The other firefighters donned their turnout gear, wondering what all the ruckus was about. As the main lights came on, someone noticed the blackened lenses. "Take off the darned glasses, Schultz. You ain't blind!"

Laughter broke the concerned silence. Schultz removed the glasses and studied them carefully. As everyone started for the poles, he ripped the paper off and ran laughing to catch up with his company.

The call turned out to be a false alarm. However word of the blind firefighter spread throughout the station house, and Schultz received a flurry of anonymous calls and serenades of "Three Blind Mice" through the remainder of the shift.

Firefighter George (Juicy) Reed rarely lets a comrade forget a mistake or an embarrassing moment. A black firefighter who has served many years with the Fire Department, Juicy is the lead-off man on Engine 23, the firefighter who hooks up the hose to the fire hydrant. He's known for his speed and quick reaction time. When he's not firefighting, he is usually playing baseball.

Juicy has a good sense of humor and a way of getting digs in on everyone. In a way, he is a paradox of a man. He isn't afraid of anything when it comes to fires, bombs or wars. But he does get a little jumpy at the thought of the supernatural. Because of that trait and his good natured way of needling others, he gets his share of pranks.

One evening at Engine 23's old station, the firefighters sat watching a horror movie that managed to catch all of us up in its suspense. One firefighter put a finger on the back of another, making him jump and yell, scaring the rest of us to death.

After the show was over, almost everyone stayed up to relay ghostly events they supposedly had heard or encountered. One fellow noticed how intently Juicy listened, and he quickly disappeared from the group. He tied a thread line string to the bell of the old 1948 Mack Engine 23 and tossed it up the back pole hole. Then he joined the men around the television table and told a made-up story about "Max," an old firefighter who died at Engine 23's station many years ago. "It is said that Max's ghost still haunts this station. Once in awhile you can hear the bell on the old pumper clang lightly. When you hear it, you'll know that Max's ghost is near you."

Juicy laughed and headed for his late night watch. Relieving his predecessor with a wave, he climbed into his position for the two-hour ordeal. He flipped through the paper and stopped to read an article with interest. Imperceptibly, the string on the old bell tightened when tugged. Suddenly, in the silence of the old station house, the bell on the antique engine clanged once, softly. Juicy dropped the paper. He turned around and, seeing nothing, slowly walked over to the pumper. He looked on top and underneath the old truck. Nothing there! Just as he turned, the bell clanged loudly twice.

"Ahhhh!" He careened into the wall, chairs and table as he made his way up the spiral steps to find us all in hysterics. That next month, every firefighter at the station was a target for Juicy's barbs and pranks, which we agreed were justified.

How do firefighters get their "real" names? Not the names from family trees. Their nicknames! Some wish they never had theirs and some love the ones they inherit or merit.

Just as every firefighter is assigned or "detailed" to a squad, ambo or truck duty — an assignment which lasts until death, retirement or being granted a transfer — firefighters are assigned names by other firefighters.

Firefighter Bill Welsh, who recently retired from Truck Company 2, claims one of my favorite names. A tall, lanky, easy-going man with a southern drawl, Bill was a great ladder truck specialist who got along with everyone and loved a practical joke.

When he was a rookie, he went right into a ladder truck company. City life was new to him and he thought Baltimore's road system resembled a plate of uncooked spaghetti — a challenge for someone from Jersey driving a Honda, never mind a country boy trying to drive a hook-and-ladder apparatus. Because he wasn't sure of the best route to take on specific calls, he depended on the regular driver.

One evening, Bill paled as a medic unit took the other driver to the infirmary, placing him off-duty. The officer, a lieutenant, told Bill the good news, "Bill, I need you up front in the driver's seat. Mack will do the tillering!" Tillering means steering the back end of the hook-and-ladder truck. Bill was somewhat relieved that he didn't have to tiller, but still didn't feel comfortable behind the steering wheel at the front of the enormous vehicle. He expressed his feelings to the lieutenant, who only nodded and said not to worry because he would tell Bill where to turn. (Some relief!) Bill sweated out the next hour.

Suddenly, a call came in for his truck. Bill jumped into the driver's seat of the 60-foot truck and sat motionless. The officer told him to go.

"Where?" Bill asked.

"Out of the station!" the officer boomed.

Bill looked straight ahead, swallowed hard, and said, "Which way?"

The lieutenant sighed and pointed right. They took off.

At every turn they had to make, the officer pointed. Sometimes his arm stretched across Bill's face as he pointed left. The officer never said a word to Bill during a run . . . he just pointed. Bill always responded by promptly turning in that direction.

One evening as the lieutenant described the situation to some firefighters in the battalion, one of them observed that Bill must have looked like a hound dog. That was it. The name Hound Dog stuck with Bill his entire career.

Juicy Reed also acquired his name as a rookie. One day some firefighters went to a field to watch him play baseball. Apparently they overheard him called "the Juice." No one knew how he got that nickname; nevertheless, the name "Juicy" stuck.

Many guys with the last name of Gibson have the privilege of being nicknamed "Hoot" after the famous cowboy. Although Lieutenant Steve Gibson on Rescue 1 is no exception, his name has been adapted somewhat with another nickname which relates to a piece of equipment on the squad . . . the Hurst tool. Because Steve became well-known for his skill and speed in using the heavy power tool, he was dubbed "Hurst Tool Hoot" or quite simply, "H.T.H."

One rookie who at first seemed to lack the firefighter instinct and drive was named "Box of Rocks."

Lieutenant Brian LaHatte, one of the sharper firefighters in the department, once made the mistake of gazing off into the distance and hesitating before answering another firefighter's question. From then on, his name was "Zero" after the Maryland State Lottery Games' air ball that was shown to be a little *slow* in their commercials on TV.

Because of our Christian zeal and commitment to help people, my partner Wayne Geldmacher and I were dubbed Billy Graham and Dr. Zhivago by Walt Schultheis.

One of the "BIG" guys at Steadman Station is known for coming into the kitchen after getting up from a night's sleep and drawing boos and hisses from those sitting at the tables. He has been named "Godzilla."

Paul Merkler is a dedicated firefighter on Engine 38. A little short and stocky, Paul can usually be found working out in the weight room. Although a Hercules he'll never be, he looks a little like Mercury under those giant weights. I had the honor of bestowing on Firefighter Merkler the name that has stuck at our station: "Mercules."

Captain Bill Goodwin commands attention wherever he goes, especially if there are ladies around. A young, intelligent, good looking man who is a serious body builder, he soon became known as "Conan."

At one time, all the companies in our station had dark blue T-shirts with Maltese crosses on the fronts. Certain companies had phrases put on the backs of their shirts. The captain of Engine 38's first name was Jerry. So his company was dubbed "Jerry's Kids." The captain of Truck 2 was named Kelly. His company became known as "Kelly's Hero's." Although the Rescue 1 team never had the phrases printed up, we were called "Conan and the Barbarians" after Captain "Conan" Goodwin.

———————

Sometimes station life is hazardous duty. The equipment is sophisticated and accidents happen. One such accident almost claimed one of the squad's finest firefighters, Charles Huber. Charlie, who resembles a short Elvis, has worked rescue squad most of his 20 some years with the Baltimore City Fire Department. Charlie is a perfectionist. On this day, the downstairs crew, which consisted of POs (pump operators) and EVDs (emergency vehicle drivers), were busy cleaning their apparatus and washing the windows on the bay doors. The giant doors were 90 percent glass, with framed joints that gave a lip of about four inches jutting out from each row of panes. To clean them effectively, a man must ascend a ladder which is propped up against the doors while they are in the down position.

Charlie finished cleaning the rescue wagon and gathered the equipment to wash the windows. He raised the ladder with the assistance of a PO and turned on the water. First he sprayed down the windows, then dunking the long-handled brush in the soapy water, he climbed the leaning ladder. Methodically, he cleaned one window at a time.

Wayne and I stood in the watch desk area, our cleaning complete. As we talked, we observed the first floor activity, waiting for the next call to come in. We looked to the Lombard Street side and saw Charlie climb the ladder. He busily scrubbed the grit-stained windows, stretching at certain points to clean every area.

As we watched, a call came in at the watch desk. The speaker box spat out the companies, including Charlie's squad unit, Rescue 1. As I wrote down the units, Wayne punched the door buttons for the called apparatus. One by one, the appropriate doors began their slow rise.

As the door of Rescue 1 rose, Charlie grabbed the sides of the ladder, dropping the brush to the floor. He couldn't believe what was happening! Wayne couldn't believe it either! Instead of stopping the door, he pointed to Charlie and said, "Look at Charlie. Look! He's bouncing down the ladder!"

I jumped up from my seat and gawked in horror. The ladder bumped and thumped as each lip from the doors passed over it. Charlie held on like a cat on a tree trunk in an earthquake, his face the picture of terror as the door rolled steadily toward the ceiling.

Finally, reality hit and Wayne punched the stop button. Two more lips and the entire ladder, along with Charlie, would have crashed to the hard cement floor. Charlie wasted no time in scampering down. He sped furiously up the steps towards us. Wayne's eyes grew large, and I held my breath as to what extreme Charlie's anger would take. He barged into the watch desk area cursing and screaming at us, more directly at Wayne. He then turned suddenly and shot into the departing squad unit. We exhaled as Rescue 1 disappeared from view.

When the squad returned, Charlie again cornered Wayne, and again after dinner, and again for about a week. But time heals all wounds . . . and nerves. At the time, it wasn't funny at all, but today he and Wayne sit down and laugh about it. We remember it as the day Charlie was almost framed.

Engine 23's old station was a very nice turn-of-the-century firehouse. It had a homey atmosphere with Engine 15, Ambulance 1 and the deputy chief based there. The old station house was a big part of the heart of the downtown, and people always stopped in casually to pay their regards and eye the modern and antique fire equipment housed there. But the life of the station house was to change forever in 1973.

The plans had been approved, the construction complete and the official word had come. Soon we would move into a brand new superstation, one of a few in the nation. The impending move was received as a mixed blessing. The new station house would be large, modern and fully automated, but we knew that we were leaving forever the neighborly pleasures of "local" firehouse life. And we would dearly miss the old station, with its heritage and relaxed openness.

Most firefighters were skeptical about the superstation concept; more companies, more men, and more equipment in one location could cause more problems and outweigh the advantages. With such a mix of operations and personalities, there were bound to be conflicts. We saddened at the thought of returning from our calls to a large, modern, antiseptic kitchen instead of the little firehouse kitchen that had heard so many thousands of stories told before ours.

We were wrong. The companies at the new Steadman Station became a tighter battalion than most others of the city. Almost like the sections of an orchestra, everyone gets along in harmony, whether working solo or together. We are never bored, and we enjoy our shifts so much we usually go home looking forward to our return.

But we could not have known all this the day we moved in. Our official move into the new superstation was heralded with a gala "Housewarming and Dedication." Elected officials from all over the city came to see this engineering feat. This was the largest fire station on the East Coast. It was three stories high and even three stories deep at the "Pumping Station" level.

After the officials left, and the crowds dwindled, 20 firefighters cleaned up and stood looking at each other. Slowly, we all eased into our routines. The first night shift came and we were bored. We pulled our chairs out on the ramp and sat watching passers-by in the warm fall air. The nice weather had brought people from outlying areas into town for dinner and a stroll. We couldn't help but notice that quite a few young women walked past the station. When someone mentioned that he was bored, I ran into the station house, returning with a handful of paper. Standing in front of the men, I handed each of them a piece. They took the paper and smiled, knowing without explanation what we were about to do. As young women passed by, we held up the signs over our heads. Marked on each one was a number from 1 to 10. It was like a toned-down version of Miss America or an Olympic gymnastics competition. It drew smiles from every young lady but one. We think she might have been the one to call and complain. "Line up!" We were told to put the signs away. We knew from that moment on, Steadman Station would be a lot of fun.

After that, we didn't waste any time settling into the new station. Instead of firefighters taking turns cooking dinners, we started a special meal system where, for five dollars per firefighter, special home-cooked menus were prepared each night of night shift. Crab Imperial, Roast Beef, Chicken Cacciatore, Spaghetti and Stuffed Pork Chops were standard fare. These heavy meals kept us full throughout the night and really helped us welcome the transition to superstation life.

Though we moved into Steadman Station in early September, by December we had enough surplus money to produce a feast for our Christmas dinner. That meal was free for anyone who came!

Steadman Station came alive that holiday season when we also carried over our traditional Christmas party for underprivileged kids. The money came from a trust fund given to Rescue 1 from a donor. Each year the firefighters put on their Santa's caps and gave kids from a certain school, along with their parents, a king's banquet and presents of clothing and toys. We took special pride in decorating our oversized kitchen in holly and wreaths. Snowflakes hung from the ceiling.

Our reward came in watching the kids' faces when they heard sleigh bells and were told to look out the big kitchen windows. Suddenly they saw Santa, Frosty and Rudolph being raised to the roof in a fire truck's snorkle basket. The kids were charged with excitement as Santa and his gang took turns to speak with each child. Over the years, the Christmas party has been replaced with a program of helping needy families in the area. But carrying over the tradition of the kids' party certainly put the spirit into Steadman Station early on.

Firehouse life isn't all fun and games. Most often it's a matter of trying to keep up your stamina. Sometimes the human body simply won't cooperate. One evening several years ago, firefighter Dan Davis and I served on the ambulance on night shift. Ours had been an extremely busy shift — in three nights we had 41 runs. This fourth night had already seen 11 runs. We were exhausted to the point of being a danger to anyone who called us for help.

At some point in the early morning we received another call. Medics at Steadman Station don't use poles because their bunk room is right over the watch desk and empties into their apparatus bay. Many newer stations do not even have poles. We groggily descended the spiral staircase and picked up our assignment sheet from the man at the watch desk. We appeared to look at it and nodded. We sped off into the night on our 53rd run with the siren and lights cutting through the predawn air.

I remember looking over at Danny. His head rested against the window as he steered the vehicle down the quiet city streets. I fought to keep my eyes open as my vision doubled, then tripled. Danny's head was nodding slowly. It seemed the night would never end.

I sat straight up. Had I dozed off? I'll never know. I reached over and turned the toggle switches for the lights off, then did the same for the sirens.

Dan lifted his sagging head, puzzled. "What are you doing?" he asked.

"We're going back to 'quarters," I replied.

He nodded willingly. "Okay," he said.

With emergency lights and sirens off, we turned and headed back to the station. The man on watch nodded, assuming we had been canceled. We slinked up the spiral staircase and slid under the covers. We had only been gone about two minutes.

When we awoke the next morning, it dawned on us what had happened. We had taken a spin, never making it to our destination. We never heard any backlash from it, which struck us as very odd. It still makes me feel uneasy to know that someone needed our help but we were too tired to respond!

———————

Exhaustion does strange things to people. One time, the last night of a four-night night shift, Van Campy had been working a part-time job during the day. By the fourth night, he was dragging. The hot summer heat makes people drink a lot of liquids. Rescue 1 had been in quarters most of the evening. Television was dull and there was no pedestrian traffic outside. Everyone was pretty burned out. They couldn't wait for morning when the shift would end. Van went to bed.

Around 1:00 a.m., a call came in for a building fire that had quickly gone to two alarms. Rescue 1 responded as assigned on the running card. When they arrived, they were greeted with a one-square-block building, one-story tall, totally engulfed in flames.

Rescue 1's assigned area was to be on the roof, helping to open up and ventilate the fire. They used their saws and axes with the ease of a surgeon carefully slicing open an infection. Van darted from one side of the roof to the other opening holes. But even Van had his limitations. The late-night blues were slowly catching up with him.

After completing their tasks, the firefighters came down the ladders and relaxed. Sweat seeped through their clothing and turnout gear while they sat on the curbside. Their wet hair made them look like battle-hardened veterans. Van sat there with two drinks in his hands from the 414 Wagon — a truck that brings refreshments to firefighters and police on working incidents. After he finished the first drinks, he went to get two more. He struggled to replace the fluid he'd lost battling the blaze wearing heavy gear in the intense muggy heat.

When the chief finally released them from the fireground, they packed up their equipment and headed home. Steadman Station looked like a place of eternal solitude when they pulled up on the ramp. Van, especially, couldn't wait to go to bed. He was so tired he only washed his face and hands saying he would shower in the morning. It was 3:30 a.m.

Charlie Huber finished up his watch duty which lasted till 4:00 a.m. He went upstairs to the kitchen and had a cup of coffee before he went to bed. After finishing, he walked down the darkened hallway to Rescue 1's bunk room. Finding his bed was difficult. The room was pitch black. He felt his way with his hands outstretched in front of him until locating the edge of his bed. He sat down, took off his shoes, pulled off his pants and removed his shirt. Slowly, he slid under the covers and felt the coolness of the sheets caressing his body.

Something startled him as he laid there trying to doze off. He saw the darkened figure of Van Campy getting up and out of bed. His eyes followed the dark figure across the bunk room floor as Van headed out toward the hallway. Charlie wondered why Van had gotten up. Except for the snores, the room was silent, and he thought Van might have gone to the kitchen. Just then, he thought he heard water running nearby. He listened intently. It was coming from the hallway! He got up and carefully maneuvered out to the long hall. He stopped in his tracks. There stood Van.

Charlie's eyes widened as he peered through the darkness. A large grin spread across his face as he realized what Van was doing. There Van stood, looking down the pole hole. What he was looking at Charlie couldn't figure out. But, he had no doubt what Van was doing down the pole hole.

Charlie quickly realized that Van was asleep, otherwise, Van wouldn't have done what he was doing. That was the watery sound Charlie had heard. Van stood silently, leaning against the pole doing what comes naturally in an unnatural place.

Charlie waited for him to finish and then proceeded to help him wake up. Van woke with a start. Charlie told him what he did. Van wouldn't believe him until Charlie showed him the puddle on the first floor and the running drips on the pole. Both men broke out in laughter.

————————

Firehouse life can even be relaxing. When we have some free time, we spend it watching movies or television, or cooking dinner or breakfast. Some firefighters lift weights in the weight room, others study the Bible, some read in the library. But here, in what many people call "the busiest firehouse in America," we almost always have a good time.

We live, laugh and even fight like brothers. Above all, we are a unit. We know that ours is a very special job. In some ways, we feel like we were each destined by God to be firefighters from Day 1 — almost like a jaguar is built for running. Whatever else it is, firefighting is work that we do well, and God knows we love it!

3 Tools of the Trade

The worldwide fascination with fire equipment spans all cultures and ages from two to 92. It fuels a multi-million dollar toy and collector industry, where recently an elaborate toy hose reel from the 1870s sold for $1 million to a private collector. Thousands of people flock to their local station houses annually to see fire equipment close up. They stretch their necks, push forward and peer around shoulders at the sparkling trucks, long ladders, funny suits and gleaming brass fire pole.

Steadman Station boasts the Big Daddy of fire poles. While most firehouses include the 20-foot, two-story variety, and many new station designs have abandoned fire poles altogether, Steadman Station sports a 30-foot giant that has caused more than one rookie to pale at first sight.

It takes a strong sense of coordination and timing (and a certain hunger for cheap thrills) to leap confidently onto an ice cold pole and drop down almost three stories in less than five seconds. Sometimes there are back-ups, pile-ups, twisted ankles and bruises. One night, for instance, a firefighter, who was experienced with shorter poles inadvertently leaped off the pole when he was still five feet above ground! He broke both ankles.

Several young men have offered us money for the chance to ride our pole! We tell them to grow up and join the fire academy.

People love unique clothing and uniforms, and turnout gear attracts almost as much attention as astronaut suits. In fact, many are made of the same material, called Nomex, because it can withstand extremely high temperatures. The advanced technology behind our turnout gear has saved many firefighters' lives.

Turnout gear usually includes:

Heavy pants with suspenders that sometimes look and feel like they belong in Ronald McDonald's closet. Called "bunkers" in other parts of the country, they are made of yellow Nomex or a chemical called "PBI" which is brown, and lined with cloth.

Turnout coat, a double fabric with Nomex or PBI on the outside and a cloth lining, that features large pockets to carry the extra equipment needed in some emergencies.

Normally turnout suits last three or four years. Once a turnout suit gets a hole in it, it is condemned. One rookie had to replace a one-month old suit after a diesel oil spill saturated him.

Fire helmet made of fiber glass, which can withstand several hundred pounds of pressure (similar to having a brick dropped on your head from six stories up). Most helmets have a plastic shield on the front for eye protection and a shorter brim replacing the old style with the long back that dipped around your shoulders and inadvertently forced the hat off your head whenever you looked up.

Gloves made of heavy duty fire-resistant cloth. A pair of gloves lasts about 18 months. Although more flexible than the gloves of 20 years ago, they feature about the same finger-point accuracy as wearing two baseball gloves.

Boots made of heavy Neoprene rubber. They make you feel as if you're walking in deep sand, but it's amazing how fast you move in them when you have to.

Air mask made of clear plastic and rubber, connected to an air bottle carried on the back. This is the firefighter's answer to Darth Vader's breathing apparatus. The air mask and air bottle together weigh almost 40 pounds.

All together, our turnout gear weighs about 66 pounds. It will accommodate temperatures of up to 500 degrees, compared with the canvas turnout suits of just 20 years. It's a feature that recently saved the life of a firefighter in Northern Baltimore.

It was about 2 a.m. when my unit, Rescue 1, was dispatched on the second alarm of a building fire. A hardware store front and an apartment unit on each side and above was "off," our lingo for "burning like hell."

As we pulled up we saw firefighters working individually, yet purposefully, like a colony of proficient ants. The blinding orange and yellow glow silhouetted each man. Ladders pressed against the structure like drawbridges allowing knights to enter a fiery castle. Hoselines slithered about the streets and sidewalks like great snakes trying to get out of the way of the charging firefighters.

As we approached the front of the building to report to the battalion chief, we could see the billowing smoke pouring through open cracks and doors. A problem was developing out front where some handlines were neglected as others were pumped into the ladder pipes. Handlines are hoselines carried into a burning building to get water inside a fire. Ladder pipes are nozzles that spew out large amounts of water from the aerial ladder of hook and ladder companies.

As gases generated by the fire built up inside, we were ordered to ventilate the front of the building. Immediately we removed the iron bars and broke the glass doors and windows behind them. Without hesitation, the air from outside rushed in and combined with the superheated gases. The already-thick smoke inside the hardware store became thicker and blacker. Without handlines readily available, the potential was great for a flashover — the point at which the entire room will burst into flames. We saw what could happen. Still insufficient handlines were available to water down the front of the building. Water with the proper ventilation can prevent a flashover by cooling down the interior. Just then a flame appeared in the distance, far into the smoke. That was all it needed.

Instantly, the rooms flashed over. Fire leaped out the windows and doors, clawing and scratching angrily at the evening stars. Men on the roof jumped back from the edge.

A young firefighter descending a 35-foot ladder made it down halfway before a massive fireball created by the flashover engulfed him. We stared in horror as his figure was engulfed in a multicolored hue. Once the trance was broken we shouted to him to either climb down or go back up the ladder. The seconds passed like entire minutes as we stood watching the motionless figure. Still no water was available to wet him down. Suddenly, he looked to the roof and sprang up the ladder like a cat scurrying up a tree.

The firefighters on the rooftop leaned over and pulled him to safety. Once up on the roof, he was taken down another aerial ladder to a waiting ambulance. They checked him over, but he soon left saying he was okay. With frayed nerves, singed hair and a slightly soiled suit, the young firefighter returned to his engine company. Had he not been wearing all his turnout gear and his mask, he would, no doubt, have been seriously burned if not killed.

Many people consider ladders the most exciting aspect of a big fire. Firefighters also find their share of excitement in them. High rise fires have necessitated longer and longer ladders. There are three types of big ladders: the aerial ladder, with rungs for ascent; the aerial tower with a basket for lifting firefighters or rescuing victims; and the aerial water tower, in Baltimore nicknamed "the Tower of Power," which sends hundreds of gallons of water per minute into a fire. All three ladders will reach a height of 100 feet, or approximately seven stories, when placed at an angle to the building. To charge up an aerial ladder in full turnout gear feels like climbing the 20-foot wall in an "Ironman Competition" with a gorilla on your back!

You remember Bill Welsh's fear in learning to steer both ends of an aerial ladder truck. Imagine having the job of sending the ladder up and aiming where it will make contact with the building, not to mention controlling its impact.

This dilemma became obvious during one of Baltimore's biggest fires.

It was a beautiful spring morning and shoppers were already bustling on the streets. The mid-morning crush of traffic was well underway.

The firefighters at the engine house on Saratoga Street, home of Engine 15 and Engine 23, were busy at their housework. Two men hung from the ledges as they washed the old-style windows. Inside the station, other firefighters mopped and swabbed floors, while pump operators were busy cleaning their apparatus. It certainly seemed like an easy-going, gorgeous day.

Suddenly a large woman with bundles in her arms ran wildly into the engine house screeching that there was smoke all over the street just around the corner from the station. She began hyperventilating and started to wobble. As they sat the mammoth lady in a chair, shopping bags and all, the old choker-tape began chopping off the numbers of a downtown firebox. Firefighters gathered around as the officer of Engine 15 read the numbers. "That's us! Everybody goes! Three hundred block of North Howard Street!"

In full turnout gear, the flagman ran out to halt the traffic as the companies rushed to their apparatus. Seconds later, two engines screamed out of their quarters, with other downtown units from nearby stations following close behind them.

Engines 23 and 15 only had to turn right and drive a half-block to Howard Street to reach the blaze. It was the Albert S. Smyth Company Jewelry Store, a popular, long-time landmark of Howard Street.

Already, thick smoke hung low over the street threatening to hide men and equipment. An orange glow penetrated the upper edges of the gloomy smoke. The chief was the first to realize the seriousness of the blaze. Immediately the call went out for a five-alarm fire. High-pressure heads, a kind of instant hydrant that connected to the high pressure system pipes in the street, were positioned on the sidewalks. Each pressure head provided 250 gallons of water per minute to each of four hoselines. As the high-pressure system was activated, men scattered about with hoses.

Within seconds, an army of firefighters besieged the flaming fortress. In the front and the back of the building, four aerial ladders and between five and ten

24- to 35-foot ground ladders stormed the walls. As aerial ladders mounted skyward, the smoke thickened and banked down to street level, making it almost impossible for firefighters to see the building, even in the bright daylight. The men had to "guess" hose streams into windows or openings. The thick smoke lifted a few inches above the street, revealing rings and jewelry floating down the gutters in the dirty water.

The smoke grew thicker than pitch, threatening all firefighting efforts. Once in awhile, a breeze blew by creating a fleeting hole where one could see the building. This happened once for Truck 2.

As they scanned for a place to put their ladder pipe, just such an opening occurred. Suddenly, frantic yelling came from the open spot and the firefighters searched for its source. There! At one of the open windows, a man leaned out waving his arms and screaming. Gone! The smoke again covered the building and the man.

The officer of Truck 2 anxiously moved the aerial ladder around to line it up within the general area where he thought he had seen the man. A firefighter waited patiently at the base of the ladder ready to dart up and rescue him. "GO!" the officer shouted.

The firefighter climbed the ladder bed with the agility of a mountain goat, counting the rungs in the blackness. He groped for the end of the ladder until he felt the assembly used for the ladder pipe. Then he reached out to the building to feel for the window or the man. Suddenly, the man shouted out in pain. The firefighter leaned forward, reaching for the sound. The smoke began to thin slightly. Then, he saw the man.

When the smoke had re-covered the hole from where they first and last saw him, the man had moved out onto the ledge, ready to jump. But now he wasn't going anywhere — at least not until the aerial ladder was moved. It had pinned him against the window ledge. Amazed, the firefighter shot down the ladder, tore off his mask and yelled to the officer, "Lift the ladder about two feet. You've trapped the victim!" Then he returned to the distraught man.

The victim was finally brought down, very slowly, cursing all the way. Once on the ground, he was taken by ambulance to the hospital for smoke inhalation.

There are three types of instant communication: telephone, telegraph, and "tell-a-fireman." Even before Truck 2 had left the fireground, practically the whole Department had heard about the man that they had pinned against the wall.

Bringing someone down a ladder is a lot like carrying a mattress down your basement steps backwards — maneuvering through a tight space with dead weight and no ability to check what's in front or below you.

Several years ago, Rescue 1 responded on the first alarm to a dwelling fire in the downtown area. The first companies on the scene found the three-story building "fully involved." People hung out the windows, clinging desperately to the sills and screaming to us.

No matter how prepared you think you are, when a firefighter sees someone in this precarious position, the call takes on new urgency. You're not just fighting a fire in a house. You're engaged in a battle of wills — yours and the fire's — as to who will claim that life.

Engine 23 grabbed a hydrant and dropped a 3-inch line to the fireground. They yanked off an 1-1/2-inch hoseline and ran it off their booster tank until the 3-inch hose could be filled with water from the hydrant, thus supplying the pumper. Armed with their hoses, the firefighters charged the enemy.

Truck 2 positioned their rig near the center of the building, directly in front of the fire. While the officer raised the aerial ladder, the firefighters pulled ground ladders from their beds and began the rigorous task of laddering (laying ladders against) the building. Other engine companies advanced to the fire's body.

Throughout the action, people screamed and shouted for help. Assurances were yelled up to them. Rescue 1 rushed to assist with the ladders.

Already a truck man had shot up a 35-foot ground ladder to the third floor. Augie Stern and Fred Ehrlich butted the ladder at the bottom. A woman at one of the windows grew more anxious as she watched the life-savers. She draped her large, bulky body out the open window waving both arms in panic.

As the firefighter on the ladder approached the window and began giving her instructions, without warning she dove out of the window toward him, almost knocking him off the ladder. In total surprise, he instinctively reached for her, managing to grab her right arm. Quickly and painfully, he leg-locked into the ladder to help prevent himself and his "charge" from falling.

The woman's eyes bulged as she dangled in midair underneath the ladder's rungs 25 feet from the ground. The firefighter strained to hold on to her, but he was slowly losing his grip. He couldn't even maneuver around to grab her with his other arm.

At the base of the ladder, Fred and Augie watched in disbelief. The other people had already been rescued. All eyes turned to the dangling duo. Fred let go of the base of the ladder and ran under the woman in a vain attempt to catch her. Augie, too, decided that two catchers would be better than one, and followed suit. They poised themselves underneath her, waiting for that inevitable moment.

Two other firefighters grabbed another ladder and ran it over to the victim. Too late! The firefighter on the ladder holding the woman lost his grip. She plummeted toward the concrete below. The only thing between her and possible death or serious injury was two very frightened firefighters.

As the gravity-drawn mass hurtled earthward, two sets of eyes grew wide, joining the third. Fred and Augie stood in a direct path of the collision. Fortunately, however, the woman hit an awning that projected out from the first floor. She slid off it like a bullet, ricocheting across Fred's upper chest and arms, sending him backwards and finally down onto the ground. As contact with his body broke the woman's fall, the remaining course of her trajectory was propelled toward Augie. Although he stood with arms wide open and received the bulky package, he wasn't positioned firmly. He wobbled backwards and backwards and backwards with her in his arms and at last went down on his back in the middle of the street.

Fred and Augie lay on the ground flabbergasted while the firefighter on the ladder, who witnessed the whole thing, roared with relieved laughter. The woman was fine. She got up and ran down the street, only to return moments later to thank everyone. She asked if the two firefighters were safe and was glad to hear they were. The fire was extinguished and everyone returned to their stations. Fred and Augie? They both asked for the "Extra Strength" Excedrin that night.

Sometimes the most dangerous part of firefighting isn't fighting the fires, it's driving the equipment through city intersections to reach them.

One beautiful Saturday evening as we sat listening to the chatter on a scanner, there was a dispatch for a reported building fire on the east side of town. No one had arrived on the scene yet. We gathered around and waited. Sometimes a firefighter can "sense" that an incident will become serious. Some say it comes after years of experience. Others say it's something in the dispatcher's voice. It's a kind of instinctive knowing that tells you that you'll soon be involved in this incident. The majority of us had that sense this day as we waited for the first arriving company to call in.

We waited for the call we sensed was coming. "Engine 41 . . . we have fire showing." The officer of the engine company called out through the radio he held in his hand. We quickly looked at each other at the watch desk. Our ears perked up as the battalion chief arrived on location, "Battalion Chief 1 . . . we have a three-story building . . . fire showing first and second floor. Battalion Chief 1 will be command post."

We anxiously awaited another update which came quickly. "Battalion Chief 1 . . . give me a second alarm." Captain Goodwin, myself and Fred took off for the Rescue Squad. The emergency vehicle driver (EVD) was already in his seat waiting for us. Rescue 1 was sent on the second alarm along with four other engine companies and two trucks. The station's big bay doors seemed to take forever to roll up. The EVD revved the engine, released the air brake and we went sailing out the door.

The traffic light at Pratt and Howard had turned yellow as Jody Chambers neared the curb to cross. She stopped and thought she heard a siren in the distance. Down the street she saw a large white and orange fire truck turn the corner a block away. She wasn't in a hurry so she decided to wait on the corner until it passed.

Ian McCloud's Mustang didn't slow up very much on I-395 as it became Howard Street downtown. At the section where the speed limit slows to 30 miles per hour, he must have been traveling at 50. He crossed Camden Street and headed for Pratt, racing to beat the yellow light that now appeared hanging at the intersection.

With sirens wailing, air horn blaring and running lights flashing, Rescue 1 peeled down the streets. Fred and I rode in the back of the squad, listening to the radio and visualizing the companies as they relayed their progress. Meanwhile up front in the cab, Captain Goodwin and the EVD could see the intersection ahead. The squad slowed as it approached the red light. The intersection appeared clear except for a young woman who waited on the corner to cross. Behind her stood a large advertising sign announcing the construction of a new building at the site. The EVD scanned both ways as he moved into the intersection. He saw the Mustang a block away and thought the car would see him and stop in time. But he misjudged the Mustang's speed.

As he neared the intersection, the EVD saw the light turn green and pressed the accelerator pedal to the floor. He wanted to gain as much momentum as possible to pull the heavy duty rescue unit down the street. The captain looked to his right and saw the Mustang speeding toward them. "He's not going to stop!" he gasped, preparing for the impact.

Ian McCloud was tired. With his windows up, air conditioner on, and a rock station blaring on his radio, he never even heard the sirens and air horn. He barreled into the intersection.

Jody Chambers' eyes were riveted on the fire truck. She never saw the Mustang fly up the road or run the light. She simply waited to cross the street.

"Watch out!" the captain hollered. Ian's automobile almost made it across the intersection, but the front wench on the rescue, which protruded out three feet, clipped his sports car and sent it sailing around in circles, veering off toward Jody.

In the back of Rescue 1, all we felt was a small thud. We looked out the rear doors and saw that we were pulling over to the left side of the road. "What's going on?" we both asked in unison as we felt the engine shut down.

We jumped out the back door and ran toward the intersection. Cars from all directions sat motionless at the light. We assumed that we had been involved in an accident with one of the vehicles. As we neared the occupants, they pointed in the opposite direction. We stopped and turned back.

Ian McCloud's Mustang had gone out of control after we struck it, spinning in circles toward the sidewalk. Jody Chambers did not see it until the second it struck her. Ian's car compressed against the huge sign before coming to a stop.

As Fred and I neared the corner, only the car was visible. The real horror came in seeing Jody's body convulsing wildly, similar to a fish pulled out of the water and thrown on the dock. She lay unconscious with only a small whimper escaping from her lips.

The captain had already called in the accident, asking for a medic unit to respond. He and the EVD now joined us. The EVD stood in shock as he realized the full impact of the accident. He started muttering something and backed away, wide eyed.

As we checked Jody for broken bones and monitored her breathing, she stilled completely. At first I thought she had died until I checked her pulse. She had a few minor cuts, and her legs were crushed but my main concern, as a former paramedic, was the condition of her neck and head. Fred held her head and we maintained traction until the medics came. Then we placed a neck collar and backboard on her.

Meanwhile the captain checked on Ian McCloud who had left his car and was walking around unhurt.

Once the medic unit came, we assisted them in packaging Jody for transport to University Hospital's trauma center. Police were now on hand directing traffic and the scene that had started out as utter chaos seemed more orderly. The accident investigation unit mapped out the area as some of the fire units that had responded to help us returned to their stations.

The police officer in charge of the investigation talked to each one of us for an account of the incident. Fred and I hadn't seen anything prior to our leaving the back of the unit. The captain wanted the EVD to talk to the police, but couldn't find him, although he had been walking around the area earlier.

He was later spotted coming out of a nearby store mumbling, an apparent victim of shock. The police tried to question him, but weren't very successful.

The captain called for another medic unit to check out the driver. Once they arrived, the paramedics decided to take him to the hospital for observation.

Who was at fault? Jody Chambers could not tell. The last thing she remembered was seeing the fire truck pass by. Ian McCloud just wanted to get through that light as quickly as possible. The EVD, who by law had the right of way, was concentrating on getting to the fire. I can't judge any of these people. All I know is that fate sometimes weaves a jumbled web. People who have never met suddenly find themselves enmeshed in the trials and tribulations of one another.

Jody Chambers survived and was sent to her home in Philadelphia several days later to recuperate. She had two broken legs. Ian McCloud was treated and released the same day having escaped without major injuries. The EVD was given leave for two weeks to recover from shock. To this day he is still haunted by the memories of that intersection. As for the fire . . . yes, it was put out.

———————

When a call comes in to respond to a traffic accident involving fire equipment, your heart jumps up and down like a spooked jackrabbit, your pulse rate skyrockets and your skin seems to melt away with perspiration. You can't get to the scene fast enough, because you know your brother firefighters may have been hurt. Considering the weight and speed of fire and rescue vehicles, injuries to civilians and firefighters can be extremely serious. Many firefighters who die in the line of duty do so in traffic accidents while responding to a call. The most critical injury is most often to the civilian or passenger in a vehicle that failed to yield the right of way to the fire equipment. Such was the case with one of the most spectacular accidents in Baltimore city history.

The Westside Fire Company received an alarm for a building fire during rush hour one morning. Engine 20 and Truck 18 sped through the bay doors to the full-box assignment, followed by their battalion chief.

Meanwhile, George Johnson sped to work. If he was late, he would be fired and his wife would never forgive him. He left a trail of rubber as he rounded the corner, weaving through the slower vehicles, sweating and cursing.

The engine driver expertly maneuvered his massive vehicle through the rush hour traffic. Only a small grassy median separated the Engine and the oncoming vehicles. Still, the operator handled the fire chariot with ease. He approached a red traffic light as the opposite light was turning from yellow to red. The driver let up on the accelerator — just in case. The traffic in front of him had pulled over allowing him to shoot straight through the intersection.

Johnson saw the light turn yellow, but determined not to be late for work, he pressed the gas pedal. He hummed with the radio. His windows were closed, and he couldn't hear the siren's wail as it rapidly closed in on him.

The EVD's eyes filled with terror as he hit the brakes. The officer next to him threw out his arms to break the impact. Johnson's car passed directly into their path.

Engine company 20 slammed into the car, shoving it across the median into the oncoming traffic, where it struck another auto. The three vehicles continued to slide with a deafening crunch of metal into the side of an MTA bus. The heap of twisted steel finally came to rest on the opposite side of the street.

Following behind, Truck 18 and Battalion Chief 7 watched the massacre in disbelief. The chief bellowed into his radio to fire communications to send help. Meanwhile, the firefighters in the other units scrambled to assist their comrades and civilians. It was a gut-wrenching feeling.

Rescue 1, responding from their downtown station, arrived to find stopped traffic, police cars, ambulances, and hundreds of people everywhere. Paramedics triaged the victims as firefighters pulled their comrades from the wreckage. The officer of the Rescue, Captain Bill Goodwin, attempted to assess the situation. More ambulances arrived to replace those carrying away the injured. Every victim had received medical attention except for the driver that ran the light.

Johnson was pinned in his car, unconscious and very near death. Rescue 1 went to work.

It was then that the Hurst tool, or "Jaws," as it is nicknamed because of its massive cutting power, was put into action. Like a giant can-opener, the powerful tool sliced through the windshield and each door post. Charlie Huber, driver of the Rescue, crawled into the backseat and pushed the severed roof up and back. Two engine company men assisted, pulling the car top off from behind.

Captain Goodwin reached down to free Johnson's legs but couldn't. The crew set up a muffler cutter unit and handed it to the captain.

Then something unbelievable happened. A high-ranking officer from the medical division ran up to where the rescue workers were struggling to free the trapped man, yelling "What's going on?! You're taking too much time! What's wrong with you?!" He jumped onto the vehicle, waving his arms violently. "All right! I want some ropes up here now. We're gonna tie them around the victim and pull him out of there! Now let's go!"

The men stood silent, stunned. The medical official had undoubtedly lost his cool. Very calmly, Captain Goodwin, an imposing presence, crawled out of the backseat, looking like a gigantic genie out of a bottle, and coolly appraised the screaming officer. "Get this clown out of here now," he said to the nearby deputy chief. Turning to the medical officer, he said, "I'm in charge of this incident and don't you tell me or my men how to do our work. When we get him free, he's all yours." The medical officer seemed to realize his mistake and meekly turned, climbed off the car, and disappeared into the flurry of activity.

The squad used the muffler cutter to slice through the accelerator pedal that trapped Johnson's leg. Finally, he was freed. Medics carried him to the waiting ambulance and transported him, priority one, to Baltimore's Shock Trauma Center. Later that afternoon, George Johnson was pronounced dead of multiple internal injuries.

Four firefighters and 11 civilians were injured in that four-vehicle crash.

A firefighter spends his career learning how to care for, repair and use his equipment. Almost as soon as he masters it, the equipment becomes obsolete and is replaced. There are additional challenges posed by a new rescue tool. It takes several weeks to train everyone in a company, so there are always periods where some have received the information and others haven't. No matter how well someone explains how to operate a new device, until you've used it the first time in a real emergency, you really don't know what you have.

One amusing incident happened not long after Rescue 1 received its air bags. These bags are used for auto extrication, hazardous material leaks, forcible entry through a door, or lifting a car off a victim. The bags are made of a heavy-duty, rubber-reinforced material that inflates to the size of a pillow when filled with air from air bottles. The air bottle contains a regulator with a supply hose to connect to the air bag. Our unit also contains a "dead man control switch" on the end of the supply hose dividing the hose into two air lines so that two bags can be filled at once. The biggest bag we have is three feet by three feet. That is important information in understanding the next incident, which shows how a lack of communication can happen at any level.

Depressed and alone, a young man decided that his life was not worth living. He had reached his emotional bottom and decided to commit suicide. He climbed the stairwell of an apartment building that stood 20 stories high and perched himself on the parapet, where he contemplated his life and his death. A passer-by, seeing him, ran inside the building to seek help. He found the manager. The manager took the elevator to the penthouse. Stepping onto the roof, his heart stopped as he saw the young man standing motionless, looking down. The assistant manager also followed him to the roof. The manager stopped him with a finger to his lips. "Go back down there and call 911. Hurry!"

Steadman Station houses the largest life net in the city. Whenever a call comes in for a jumper anywhere in Baltimore, companies from Steadman Station are dispatched because we are the only ones trained in erecting it. This is not the typical round net with a red spot in the middle that many people have seen in films. Approximately 25 by 25 feet and supported by poles and ropes, the net is very cumbersome and takes at least four companies of 16 men more than 15 minutes to raise.

Just before this incident, Rescue 1 had received their air bags. We were still training with them when the call came in. "Officer of Rescue 1," the watchman called out over the station intercom, "you've got a phone call at the watch desk. It's communications."

"We've got a jumper," the officer from communications began, "and we're gonna need the net. But the chief wants to use the new air bags. Can you get them together and get up here?" The rescue officer smiled to himself, "You want our air bags for a jumper?" "That's right. The chief wants you to take them over there now." "Okay, but that's not what they're used for."

The companies responded with the air bags and the net. After several minutes running without lights or sirens to avoid startling the victim, everyone arrived on location. Police surrounded the building and kept curious people at bay. The deputy chief came up to greet the rescue officer. "Hello, son. I thought we could use this opportunity to try out the new air bags." The lieutenant paused to explain that the bags were not for jumpers, but decided instead to send one of his men to the back of the wagon to bring the biggest air bag he could find to the chief. "Should we put an 'X' on it, sir?" the lieutenant smiled. The chief looked bewildered when he realized how small they were. "Well these certainly aren't going to work for this," he said. "I guess we'll have to put the net up. Did you bring it with you?" The lieutenant reassured the chief that they had. "Well, it sure is nice to be with someone who thinks ahead," the captain said nodding to the lieutenant. "It's all yours."

The companies moved quickly to erect the massive mesh trampoline. Just as it was almost in place, police psychiatrists and a crisis intervention team coaxed the young man away from the edge of the roof and persuaded him not to jump.

This story shows a rare but potentially fatal lack of communication from the top down. Lucky for the squad, this story had a happy ending.

Sometimes equipment that looks or sounds similar presents its own challenge, especially in the heat of an emergency. This happened once to my friend Fred Ehrlich and I as we served on ambo duty. Fred takes pride in doing good work, and will usually let you know it. This characteristic made the next situation particularly frustrating for Fred, and me!

"Medic 1, respond to an auto accident . . . Russell and Hamburg Streets . . . Acknowledge!" We repeated the address and flipped on the lights and siren, zigzagging through the traffic to reach what was one of the most dangerous intersections in Baltimore. We listened to the engine company already on the scene call in, "Send at least three more medic units. We have a multi-vehicular accident with several victims."

As we approached the tangled masses of metal, it was quite evident that there were serious injuries. One firefighter desperately waved his arm and called us over. "This guy's not breathing!" The man's color told me things were critical. Dodging glass and metal, I climbed through the shattered rear window into the back seat.

The victim was a 50-year-old, heavy-set white man whose limp body laid up against the steering column. The steering wheel had been shoved upward against the dash when his ribs and sternum crashed against it. A seat belt might have protected him had it been used. I looked out the window and scanned the scene for nearby firefighters who could assist, but they were all busy with victims. I could hear the sounds of other arriving units.

I leaned over the seat and pulled the man back so I could begin cardiopulmonary resuscitation (CPR). It was not the most comfortable position, as I had to contort myself to reach over and blow into his mouth while stretching to compress his chest, all while trying to hold his head to keep the airway open.

Fred was busy trying to reach other victims when I yelled to him above the sirens to bring an esophageal airway (EOA). He ran over to the medical bag, searching, until he found an oropharyngeal airway. Shaped like a question mark, this airway keeps the tongue from falling back, forcing the natural airway to close. He reached into the car and handed it to me.

The EOA, on the other hand, is a long tube with a blow-up bubble on one end. It is slid down the esophagus and inflated with 35cc of air to prevent the stomach from aspirating its contents while CPR is being administered. We had only received this new piece of equipment two weeks before this incident. I thought Fred had been versed in its operation. He wasn't.

"NOT THAT ONE!" I shouted, "The esophageal airway!" He obediently took it back and scanned the medical kit again and again and found a larger oropharyngeal. He slipped it to me. I reached for it and again yelled the same thing. I was frantic because I couldn't get adequate oxygen to the man.

As before, he took the airway back and searched again. Finally I screamed, "Come on, give me the EOA!" I learned a valuable lesson that day: Frustration begets violence. Fred looked at me in a way I've never seen him look before. He threw the medical kit in the car and blurted out, "Find it yourself!" Then Fred left to aid the other victims.

Two other firefighters attempted to assist me in reviving the patient. Fred rendered medical attention to a man lying near oil on the roadway.

We counted six people injured and one dead — the man in the car never revived. Approximately two hours after we had returned to our station, Fred and I again received a call to the same address. It was difficult to return to the scene of such frustration. This time there was only a woman standing near the bus stop holding a hub cap. We made the mistake of asking her if she had seen someone hurt. The woman immediately complained that she had been hit in the leg by a hub cap from the accident, and now she was holding it for proof. She had no visible injuries, so we returned to our station house. Finally, we both shook our heads and laughed. Fred has since become well versed on the EOA.

Back in the mid-1970s, EMS (emergency medical service) was an up and coming service. The popular TV show *Emergency* enormously advanced the funding for emergency care in the United States. The Baltimore City Fire Department was no exception. EMT and CRT courses were instituted with intensive hospital training and on-going in-service courses. Piece by piece, units were supplied with new equipment or given supplies to add to their inventories. Among these were intravenous solutions, or IVs.

I was one of the first paramedics to use an IV in the field. It seemed as if everyone was waiting to see who would be first. At that time, we used butterfly needles instead of the catheters we use now.

I assured myself that when the call came, I would do what had to be done. Little did I know it would come within a day of when we received our supplies.

Ulf Karrlson, a 22-year-old Swede who had been working on ships since he was 17 years old, had finally landed his first trip to the United States. A good worker and a virile, young man, he worked right along with the other men on board.

As the cargo to the huge container ship was unloaded, Ulf stepped to his left to ask a question of one of his shipmates. He did not see the large crate swinging toward him. Just as he turned to go back to his position, the crate, moving fairly quickly, struck him in the chest, lifting him up and dropping him down into a 50-foot deep hold on the ship. His scream startled everyone as men scattered toward the hold. There, on the deck below, lay Ulf . . . unconscious.

Firefighter Dan Davis from Engine 23 and I were leaving University Hospital when the call came in for an injured man on board a ship at the Locust Point Marine Terminal. Engine 17 and Truck 19 were also there when we arrived.

The firefighters came running, telling us to bring our EMS "stuff." They explained what had happened to the victim and described his injuries as best they could. As Dan and I reached for the appropriate equipment, the firefighters pulled the stretcher and backboard to the side of the ship.

We climbed up the gangway, which shook crazily as we passed. Crew members led us to the hold. We looked down and saw Ulf's broken body lying on the deck. He was covered with blankets, surrounded by concerned friends. We inched down the steep ladder to the deck below carrying the heavy equipment.

As I approached Ulf, I could see the life draining from him. I took his vitals, and he let out a low moan. His abdomen was hard as a rock from the blood collecting within. He had two broken legs, both at the lower tib-fib region. His clavicle was broken and partially protruding from the right side. Blood seeped from his left ear and one pupil was dilated. His blood pressure was extremely low and dropping rapidly. An IV?

I felt as if the whole world were watching me. Inside I was a case of shattered nerves. But I knew if I were going to help Ulf, I had to get a line in his veins with the drugs that would bring his pressure up and keep his circulatory system from collapsing. Once it collapsed, the only way to get a line into him would be by a Cut-Down, which is something only a hospital can do.

"Dan, hand me a D5W, IV set-up!" I shouted urgently. He responded immediately. I attached the line and bag and prepped Ulf's hand for venipuncture. I felt like a quarterback in a huddle, looking up and seeing a circle of heads watching me.

Slowly, I took a deep breath and penetrated Ulf's hand. Luckily, I had a blood return in the small tube. Quickly I attached the long line and opened the IV while removing the rubber tourniquet from his upper arm. The solution flowed in.

We readied Ulf for transport. Instead of using a backboard, we placed Ulf on an orthopedic (Scoop) stretcher, which disconnects in the middle to literally "scoop up" the patient. This stretcher was then strapped into a Stokes basket, a wire mesh stretcher used to fit through tight spaces. We then placed a collar on his neck and stabilized him. Before we sent him to the upper deck, I monitored his blood pressure. It had only gone up 10 points systolic to 70.

While oxygen flowed to Ulf, the crane that had knocked him into the hold now attached its hooks to the Stokes basket. Painstakingly, it lifted Ulf to the dock alongside the ship. Dan and I hastily made our way up the ladder and down the gangway. We requested a firefighter from Engine 17 to drive to South Baltimore Hospital while we worked on our patient.

On the way, we "red-phoned" to the hospital with Ulf's condition. Doctors and nurses were waiting when we arrived. They worked feverishly to try to elevate his blood pressure. Blood poured into tubes set up from his stomach-tap.

No matter what they did, Ulf's condition continued to deteriorate.

We received another call and had to leave while the emergency room (ER) staff worked on Ulf. Within two hours after the crane had knocked him down into the container hold, he died.

A doctor at the ER called to tell us that we had done a good job. It was a sorry victory. Whenever we lose a patient, especially such a young one, any sense of pride in having done a good job quickly dissipates. We begin to wonder if there was anything else we could have done. We gave our best, but sometimes it's not enough.

The construction crew had their orders to work in a 20-foot-deep hole near a new road site. They readied the equipment as one man strapped on his rope harness and descended. The next worker followed slowly, maneuvering carefully in the cramped space. Without warning, the bottom man went limp and dropped. The second man collapsed and fell directly on top of him. The topside crew sent a third man to investigate. He, too, became unconscious and fell. Their foreman ran to the trailer and called the fire department.

It had been a busy day and Wayne and I felt it would never end. We had darted back and forth across the city more times than I could count, like riders on a mad calliope; as soon as we would return to the station, we were sent out again.

We dropped off our last patient at a southeast hospital, and tried in vain to get back to the station to eat lunch. We listened to the radio chatter, subconsciously dreading the thought of another run.

"Medic 15 . . ." the radio spat, "respond to I-95 and Washington Boulevard . . . job site, a man overcome by a gas leak. Rescue units are responding with you."

Whew. Not us.

We listened with mounting apprehension, however, as we heard Medic 15's urgent plea for more units. Medic 12 was called next, then us, Medic 1.

"Let's go," Wayne said.

We broke through the downtown traffic and headed southwest. It took us almost eight minutes to cross town . . . not bad. An old high school buddy, Jim Boyer, ran to us when we arrived. "Grab all your telemetry equipment and bring it over!" he shouted. "Three men are down. The other medics are working on them now."

It looked like a disaster. None of the other medics had time to get their telemetry or advanced life support equipment (ALS)! They were caught up in simply maintaining basic life support. It was amazing what two extra sets of hands could do.

Upon arriving at the scene, the workers informed Captain Joe Clawson that three men lay in the hole, approximately 20-feet deep. He ordered three men to don air masks and proceed with the rescue.

While the men prepared, Captain Clawson descended the access ladder with only a handlight to a depth of about six feet to assess the situation. Staying a total time of approximately 15 seconds, he ascended the ladder, permitting the prepared firefighters to begin the rescue.

The medics administered a two-man CPR and probed throats with airways and oxygen. They inserted catheters and IVs to help prevent vascular collapse.

A lieutenant gathered information and vital signs for each patient we were treating. He handed it to me. I called in the reports, "Patient 1 . . ." and rattled off the statistics for each victim. The hospital advised defibrillation. We went to work.

At one point, my defibrillator refused to recharge, requiring immense technical skill to fix it — I whacked it.

Looking around, I felt helpless. All the medics and all the advanced technology, and it looked as if we were losing. The agony was beginning to show on the faces of the men as they struggled against hopeless odds.

Other firefighters lugged stretchers across the muddy terrain, bearing long backboards to assist the CPR. Three medic units backed up as close as they could to the scene. Medic 15 went first, slowly loading the patient into the back of the ambo. They sped down the highway as the men in the back continued ALS on their patient.

Medic 12 was next. But the ambulance wouldn't start! Someone started our unit, Medic 1, and gave 12 a hot-shot. They loaded the patient quickly and roared away.

We went last, moving our patient inside as two firefighters jumped in with us. We alternated administering CPR as another firefighter drove our unit.

Captain Clawson stayed behind to supervise the cleanup and to await the health department analysis of the gas.

We admitted our patient to a west side hospital and watched them work on him frantically. Respiratory therapy arrived. They hooked up a respirator, stabilized him and moved him to Intensive Care. He died the next day. The other two men died shortly after their arrival at the other hospitals.

The Health Department report made front page news the next day. The three men had died from "sewer gas."

Among the various tools of the trade are a few that occasionally are used for recreational diversion. Working in the ambulance service forces you to create your own fun, often within the confines of the cab. For example, Wayne and I returned from a hospital on a wintery day. Mounds of gray, two-day-old snow sat on the sidewalks defying the sun.

As we drove down the street we saw a large dog proudly standing on top of one of the mounds as if playing "King of the Mountain." He confidently tore into a bag of trash he had commandeered.

Grinning mischievously, Wayne reached for the microphone and switched it to the PA system. He raised it to his mouth as we passed the dog. "Woof, woof!" he barked out in a pretty good canine imitation. The dog's head jerked up, startled by what probably sounded like the largest dog in the world, and he slid clumsily down the mound of snow and bounded off. He ran so fast we couldn't even see him in our rear mirrors — even if we had been able to stop laughing long enough to keep him in focus.

Wayne has a thing about microphones. Once, while returning from a call and driving through one of the busiest intersections in Baltimore, at Howard and Lexington Streets, he calmly picked up the microphone, placed it discreetly next to his mouth so no one would see it, and sang out a tune from an old cat food commercial.

"Meow, meow, meow, meow . . . meow, meow, meow, meow . . ." he went on and on. He couldn't look at me because I was hysterical and he didn't want to give away his secret to the stunned pedestrians who looked about in amazement, laughing and trying to figure out where the insane jingle was coming from. A block later, he couldn't hold it in any more.

During Halloween it's Trick or Treat. Unfortunately, firefighters can't always give treats. In fact, most of them would prefer a good trick — prank, that is.

One Halloween night several years ago, a fire station in a residential area had received several young trick-or-treaters during the crisp, clear October night. The men kept the big doors and the side door closed to conserve heat. There was little chatter on the radios. No major fires, assists or medic standbys in progress.

After two satisfied children and a parent went out the side door, an alarm came in for a building three blocks away. The engine company mounted up and rolled out the big door with lights and siren. Upon arrival on location, they investigated the premises with another engine and truck company and found it to be a false alarm. With that resolved, they all went back in service, proceeding to their respective stations.

Halloween is one night that requires extra caution when driving. Since many of the costumes make it especially difficult to see the children in the dark, the men on the engine company took their time returning.

As they sat at a red light, they noticed a large group of kids accompanied by some adults, trick-or-treating down the sidewalk. A few words were exchanged between the pump operator and the officer. Smiles leaped upon their faces simultaneously. They advised the two firefighters in the back of their plans.

The lieutenant picked up the public address microphone. As the kids neared them, he placed the mike near his mouth and spouted out a slow, deep, and long "BOOOOO!"

The kids stopped in their tracks. The adults looked around. All of a sudden, the children scattered like bats with their parents in fast pursuit. Within seconds, the street was empty.

The lieutenant and engine crew laughed hysterically as they proceeded back to the station.

Later on that evening the man on watch noticed a glow outside the doors to the engine house. He jumped from his chair to the portal to investigate. To his astonishment, there was a small, brown bag set on fire right in front of the doorway. He flung open the doors and began jumping on the small fire, which by now had totally consumed the paper product. But not the brown product in it!

Someone, possibly from the group scared at the traffic light, had returned a trick with a trick. They had placed dog manure in the bag and set in on fire. The firefighter was not allowed back into the firehouse until he cleaned up. He took off his shoes and scraped them angrily. He called the crew down to the watch desk to explain to them what had happened. They were, of course, most sympathetic. As they wiped the tears of laughter from their eyes, another alarm came in to the same building as earlier. Again, it was a false alarm. Some tricks just aren't that funny.

Then, the pièce de résistance. Guests at a busy hotel across the street kept seeing the curtains open and close at the fire station. A man in one hotel room just happened to have a pair of binoculars with him. As he peered through them, he found himself looking at the very end of another pair of binoculars, from inside the station. We were all called to "Line up!" and given a most eloquent lecture on the just and proper use of fire department equipment.

4 Ambos: Love 'em or Leave 'em

Ambulance duty. Firefighters love it or hate it. Here you see the most devastating human injuries and personal tragedies: the aftermath of gunfights, maimings from power tools, families chopped up in tangled automobiles, toddlers with bodies bruised by human fists.

On ambo, your responsibility is to administer the first medical aid, stabilize the patient, serve as the physician's temporary hands, and deliver the injured person rapidly and safely to hospital care. Until then, that whole life is in *your* hands.

Ambulance duty is also where you deal with the wanton misuse of emergency personnel, answering false calls or non-emergency cases from people looking for everything from free medical taxi service, to an audience for a dramatic display, to simply some company on a lonely evening when no one else will come. I have even heard of paramedics who responded to an emergency call only to find a prostitute looking to showcase her wares.

Unlike fire duty or rescue squad, on ambo, work is completed in minutes; and in the urgency of the moment, there is no time for accepting handshakes. You often miss out on the personal satisfaction that comes when you see a victim walk away healthy and happy, and you rarely know if people recover after you deliver them to the hospital.

But on ambo, you have the thrill of knowing that it is an assignment where personal lifesaving skills are put to the ultimate test and you gain satisfaction from individual effort.

Back in the 1970s when I joined the fire service, firefighters could wear several hats. I was one of several who volunteered for paramedic training, an eight-week intensive program that certified us for ambo duty. Being both a firefighter and a paramedic was possible until the mid-1980's. Today the department only hires certified professional paramedics who do not firefight. Nevertheless, the opportunity to be both gave me experiences I shall never forget.

In Baltimore, a team of two paramedics is assigned to an ambulance to serve one of three shifts. Assignments last until you die or put in for a transfer. When a paramedic takes a vacation or is ill, another firefighter fills in until he returns.

Paramedics are only as good as their teamwork and their ability to support each other, which, like in marriage, is difficult when the pressures are constant and the quarters are tight.

Every paramedic hopes for a partner like Wayne Geldmacher, my partner for 10 years. Wayne is a thorough professional who knows what equipment you want before you ask for it, is as organized as a tax accountant, and is as good spirited as a department store Santa.

You especially hope for a partner who keeps his cool, even when threatened as Wayne once was at knife point for trying to help a man's mother. With arms outstretched, he calmly backed away and talked to the man until the police arrived.

A good ambo partner is also forgiving. Once Wayne and firefighter Brian LaHatte followed a man upstairs to help his wife. Suddenly the man turned and told Wayne he had a bomb in his hands and would blow them both up. Wayne discreetly signaled to Brian to get the police. But Brian didn't hear the man threaten Wayne. Wayne was so calm, Brian thought he was signaling for a stretcher. After several tense minutes, Brian trotted back with the stretcher, wondering why Wayne looked so perturbed. Fortunately, Wayne had already calmed the man only to discover that the bomb threat was a hoax.

The best thing about a good partner is his ability to share the unparalleled joys and unfathomable sorrows of ambo duty. Wayne has been that kind of spiritual and moral support for those of us who know and work with him.

Tragedies come year round, but fatal fires and accidents are especially difficult during the holidays. No matter what festivities a firefighter and his family plan together, some tragic incident will happen while on duty that will take the joy away. This was the case for Wayne and I on New Year's Eve about eight years ago, while we were assigned to Medic Unit 1.

It was a cold night, and the city air carried the distinct smell of furnaces, fireplaces and stoves working overtime.

TURNOUT

That New Year's eve had proven to be a busy one for the medic units in the city. But strangely, at around 2:00 a.m., everything seemed to calm down. Most paramedics took full advantage of the lull and crawled into their bunks. Wayne and I collapsed from the rush of the past few hours, and sleep overtook us quickly.

Meanwhile, only a few blocks away, the Bellini children were awake and playing quietly in their bedroom. Eleven-year-old Jason held up a pack of matches. His little four-year-old brother, Jimmy, watched in awe as Jason struggled to strike the match against the matchbook. Suddenly, the orange flame bounced around the cardboard stick. Quickly, Jason tried to blow out the match before it burned his fingers. He was too late. His reflex flicked away the hot match on the carpeted floor. He haphazardly searched for it but soon gave up. Telling his little brother to go to sleep and not to say anything, he, too, crawled under the covers. Soon they fell asleep.

Wayne and I awoke abruptly when we heard the call come in. We shared quarters with Battalion Chief 5, Engine Company 23, Engine Company 38, Truck Company 2, Rescue Company 1 and Air Flex 1. The apparatus sped off to a house fire southwest of the station. We hurried to the watch desk to monitor any calls that might come in because no one else was in the station except us and the Air Flex unit. The Air Flex unit supplies air bottles, lights, and foam and goes to all working fires.

Within minutes we heard Engine 38 call in that fire and smoke were coming from the dwelling. When Air Flex 1 rolled out, Wayne and I were the only people left in the station. We listened and waited.

"Medic 5 and Medic 1, respond on the fireground . . . " The dispatcher's voice had a sense of urgency, "People are reported trapped."

Nothing is more horrifying than to come face to face with fire and have no place to run. We took off immediately, siren blaring up and down the scale.

As we approached the fireground, men from Truck 13 ran toward us carrying the limp body of an 11-year-old boy. The firefighter holding the child was blowing into his mouth while another raced alongside compressing the child's chest.

We hopped out and ran to meet them, carefully placing the boy's body across the hood of the ambo and taking his vital signs. No respiration or heartbeat!

Meanwhile, the other units carried out a man and woman; Medic 5 had hustled out the little brother. It was a tragic sight — the family of four laying out in front of their flame-torn home as we struggled to save their lives.

We transferred the older boy to the back of our ambo and cut off his burnt clothing. Our first priority was to maintain artificial respiration. Two firefighters continued the cardiopulmonary resuscitation (CPR) while I hooked up the advanced life support (ALS) equipment and Wayne established an intravenous line.

The screen on the heart monitor showed the boy's heart was fibrillating, or as we say, it was acting like a bag of worms. I fired up the monitor and shocked him, causing his body to jerk from the stretcher. I scanned the monitor screen — nothing! Wayne glanced up at me with a heartfelt look. The monitor had gone to asystole, indicating a dying heart. "Continue CPR!" he shouted to the firefighters.

Another firefighter moved into the driver's seat of the ambo and was ready to take off at our signal.

As the firefighters continued CPR, Wayne and I examined the child. Although second and third-degree burns mottled his body, it appeared that it was the smoke that had won the battle for his life. The monitor line was still flat.

As we took instructions over the radio from the physician-in-charge and followed his orders, we fought back the impulse to drop the stabilizing measures and promptly take off for the hospital. But under Maryland protocols, we were bound to try everything possible to stabilize the patient before attempting to move him. After administering the necessary drugs via the IV line, we got our okay. "Hit it!" we shouted to the driver.

Beyond administering CPR and monitoring the boy during transport, our hands were tied. We felt helpless. We wanted to perform a miracle to make the boy revive, but realistically, we could see that the battle was lost. We continued to do our best knowing it was all we could do. His young life was in the Lord's hands.

The Emergency Room team was waiting for us as we arrived at University Hospital. Even before we stopped, the back doors of the ambo were thrust open. We pulled out the stretcher with the boy and charged through the Emergency Room area, literally pushing people out of the way as we rushed through the double doors to the "arrest area."

As the physicians took over, Wayne and I completed our paperwork and waited to hear the fate of our patient. Finally, the team leader came out to tell us that the boy didn't make it. Neither did his parents or his little brother. For the Bellinis, there would be no "Happy New Year!" The same was true for Wayne and me.

———

One constant in ambo work is the likelihood that you'll have to administer cardiopulmonary resuscitation (CPR). The training in this life-sustaining technique is particularly important, and we were taught the techniques using dummies and simulations. Still nothing can prepare you for your first time. One of my earliest experiences was a call to revive a city sheriff who collapsed in a courtroom during a trial. We had *just* received our defibrillator and heart monitors and completed the required training. The sheriff lay motionless on the courtroom floor as I bent over him to begin the CPR. I used an airway and a mask — aware of all the eyes that were on me — and worked as quickly as possible to get oxygen to my patient. There's nothing like demonstrating CPR with new equipment, on a real patient in a real crisis who happens to be a law officer — right in front of the entire legal profession! Fortunately I did everything right, and the sheriff lived.

Giving CPR is strenuous work. Usually, two medics administer the technique to a victim, with one ventilating (administering the puffs of air) while the other compresses the chest, hooks up any needed IVs or the ALS, or calls for additional help.

Former paramedic Charlie Grantland tells of one of the strangest CPR incidents on record. His ambo unit responded to a call for a non-breathing patient. As they sped to the location, they realized it was a familiar address — a doctor's office!

They rushed through the waiting room, startling the patients who were reading magazines. The receptionist opened the door to the examination rooms and pointed the way.

A woman in her sixties lay unconscious on the examination table, limp and not breathing. Charlie checked for a pulse as the doctor related the information he had. No pulse! Charlie ordered Dave Green, the other paramedic, to start oxygen therapy and to get an engine company to the scene for assistance as he began compressions on the lady's chest.

Charlie had turned to ask the doctor a question when he heard a thud from behind him. The doctor had collapsed unconscious on the floor! Fainted, thought Charlie.

Dave knelt down to check on the doctor while still pushing oxygen into the woman.

"Oh, my God," Dave said. "He has no pulse!"

Dave immediately began one-man CPR on the patient-doctor, while Charlie continued to work on the woman. They had their hands full. Sweating, his blood pressure throbbing in his eardrums, Charlie grabbed his radio in one hand while continuing to pump with the other. "Medic 1" he screamed. "Dispatch another paramedic unit for another cardiac arrest . . . and another engine company!"

Finally, help arrived. Charlie and Dave caught their breath while the other medics started intravenous fluids and began drug therapy. The two ambos took their patients to different hospitals so as not to tax either facility with two full-arrests.

After delivering the woman to the hospital, Charlie and Dave collapsed into the chairs in the ambo room, completely exhausted.

Giving CPR for 30 minutes requires as much energy as swimming a butterfly stroke across a pool 25 times with 5-pound weights on each arm. They wiped the perspiration from their foreheads, filled out their paperwork and resupplied their med kits. Then both men sat, eyes closed, waiting.

A nurse approached them. "Call on line two," she said.

It was the other paramedic unit. The doctor had been pronounced DOA.

They replaced their equipment and stretcher in the ambulance and returned to check on the woman's condition. The hospital staff had already begun to clean up the arrest area and put the life support equipment away. Their patient lay on the gurney. She, too, had died.

One of the advantages of the popularity of CPR classes has been that a great many heart attack victims have been helped by bystanders while others called "911." But not every "angel of mercy" can be trusted.

One day, for instance, a very large lady walked down Howard Street with arms full of Christmas packages. She puffed and groaned as she carried the heavy load across the street, packages bobbing with every step. She peered through the boxes to see where she was going. She spotted the curb six feet away but never saw the pothole. Suddenly, packages flew into the air like brightly colored birds as she fell onto the street.

Wayne pulled up to the busy intersection, grabbed his arrest equipment, and with the EMT, pushed his way through the gawking crowd of holiday shoppers.

The fallen shopper lay sprawled in the street surrounded by her many packages. Another woman was kneeling beside her administering CPR while a police officer looked on. The woman identified herself as a doctor while continuing to pump on the woman's chest.

Wayne felt for a pulse and was surprised to find a strong, bounding one. "Hold it!" he shouted to the woman pumping the chest. "Let me take a look," he declared. The woman retreated.

"Miss, can you hear me?" Wayne asked.

The lady's eyes fluttered. "Yes," she muttered weakly.

"Are you okay?"

She opened her eyes. "I'll be fine as long as that woman stops pumping my chest!"

Wayne could not hold back a smile. He turned to speak to the other woman, but she was gone.

They sat the victim up. She explained how she had stumbled and fallen, hitting her head on the asphalt. She had regained consciousness to find herself an unwilling victim of cardiopulmonary resuscitation. Wayne helped her to her feet.

"Wait a minute," she said. "Where's my pocketbook?"

It, too, was gone. The "doctor" administering CPR had picked it up and disappeared into the crowd.

The patient was taken to the hospital, treated for a bump on the head and a sore chest, and released.

It is easy for a firefighter-turned-paramedic to forget which hat he is or, in this case, *isn't*, wearing. A medic's fervor to save a life can instantly combine with the firefighter's courage to face flames, causing him to charge headlong into hell without protective clothing.

The call came in for Medic 1 early in the day shift — a simple sick case in the 700 block of Harlem Avenue, on the west side of Baltimore. Paramedics Ted Belt and Bob McCurdy hit their lights and siren, and their unit wailed out of quarters toward their destination with an ETA (estimated time of arrival) of four minutes.

About the same time, "Mr. Bill," as he was fondly known in the neighborhood, was sound asleep in the middle bedroom of his three-story brick rowhouse. Althea, his wife, went into the kitchen to turn up the gas burners on the stove. It was their way of keeping warm in the December chill. Joey, Mr. Bill's brother, slept in the front room on the sofa. As Althea turned up the burners, her arm brushed against the curtains that hung at the kitchen window, pushing them over the high jet flames. She snuffed the flames out quickly and went back to bed to join Bill. As she dozed off, a spark, unknowingly left smoldering in the curtain material, began to grow.

A block away, Ted and Bob arrived at their call. Each one zipped up his jacket before getting out and heading toward their patient. He was a tall, black man in his sixties who complained of feeling sick for several days. They took his vital signs, checked his medications and asked some questions. With this phase completed, they asked the patient to dress. Then they helped him into the ambulance and began their pre-transport routine.

As they prepped their patient for transport, Bob happened to glance out the back window, "Oh, no!" he hollered. "There's smoke coming from that house,

Ted!" Ted peered out the window as Bob jumped out the side door and called the fire in on the radio. Ted described the scene to the strapped-in patient. "I'll check to see if anyone's in the house," he told the patient. "I'll be right back!"

The patient, who had been very cooperative, said, "Go ahead. I'll be all right."

With that, Ted darted out of the ambo and headed for the house.

Bob saw Ted run toward the house as he talked to dispatch, "Communications, this is Medic 1. We have a dwelling fire in the 600 block of Harlem Avenue. Heavy smoke coming from the second and third floors. Dispatch companies to this location. We'll be standing by with our patient."

As Ted neared the intersection, a man, out of breath, met him. "Hey, call the Fire Department! The house is on fire and there's people in there!"

Ted told the excited man that they had already called the fire in and units were on the way. Then he ran past the people already gathering in front of the burning house to watch the fire. The front door was open as wisps of smoke emerged intermittently. "Is anyone still in there?" Ted urgently called, his adrenalin rushing. As if in unison, several occupants shouted, "YES!"

Ted looked up at the tall, three-story dwelling as smoke billowed from the second and third floor windows. Charging up the steps, he entered the narrow hallway. Another man had already entered the passageway and was busy helping some people out. Ted assisted a man who seemed to be in shock and escorted him from the smoke-laden building to the cool, December air outside and over to the steps next door. The other Samaritan brought out an elderly woman who was screaming that her husband was still inside.

Ted grabbed his portable radio. "This is Medic 1. Send two more medic units and be advised we still have a person trapped."

The urgency in his voice caught the dispatcher, "OK, Medic 1. Two more medic units are being sent. Companies should be there momentarily."

Now he could hear the wail of the sirens in the distance. They still seemed so far away. Bob joined him, and they advanced into the blackened hallway. Smoke grew thicker and deadlier by the moment. Fire had already broken free from the upper floors and seemed to snarl out the windows, snapping at the air for oxygen.

They proceeded cautiously up the staircase. Without any warning, the steps exploded in a ball of fire which blew over their heads as they ducked. They could hear the man above them yelling for help. "Go to the window." Ted called out at the top of his lungs. "Go to the window. Firefighters will be there soon!"

Instead the old man continued yelling and screaming. His cries tore Ted and Bob apart. Ted repeated his command two or three times.

Bob darted out the door and around back to find another way to reach the victim. As he disappeared, a shower of sparks cascaded in front of Ted, as walls and ceiling materials crashed down around him. Ted continued calling to the old man as he backed away, but the smoke became so thick he had to retreat to the outside. Both firefighters had forgotten that as medics they wore no protective clothing.

More companies arrived. Hoses charged and the ladders flew up against the building. Bob came back around front, out of breath. "There's no way in, Ted," he croaked. "This place is gone."

They walked back and leaned against an automobile, watching the firefighters attempt the rescue. They, too, were beaten back by flames until the man inside could be heard no more.

Slowly, Bob and Ted turned and walked back to their medic unit to check on their patient. He was still waiting for them and obviously okay. "We'll be leaving in a few minutes, sir," Bob said.

The battalion chief came over and told them that one of the other medic units would take their patient. He wanted them to stand by and talk to the Fire Investigation Bureau (FIB).

Ted watched the fire. He knew that by now the old man was dead. Still, he kept hearing the agonized cries of the faceless victim. He had tried. Bob had tried. Even the neighbors tried. No one could save the old man. Mr. Bill's body was found on the second floor, two feet from the front window.

Bob and Ted were given departmental commendations for their valiant efforts. Paramedics aren't issued turnout gear in Baltimore City. They had run into the burning building without *any* protection. But on this day, it didn't matter to them. Cries for help were heard and they risked their lives to answer them. They still carry the burden of Mr. Bill today even though they know they gave their best.

Much of a medic's duty in Baltimore involves transporting people and equipment up and down the stairs of three-story rowhouses or high-rise apartments or office buildings with broken-down or non-existent elevators. It's hard work, even for the strongest.

One such situation led to the most embarrassing moment of my career.

It was late summer 1983. Firefighter Tim Reilly was my partner for the night on Medic 1. We had been steadily busy throughout the night.

As the evening progressed, we responded to a call for a sick case on the west side of town. We arrived to see that the house sat high up on a hill, one of a long row of look-a-likes. Cascading down to street level was a never-ending flight of steep, concrete steps. Tim looked at me and said, "I sure hope this patient can walk!" I agreed. "At least we don't have to carry anyone up them!"

A sweet elderly lady answered the door and directed us upstairs. "It's my sister. She's been throwing up for three days now and can't keep anything down. I'm really concerned."

"How old is she?" I inquired. "She's 73," the woman said.

Under Baltimore City Fire Department policy, anyone who is under three or over 60 years of age must go to the hospital regardless of what's wrong, even if the emergency medical services brought by an ambulance are not needed.

We took her vital signs, which were good, and observed her slight size. She wouldn't be too heavy to carry down all those steps. Besides, they were two sweet ladies so we wouldn't mind the extra effort. With vitals okay, we used the stair chair to bring the sick sister down to the first floor of her house. Then we transferred her to the stretcher and carefully carried her outside and down the cement steps to the ambulance. No problem. We secured her in the ambo and put her belongings on the bench seat.

As I worked on the patient, prepping her for transport, Tim went back to the house to assist the elderly sister to our unit. The lady was having trouble finding her keys to lock up the house. I waited for several minutes.

Impatience took over. I peeked out the side door window and saw Tim and the sister fiddling with the lock at the front door of the house. Having made sure my patient was okay, I told her I was going to assist my partner. She nodded.

I put my hand on the ambo door and using the handle for a brace, I stepped out. Just as my left foot neared the ground, the handle broke off, releasing the full weight of my body onto my left ankle. My leg buckled and I very convenient-ly sat down on it. The only problem was that my ankle went one way and my foot went the other! Pain shot through me.

Tim and the lady headed down the steps just in time to see me collapse. Sitting helplessly in the gutter, I could hear the lady laugh as she said to Timmy, "Look at him! He fell out of the ambulance!"

Tim, a normally considerate and very compassionate fellow, didn't just laugh with her. He ROARED! There I was, sitting in the street, in pain, and all I could hear was laughter.

Slowly I pulled myself up. I told them I was a little sore but should be okay. We helped the sister in the back and I climbed in behind her. Finally, we left for the hospital.

My leg began to hurt badly, the kind of hurt where your stomach feels as if it is in your ears. I called to Tim through the back window to the cab, telling him that after we finished we should go to the department infirmary.

When we arrived at the hospital, Tim came around and opened the back doors. The sister stepped out and I followed ... very slowly! We pulled the stretcher out and set it down. As we began to push it toward the emergency room, an excruciating pain stabbed through my left ankle. I knew at that point my leg was broken.

"Tim," I said, "I can't go on anymore." The hospital crew took over, and the patient was delivered as I hobbled back to the unit. When Tim returned, I said, "Let's go right to Mercy Hospital. I think my leg's broken."

He started laughing and joking about it. Firefighters go to Mercy Hospital whenever they are sick or injured, unless it is a matter of life or death and another hospital is closer. We proceeded to Mercy.

Compassionate Timmy joked about my predicament all the way to the hospital — or I should say out of the way. For some reason, we had to ride by our firehouse so he could yell to everyone, "Hey, Bill Hall fell out of the ambo and broke his leg!"

At Mercy I was put in a wheelchair and rolled directly to X-ray. The medical lieutenant arrived to ask questions, with a big smile on his face. He inquired whether I wanted him to call my wife and let her know what had happened. I said, "Yes," relieved not to do it, "but tell her quickly so she doesn't think something terrible happened to me."

Compassion was everywhere. When he called Carol, she burst into laughter. She told me later that all she could see was an ambulance going down the street, the doors opening, and Bill Hall falling out. She just couldn't help it. It sounded so funny, especially the *way* he told her I fell out of the ambo and went "Boom!"

With my leg in a cast and a pair of crutches beside me, I was returned in "my" ambulance to be transported home by Tim and another paramedic. Before we left the hospital, I called Carol to tell her I was being brought home in the ambo. She was still laughing ... two hours later! She even said the girls wanted to stay up to see daddy's leg! Compassion!

Occasionally, Fred Ehrlich was detailed to ambo duty as a driver. Fred has a knack for being nearby whenever you needed him — like Mighty Mouse! When he sits, his feet tap the floor rapidly. He could power a windmill with that nervous energy.

Fred is one of the best drivers in the business, but to be perfectly honest about it, Fred likes ambo duty about as much as I like a root canal without anesthesia. He'd rather be fighting fires. He especially dislikes having to carry

Ladder pipes pour gallons of water into the burning inferno in a vain attempt to halt the fire.

Courtesy of Howard Meile

Courtesy of Jim Atkinson

(**1**) *Water tower attacks the fire from the opposite side of the building.*
(**2**) *Tons of debris from the wall collapse onto the street and apparatus.*

Top: *Typical rescue call. Firefighters attempt to release a child's head caught in the railing.*
Bottom: *Firefighters' compassion isn't limited to the human species. Here a firefighter gives oxygen to a dog overcome by smoke in a house fire.*

Courtesy of Dave Schmitt

Courtesy of Bill Britcher

(1) *Investigators from City, State, and Federal agencies search the wreckage of the "chopper" for clues to determine the cause of the crash.*

(2) *A victim of inner city violence.*

(3) *Members of Rescue 1 scan the accident scene after retrieving victims from the automobile.*

Courtesy of Bill Britcher

Courtesy of Howard Meile

(1) *Fully involved basement fire in a rowhouse.*

(2) *Many house fires begin in the bedroom. Here, firefighters overhaul a bedroom, throwing a burned mattress out of the window.*

(3) *Firefighters battle a smokey building fire downtown.*

(4) *Firefighters prepare to enter wood-frame dwelling to get to the seat of the fire.*

①

Photos 1 through 4 show the sequence of events in a developing fire. This fire flashed over as firefighters were beginning to ventilate.

②

Courtesy of Dave Schmitt

③

④

Courtesy of Dave Schmitt

73

Courtesy of Howard Meile

(1) *Firefighters try to pack a frozen hose back on their pumper.*
(2) *The end result. The hose must be taken back to the station to thaw out and then be repacked.*
(3) *Large upper section of this building begins to fall to the street below. No one was injured.*
(4) *Multi-vehicular collision involving Engine 20.*

Courtesy of Howard Meile

Courtesy of Douglas Wagerman

Courtesy of Bill Britcher

(1) *"A" team poses for photo at rear of Rescue 1.* **Left to right:** *Douglas Wagerman, Bill Hall, Bob Wagner, and Art Cate.*

(2) *The watch desk, the hub of activity at Steadman Station, is manned by firefighter Tim Reilly.*

(3) *Tim Reilly doing what firefighters do best . . . looking for something to eat.*

(4) *Retired firefighter Frank Kelly visits Steadman Station frequently. Here he sits in E-38's office.*

76   Courtesy of Bill Hall

(1) *Firefighters horse around on a 1923 Ahrens-Fox pumper stored at Steadman Station, affectionately known as the "Superhouse."*

(2) *Former captain of Rescue 1, Chief Bill Goodwin, stands next to his first love.*

(3) *Firefighter Fred Ehrlich checks his work schedule.*

(4) *Captain Joe Brocato loves his new assignment on Rescue 1. Here he completes monthly reports.*

(5) *"A" shift poses with two new grills in the kitchen.*

③

Courtesy of Bill Hall

Courtesy of Bill Hall

⑤

④

Courtesy of Bill Hall

Courtesy of Bill Britcher

77

78

1) *Firefighter George "Juicy" Reed reaches for his dress hat while getting ready for semi-annual inspection.*
2) *Lieutenant Steve "Hoot" Gibson works on performance evaluation reports for Rescue 1.* (3) *Firefighter erry Hughes makes an "important" phone call while relaxing in kitchen.* (4) *Long-time partner and friend Vayne Geldmacher poses next to long-time acquaintance, Medic 1.* (5) *Lieutenant Bob Scarpati goes hrough Rescue 1's company files.* (6) *Firefighter Paul Merkler washes down E-38 at Steadman Station.*
7) *Battalion Chief Donald Heinbuch. His greatest fire was the Pigtown Fire. He said it challenged every skill e had been taught.* (8) *Fire blows out the second story of a rowhouse as firefighters begin to advance lines.*
9) *Firefighter "turning out" down the brass pole at Steadman Station.* (10) *Lombard Street side of teadman Fire Station with Rescue 1 poised on ramp.*

Firefighters hose down debris in the aftermath of a spectacular building fire. The new ladder truck on the left was destroyed by a falling wall.

anyone to or from the ambo. Its understandable, considering his short, stocky build. And, after 20 years, he feels it is a job better left to younger men.

His feelings were never so evident as 10 years ago. After two strenuous nights, I should have known something strange would happen because he became so quiet. Usually, he is very boisterous and rowdy, but when Fred is quiet, expect him to be impatient and ornery.

Medic 1 responded to a call for a shooting victim on the seventh floor of a low-income public housing unit that stretched up 11 stories. Fred drove intently, anticipating the action. We had no trouble finding the address; blue flashing lights lit the way. Even as we arrived, more police pulled up. I only hoped the shooting was over.

We gathered up our equipment and loaded it onto the stretcher. Pushing it toward the building, we looked up through the chain link fencing to see police and passers-by gathering on the open seventh floor hallway.

Dadburnit! The elevators were both out of order. Fred muttered under his breath as I pushed the stretcher into the guard booth, then we loaded ourselves with our basics to ascend the urine-stained stairwells. Fred complained the whole time.

The seventh floor appeared to be in a state of chaos. An officer informed us that a young man had been shot in his left leg, possibly two times. We approached the mob cautiously. The fellow was lying on the hallway floor, bleeding from a leg wound, while his mother cradled him in her lap. She sobbed as she rocked him, crying, "My baby's gonna be all right."

I knelt down and checked the boy's responsiveness. It was good. His blood pressure and pulse were fair. He didn't seem to be in any immediate danger. The wounds were made by a single .22 caliber bullet. It had made an entrance and an exit, but was nowhere to be found. He was lucky, the bullet had just missed the femoral artery.

I began to prep him for transport, first the bandage, then the IV of Ringer's lactate solution. He appeared in little distress. I told Fred that I would run down and carry up the stair chair and also set the stretcher at the bottom of the steps. That way, we could carry him down more easily and, when at the first floor, place him on the stretcher and wheel him out. A little less work, but still a long way down and over to the ambo.

Fred stood by with the patient as I left to get the stair chair — seven flights down and seven flights up, just to get the patient and go seven flights down again. Going down is a heck of a lot easier than going up. I pulled the stair chair from the back of the ambo unit and headed back to the building, where I picked up the stretcher at the guard booth.

When I reached the bottom of the steps I couldn't believe my eyes! Coming down the steps before me was Fred, the victim and his mother. The boy was even carrying his own IV bag. All the while, his mother yelled at him, "You heard the man. Walk! Or your leg will stiffen up and you'll have a real problem. Now get movin'. Listen to the man. He knows what he's talking about."

I frowned at Fred and said, "Let's get him on the stretcher. Now!"

He obliged. We transported the young man to the hospital where the leg was bandaged and he was released.

I couldn't believe Fred would do that. His objective was to get the boy down as quickly as possible. He felt it would have taken forever to transport him down seven flights. "But the IV bag, Fred. Why did you make him carry his own IV bag?" I inquired.

"It gave him something to keep his mind on, Bill!"

That was pure Fred.

In the 1960s and 1970s, the Baltimore City Fire Department provided transportation from the hospital's helipad to the Shock Trauma Center of University Hospital. To do this, an ambulance was dispatched to the top of the public parking garage near the hospital where it would meet an incoming helicopter. Usually the estimated time of arrival (ETA) of the helicopter meshed with that of the arriving ambulance. The patient was then transferred from the helicopter to the waiting ambulance which would race through the parking garage and over to the nearby hospital. It sounds complicated, but it was better than driving an ambulance across the city from out in the surrounding counties.

To accomplish this feat of driving skill, the driver was forced to drive up the "down" ramp to the roof because the "up" ramp was not designed for an ambulance to fit through. By the time the ambo reached the top, the driver was not only dizzy but also partially deaf from the echo of the sirens on the concrete walls.

On this particular night, Fred was driving and a little irritable. We had been extremely busy that shift. Neither of us wanted to be on a run to the helipad. First of all, it was keeping us from our street runs. Secondly, Fred had a headache. When Fred has a headache, stand back. He's as much fun as a bathtub full of barracudas.

We received the call to our station, which was only three blocks away, with a given ETA of two minutes. It always amazes me that a helicopter could be as close as two minutes away yet unknown to us. Dispatch insists that is all the warning they receive. Off we went, with lights flashing and siren blaring. We arrived at the garage in less than a minute, only to wait five minutes for the guard on duty to shuffle cars out of the way and raise the gate.

Then we moved across the ground level and began our ascent. In this garage, running up the "down ramp" guaranteed a surprise. Whoops! A car swooped down on us. Siren, horn, lights. It didn't matter. The car came halfway down before it stopped. We sat and waited for the driver to back up so we could continue. The car crept slowly back up the ramp, afraid of hitting the sides.

We were already running late so I left the siren on, trying to force the auto to speed up. "How 'bout turning that thing off?" Fred blurted.

Maybe it was unkind of me, but Fred had been particularly prankish lately, and I couldn't pass up the chance to needle him. I flipped the siren back and forth from "wail" to "yelp." "Nah, Fred. We've got to keep it on so no one will hit us!"

"I'm telling you, Bill. I have a headache. Turn it off or I'll stop the ambo, get out and walk upstairs." Through the open windows, we heard the whoosh, whoosh, whoosh of the chopper blades spinning as it neared the roof.

Suddenly, Fred hit the brakes, put the ambo in park, threw open his door, jumped out, and proceeded to walk down the ramp leaving the ambo and me sitting on the ramp.

The swishing of the blades grew in intensity.

"Fred! Get back in here!" I scolded.

"Are you gonna stop?" he asked.

"Yea, Fred. Come on. They're on the roof!"

He returned to the driver's seat, muttering under his breath. We arrived on the rooftop as the chopper touched down. After assisting the medical team in completing the call, Fred took some aspirin and we returned to our busy street runs.

As I mentioned, Medic 1 was usually called first to transport patients from the helipad to Shock Trauma because we were only two blocks away.

Many times we arrived on the roof to find no helicopter. An ETA of two to four minutes for the helicopter sometimes extended to an hour. Although that was rare, it did happen. Usually the first person to join us on the parking garage roof was a hospital policeman. His job was to man the rooftop CO_2 extinguisher as the chopper landed. It was a token gesture because if the helicopter were to crash on the roof, no one up there would survive.

Next, the trauma team arrived: two nurses and a doctor, sometimes more if there was more than one patient. Often, the group of us sat on the roof swapping medical "war" stories as we waited for the helicopter. Eventually someone would spot the dot in the sky. At night it appeared as a small moving star of light. We would all stand ready as a Bell-Ranger helicopter with two Maryland State Police Troopers and their patient(s) landed.

On this particular night, we awaited the arrival of what Shock Trauma officials dubbed a RTA (road traffic accident) victim, who had massive injuries, including a gaping hole in his chest, and who had suffered a cardiac arrest. As we perched on the slanted wall, we spotted the floodlight of the chopper. Almost in unison, everyone stood and took their positions. The Bell-Ranger moved in and over the large helipad. I often thought how small the roof must look to the pilot. He hovered for a moment as the winds created by the rotating blades caused a maelstrom on the roof. With the soft touch of an artist finishing a portrait, he let the helicopter settle on the pad.

The medical team and our team ran over to the chopper, ducking our heads to avoid decapitation by the rotating blades. The EMT policeman on the helicopter ran around from the right side and opened the left passenger doors. The assistant and I took one end each of the fold-up stretcher with the patient and slowly removed it from the mercy vehicle. We laid it on our ambulance stretcher. A nurse straddled the patient while administering CPR to his chest. The doctor checked the victim over as we all ran over to the ambulance. The whooshing sound of the blades began to die out as the chopper was shut down.

We lifted the patient into the back of the ambulance as medical people worked feverishly. One nurse stripped down the man as another continued CPR. I jumped in the back to assist if needed. My driver sat fast, waiting for the doctor to give the order to transport.

While we worked on the patient, the doctor saw he was losing the battle. The patient's open chest wound made an easy port of call. The doctor used a pair of rib-spreaders to widen the hole. Then he poked his hand into the man's chest cavity, searching for the vital organ. He had to get the pulse back. The surgeon's hand grabbed the heart and he began squeezing it in a rhythmic pattern. The portable scope matched his tempo. The doctor then signaled me to tell the driver to take off. He obeyed immediately.

As we spiraled down the parking garage ramp, holding on at times due to the whirlpool effect, the doctor continued to massage the patient's heart. As his hand began to tire, he saw my apparent interest in the procedure. "Here, do you want to take over?" he questioned. I must have given him a look of "What?" He again asked. "Sure!" I said. "What do you want me to do?" The nurse helped me into a surgical glove.

Have you ever held a balloon full of hot water? That's how the human heart feels. I felt the heart pulsate slightly in my hand. I squeezed it gently and consistently. I just couldn't believe that I was giving open heart massage. It was truly a fascinating experience. I focused on the patient. We knew hope was running out. The heart was not responding. Yet we had to work with the chance that he might make it.

We reached the bottom level and rode into the street, ending up at the ramp we would use to move the patient to the fourth floor operating room. We transferred the patient to a hospital bed and hoped that somehow he might live. But during surgery, the patient died. We cleaned up our equipment and the back of the unit. I could still feel the pulsating heart in my hand, as though I had touched life itself. I felt a curious mixture of sadness and wonder as I signaled "thank you" to the doctor for an experience I would never forget.

Everyday throughout the world, emergency vehicle drivers (EVDs) respond to circumstances which require speed, precision, and common sense. For the number of vehicles in use, their accident rate is low. Considering the fact that they have to weave through heavy traffic, red lights, zig-zagging obstacle courses in every possible stage of repair and still get to their destination within minutes, they fair pretty well. EVDs are professionals. They have to be cautious and alert. It's their livelihood. But no matter how careful they want to be, there is always the unknown element . . . the behavior of other drivers.

One patient had the ride of his life in a Baltimore City ambulance.

A few years back, Firefighter Jim Catterton was detailed to Medic 4 on the west side of Baltimore City. He and paramedic Al Smith had been at a rolling boil all day. Medic 4 is one of the top five units in the city. They are housed with Truck 4, Engine 13, and Battalion Chief 4. In one year, they numbered well over 7,000 runs.

On this particular day, they had a call for a person having a seizure. As they sped to their incident, Jim used caution to assure their safety. Jim is also an Emergency Medical Technician (EMT) which allows him to give advanced first aid to victims, but not at a paramedical level. Any advanced support would be done by the medic.

They arrived at a house to find a tall, black man unconscious and post-ectal. This meant he was coming out of the seizure but was still unresponsive. As his body quivered from the violent tremors, the medic took his vital signs. His blood pressure was pretty high, 260/130.

Al had Jim set up an IV of D5W for him. Jim went to work as he had done many times before. He inserted the needle and catheter into a large, protruding vein in the victim's left arm. As he did so, the man suffered another grand mal or severe seizure. Al lost the vein. The needle popped out allowing a trail of blood to flow freely until the opening could be covered. Nothing could be done until the seizure subsided.

The man wrenched and shook with uncontrollable force, his body saturated with sweat from the violent eruption. Just as suddenly, the seizure stopped and his body began to rest. The bleeding in his arm stopped. Al inserted another needle. Success! Jim helped Al secure the IV to the man's arm to allow the liquid to enter the man's body. They told members of his family they would be right back. They retrieved a wheeled stretcher from the ambo and secured the patient to it. Slowly, they rolled it to the front door. As they started to lift the litter to carry it over the steps to the medic unit, the patient again went into another grand mal seizure. His tremors were so violent that they had to put the litter down and wait for them to subside.

At last it was over. They hurried the patient into the back of the unit. The medic called on the hospital box (EMRC Radio) to Bon Secours Hospital and advised them of their status. Multiple seizures back to back, such as he had, constitute a true emergency because of the strain they exert on the body and heart. "Transport as soon as possible" was the order from the doctor. Al gave a three- to four-minute ETA.

Jim accelerated reasonably as he drove west on Franklin Street. With lights and siren on, he guided the ambulance through the city traffic. Ahead was the intersection of Franklin Street and Fulton Avenue.

At the same time, Carl Woods was driving his green 1962 Chevy Impala north on Fulton Avenue toward the same intersection. The 60-year-old man had been driving for 40 years. But recently he had been involved in several minor fender benders. Fulton Avenue was one way and didn't have much traffic. Carl felt the incentive to go a little faster. He had encountered green lights as he sped north on the two-lane road. As he neared the intersection, he thought he heard a siren. Up ahead in the left lane another car had stopped at a red traffic light.

As the ambo neared the intersection, Jim saw the auto sitting stationary. He also saw the glow of the amber light ahead of him. Next it would be red. He began slowing up, while noting that the car was still sitting, obviously seeing him approach. The light changed to red. Jim was almost at a dead stop.

Carl Woods' auto closed in on the car in the left lane. He also noted that the light ahead had changed to green. Impatience caused him to veer into the right lane around the sitting car which had his full focus. His big gas guzzler rolled onward into the intersection.

Because Jim saw Carl's vehicle coming up behind the standing vehicle, he assumed Carl would stop and the ambo would have a clear shot. The medic unit, with lights flashing and siren wailing, entered the crossing.

Carl's Impala crushed the driver's side of the box (back section of the ambulance) sending the paramedic sailing across the patient and back up again. Jim's head and left side slammed into the door. The gas guzzler kept pushing. The sheer weight and force of the impact shifted the speeding weight of the medic unit. It was too much. The ambulance rolled onto its side, sending the occupants flying. Again it rolled, ending up on its roof. It continued to slide due to the weight of Carl Woods' car pushing against it until the ambo stopped on the corner of a sidewalk. Tires continued spinning as the inhabitants came to rest inside.

Woods' car was crushed in the front and right side as its weight shifted it around after the impact. After the noise had stopped, Carl Woods looked up and shook his head. The total incident had taken about 10 to 15 seconds.

Hanging upside-down, Jim had enough clarity to unhook his seat belt and maneuver around in the cab until he could reach for the microphone. "Medic 4 to communication." Dispatch came back, "Come in Medic 4." Jim continued, "We've been involved in an accident at Franklin and Fulton. We have a patient on board. Dispatch units to our location." The dispatcher could feel the urgency in Jim's voice. Instantly units were sent to the scene.

When they arrived, they found Medic 4 on its back, tires reaching for the sky. Pressed into its side was the green Impala. Its occupant had been able to get out and was walking around. A medic checked him out. The fire company pulled off a hoseline in case of a fire.

In the back of Medic 4, Al had been able to get the patient undone and was working on him when units opened the back doors. Luckily for the patient, he had been strapped to the stretcher. Aside from a few minor cuts and bruises everyone was okay. It was miraculous that no one had been killed. The impact alone could have been lethal.

When the case went to court, Carl Woods was found guilty of failing to yield the right-of-way. When the judge asked him why the accident happened, Woods said, "The ambulance was going too fast."

Nothing aggravates a paramedic more than arriving at the scene of an emergency to find people pretending to need medical attention. Their obviousness gives these impostors away. Whenever we compromise our suspicions and transport such cases to the Emergency Room only to learn it was hoax, we become angry with ourselves.

At the scene of a very minor car accident one man informed me that he hurt his neck and back. I examined him, found everything to be normal, and asked him to describe what happened. With a touch of drama, he provided me with an explicit oral and physical reconstruction of the accident. I was astounded at the extent of the injuries he described. He whipped his head back and forth, snapping his neck repeatedly, to be sure I could visualize how severely he had suffered.

After the performance I was tempted to applaud but instead asked, "Could you show this police officer what happened, just for the record?" He gave a command performance. The officer turned to me with a smile and said sarcastically, "He's really injured, isn't he?" I told the man he could see his family doctor or go to the ER on his own. He was upset. If the fire service gave away "Oscars" or "Emmys" for outstanding performances in attempted public deception, he certainly would have been the "Best Actor" recipient — hands down!

During my years as a paramedic, I was repeatedly impressed at the physical endurance of the Baltimore taxi driver. Although I hardly ever treated or transported an injured taxi driver, his passengers almost always claimed to have "near fatal" injuries requiring emergency transportation.

One woman had been traveling in a cab with her five-year-old son when the cab was involved in a very minor fender-bender, with little damage. When we arrived on the scene, we observed the woman engaged in serious conversation with her son. No sooner did we approach the taxi than the woman began moaning. She advised us that she had sustained neck and back injuries.

I slid sideways into the back seat of the taxi and inquired further about her injuries. She complained that she was experiencing neck and back pain so severe that she was unable to walk. I knew by her response that something was amiss. The small boy clung to his mother and peered at me like a frightened doe. I asked him where he hurt. He didn't respond at first, but after several patient attempts he hesitantly smiled. Each time I directed a question to the boy, his mother tried to answer for him. Before responding to any of my questions, he would wait for her prompting.

With frustration mounting, I asked the boy's mother if she could stand outside the cab for a few moments while I completed my examination of her son. Disgruntled, she nodded in agreement and slowly removed herself from the cab.

Using my very best "Donald Duck" voice, I again directed routine questions at the little boy. "Do you hurt anywhere?" I lisped.

Wide-eyed and attentive, the little boy quickly responded, "No, I don't hurt no where. Mommy said I hurt everywhere, but I don't." I reconfirmed his response and then slid from the taxi's seat to confront the boy's mother. I repeated her son's conversation with me.

I cannot say that mom was pleased with her son's honesty and candor. In her shock and dismay at the sudden turn in events, she forgot her nearly debilitating injuries and began a tirade about our inability to adequately serve the citizens of Baltimore. She continued with a claim that she would be contacting the mayor about our negligent behavior, demanding our badge numbers for her report. During this lengthy outburst of displeasure she was physically demonstrative, flailing her arms, stomping her feet, and gesturing wildly. Suddenly she realized what her performance had cost her. She disgustedly slid back into the cab. My last glance saw her slouched in the seat, with her arms crossed and lower lip protruding at a dramatic angle.

The worst abuse of paramedic time and attention I can remember involved not one or two but a bus-load of phonies. The Metropolitan Transit Authority (MTA) bus driver had negotiated this particular route for years, and knew it like the back of his hand. It turned and traversed through a large section of the city. On this particular rainy day, he drove slowly because of the slick roads. "Good, an easy day," he thought as he viewed the nearly empty seats on the bus.

As he neared one of those turns where the front of the bus seems to meet the back, he faced a slow-moving vehicle. As he stopped, he watched the car go into a slow skid and come to rest gently against his front fender.

The bus driver picked up the radio and notified his dispatcher that the accident was minor and an ambulance was not needed. He did not know that this comment was premature, since the incident had occurred in front of a fully inhabited apartment complex.

The driver inquired if anyone needed medical care. Six of the seven passengers raised their hands. He disgustedly contacted the dispatcher to change his original transmission and request an ambulance.

We received the call at approximately two in the afternoon. Sometime between the call for the ambulance and our arrival on the scene, something peculiar happened. Although the bus driver had obviously not made any more stops, we arrived to find 15 injured persons on board the bus.

Apparently while the driver had been recounting the accident to the police, a passenger had opened the back door, allowing many persons to climb in, occupy the previously empty seats and feign injury. Obviously, these people weren't looking for a place to sit down. They were looking for a way to make some easy money at the expense of the city.

After checking everyone out, we decided to transport two of the "victims" to the hospital for observation. We instructed the other passengers to file claims with the MTA for accidental injuries resulting from the bus collision, and to see their own doctors. Situations like this are contributing factors to paramedic "Burn Out." They cannot be avoided, but they eat away at your self-control.

Burn out is one thing. Having your lights knocked out is another. Nathaniel . . . the name still sends shivers through me.

I encountered Big Nat during my early years in the ambulance service. A unique individual, his physical presence was commanding. This black man stood 6 feet 5 inches tall and weighed approximately 250 pounds. His background was sketchy but acquaintances agreed that he served in the Vietnam war and had been mentally unstable ever since. On our first encounter, he scared the wits out of me.

I was detailed to Medic 4 for a night shift. Being there assured me that I would be suffering for sleep long before the shift was completed.

For the next four nights, I was detailed with a compatible firefighter, which helped to make the shift more tolerable.

As expected we did not fall short of the anticipated volume of calls that night. Immediately after returning to service from a false call, communications notified us of a seizure at North Avenue and Charles Street. We whipped on the lights and siren, and took off for our destination.

As we approached our location, we could see a large crowd which had gathered on the concrete median that divided the wide boulevard. Faces glowed from the revolving light of a police cruiser. The firefighter pulled the ambo right up to the victim, using the vehicle to clear the crowd. Gathering up our equipment we rushed over to the patient.

Our initial assessment of his outward appearance indicated that he probably was experiencing a seizure. White drool flowed from his mouth as he ground his teeth together.

A preliminary exam found no injury or life-threatening conditions. His vital signs were satisfactory except for slightly elevated blood pressure and a pulse which was fast.

After the man had totally relaxed from the body-wracking seizure, I snapped an ammonia capsule and placed it under his nose. The fumes entered his nostrils and he began to stir.

Suddenly, he bolted upright into a sitting position. The crowd backed away en masse. He sat there snorting, spewing mucous and wiping it away with the back of his hand.

I tried communicating with him to measure alertness. Generally, after a seizure, a person is groggy and unable to answer simple questions. I finally obtained his name . . . "Nat." It matched the name stenciled on his worn army jacket, probably a remnant from his years of military service. Our conversation did not progress well. I was unable to get sensible answers to my questions. I decided it would be best to prepare him for transport to the hospital.

The crowd, sensing that little excitement was about to happen, had dwindled to nothing. The police officer who had responded to the call was still available to assist us if needed.

Carefully we helped Nat onto the stretcher and lifted him into the medic unit. As I climbed into the back, Nat passed out again but did not go into a seizure. Everyone took their assigned positions, the firefighter in the driver's seat and I in the back. After being told everything was okay, the police officer saluted as the ambo doors closed and we left.

I indicated to the driver that he could proceed to the hospital. He started down the road as I prepared to complete my paperwork. I sat on the bench seat writing my report while periodically looking up to check Nat. He slept like a baby. I had almost completed my report on what, at this point, seemed to be a routine call.

Suddenly, I heard a long, low growl. My body stiffened, as my eyes traveled to the patient. I heard a louder growl. It was coming from Nat and it wasn't his stomach. My entire body tensed as I observed his arms getting rigid. Very slowly and methodically I slid forward toward the cab window to be closer to the driver in case I needed help.

The growls turned into a roar which filled the back of the ambo and spilled into the front cab. The firefighter slowed and asked what was wrong. I was too puzzled and startled to even answer. Just then, as if in a clip from *King Kong,* the strap across Nat's chest tightened and snapped in half. At that point, I knew I was in *big* trouble.

I bellowed to the firefighter to stop the ambo! He turned in time to observe the patient, who with the eyes like a trapped animal, reared up on the stretcher. Another roar blasted from his throat. "Stop the ambo now!" I hollered. The driver slammed on the brakes, throwing Nat off balance and allowing me to reach the door. In my panic I didn't even think of using the side door.

Sometimes miracles *do* happen and the Lord *is* watching. Throwing open the rear door, I found myself facing a large police van right behind the ambo. The driver had seen our brake lights coming on and off, and decided we might need assistance. As I leaped from the ambo, the officers had already left the police van. "I've got a live one back there," I shouted. Nat was coming out right behind me. As Nat jumped from the ambulance he suddenly stopped. A strap was still attached to his leg and the stretcher. The stretcher had wedged in the door and held him in check.

The police didn't need much to subdue him. They didn't want to get hurt either. Nat was brought under control without any injury.

Because of all of the equipment in the ambulance which could be used as weapons, we all agreed that Nat should be transported to the hospital in the police van. I was greatly relieved. With Nat en route to the hospital for observation, we returned to the station. A message had been transmitted to the EMS lieutenant and we received the orders we already knew were there, "Okay, men. Write another report."

5 Second to None

To many people, the Squad team represents the elite of the fire service. Their knowledge and energy has earned them the reputation of being "the firefighters that firefighters call."

Baltimore has one Rescue Squad unit, a white, box-shaped piece of equipment with the invincible power of a Sherman tank. It serves a population of over 800,000 people. Because of its unique position in Baltimore's Fire Service, the rescue team enjoys the motto: "Rescue 1, Second to None."

The Squad apparatus is manned by three four-man shifts, each consisting of an officer, an EVD, and two firefighters. I've had the pleasure of serving on this remarkable team for the most exciting, fulfilling and downright thrilling six years of my life.

Realistically, the Rescue Squad unit itself is little more than a 17-ton tool chest containing extrication tools for getting people out of cars. These include the Hurst tool, air bags and portapower tools; a variety of saws, air chisels and hand tools; two large fans to pull smoke out and clear hallways after a fire; elevator tools; basic first aid kits; oxygen and airways; and many more.

So what makes the Rescue Squad so special? The strange and awesome calls, from retrieving a child out of a sewer pipe to removing invalids from burning buildings, from prying a pressman from printing press rollers to freeing passengers from an overturned bus. The main thing about the Rescue Squad is that there is no main thing. It is a service designed for the out-of-the-ordinary problem.

Rescue technicians love the unexpected, the bizarre, the challenge. Always new, the job requires imagination, physical strength, technical skill, and powerful equipment all working together in crisis situations that often defy the imagina-

93

tion. Hydraulic tools like "Jaws" or the "O" cutter, similar to a big pair of scissors, present their own element of danger. If mishandled, they can easily maim the victim, you, or others nearby.

The best part of Squad duty is the immediate rewards. After 20 years in firefighting, a simple "thank you" is still meaningful.

Much of Squad duty involves "automotive can opening" — using sophisticated metal cutting tools to sever the roofs of wrecked cars in order to reach the victims and remove them safely.

In the late spring of 1990, we responded to a vehicular accident call in West Baltimore one evening. Speed was the culprit as usual.

The driver of a compact car had raced across town dodging in and out of the night traffic. He did not see the mid-sized car as it approached the intersection ahead. Nor did he see the stop sign as he flew past.

The women in the car saw him coming towards them and shrieked, acutely aware that nothing but a thin sheath of painted metal stood between them and the rapidly approaching 2000-pound torpedo. They had not buckled their seat belts. The meteoric impact completely sheared off the hood of the man's car, hurling it across the wide city street. His head bounced repeatedly against the windshield, as the passenger side of his car folded into a "V."

The other car flipped over several times, violently tossing the three women, as if they were ice cubes in a blender. Around, around and upside down. The man's car careened into it as both cars came to rest 2-feet apart. The women's car lay rocking on its passenger side on the sidewalk, inches from a corner rowhouse.

I was driving Rescue 1 that night. Our sirens shattered the quiet night air as we bounded up Pennsylvania Avenue and cut through the ebony streets. I had been in a deep sleep when the call came in, and as my blurry eyes tried to focus, the evening lights cast false images that drove my foot to the brake out of caution. The siren, air horn and radio chatter threatened to confuse me as I concentrated on the safest route possible, while trying to shake the sleep from my head.

Despite the late hour, dozens of bystanders encircled the intersection. I pulled the wagon as close as possible without nudging people. Lieutenant Gibson hopped out to investigate as I put the wheel chocks down. Doug Wagerman and Art Cate, a rookie, ran to the lieutenant for their instructions.

We categorize civilians on the scene into two types: those that know what they are doing and jump in to help, and those that hang around hoping to see something spectacular that they can't find on late night TV. The latter hinder emergency services and place victims at a greater risk.

The precarious position of the wrecked vehicles posed a serious danger not only to the still-trapped passengers, but to nearby civilians. We could not believe that the police allowed so many people to come so close to the accident site. Five or six civilians had stepped forward to hold up the women's vehicle so it wouldn't topple over, while dozens more stood closely behind to watch them. We literally had to push people out of the way to reach the victims.

The lieutenant called for cribbing — blocks of wood to press under the passenger side to stabilize the auto. Several civilians helped us carry the wood.

As other fire units arrived on the scene to assist, the lieutenant sent me for some air bags to reinforce the cribbing. These are metal-reinforced rubber sacks of various sizes that inflate with air into pillow-shaped cushions that lift and support heavy objects. We shoved them under the sides of the wreck for stabilization. After inflating the bags, I ran back to Rescue 1 for the Hurst tool assembly, or "highway hookup," and started the generator. I passed the tools as needed to the lieutenant, Doug and Art. The deafening rumble of the generator forced some of the wreck-watchers to back away.

Meanwhile, Doug secured a "come-along," a portable jack with a metal rope, from the axle of the overturned vehicle to a nearby police car to ensure that, with all the rocking and rolling, the car didn't fall over the other way.

Lieutenant Gibson used the "O" cutter, or shears, to cut the door posts on the driver's side. A little crimp here and there, and in seconds we were ready to peel back the roof. We anticipated a problem. One victim lay directly in the crease of the roof and the passenger side of the car. If we were not careful, we could cut or pinch her while prying the roof.

Using the utmost caution and moving as slowly as humanly possible, careful not to breathe, sweat or do anything else that would shake or jitter the assembly, we lifted the roof from the car.

Medics worked quickly to remove the man and the two other women to the ambos. They brought over a long wooden backboard and we assisted them in stabilizing the lone patient. Carefully dodging glass and torn metal, they gently lifted her out and carried her to the one remaining ambulance, which took off for University Hospital.

The man suffered the worst of the injuries, and they were minor. The women were listed in good condition and soon released. Just when you think you've seen it all!

People often say that miracles never cease. In the Fire Department, we witness these miracles frequently. Each one strikes us the same way — we shake our heads and wonder at the ways of God or the quirks of destiny. One such incident happened a few years ago just off Interstate 95.

Charlotte Waters was headed home from the market in her mid-sized car. She sang along with her car radio as she cruised through the city streets at the posted speed.

Ralph Morgan, a trucker, had been handling big rigs for nearly 15 years. He specialized in 18-wheelers and maneuvered them like a snake moving through water. When he climbed into the cab, he became part of the rig.

Ralph motored up I-95 from his point of origin in Virginia, traveling well above the speed limit. He watched the traffic in front, behind and on both sides. His CB chattered out warnings of "bears" (police) up ahead. He heeded the advice, yet still he held the pedal to the metal. As he came out of the Fort McHenry Tunnel he sped along well above the accepted speed limit.

Charlotte lived in southeast Baltimore, the port area of the city. Heavy truck traffic was familiar to the residents of this part of town. Every day, hundreds of the lumbering giants checkered the area as they headed to and from the shipping docks. Charlotte, like so many of her neighbors, hardly noticed the truckers. This was her way of life.

As she approached an intersection below I-95, she came to a complete stop at the light. She waited for the light to change, while the rumblings of heavy trucks continued above her on the large interstate.

Meanwhile, Rescue 1 stood in its quarters, having just returned from an elevator emergency. Everyone had resumed their normal routine of housework and in-quarters training.

Back at the intersection, Ralph neared the off-ramp, downshifting to meet the curve at a safe speed. But Ralph was traveling too fast. As he entered the curve, the trailer pushed against the tractor. He pressed down more firmly on the brakes to slow his descent, but was unable to reduce his speed. Contact with the curved concrete wall of the ramp helped slow the rig, but the excessive speed caused Ralph to lose control. Guided by the concrete barrier, the monstrous tractor trailer lifted off the ramp and, like a giant jumbo jet, became airborne and then hurled toward the ground 20 feet below. Charlotte's car sat patiently at the light, directly in the path of Ralph's falling truck. She never knew what hit her.

Rescue 1 responded to the call for a vehicular accident, increasing speed when the arriving units asked for the estimated time of arrival (ETA), an indication of a working rescue. As they approached the accident scene, heads shook in disbelief. No one could live through this!

As the men jumped from their unit and raced over to peer into the wreckage, the on-scene officer in charge (OIC) updated them on the accident and the condition of the victims.

The tractor section of Ralph's rig lay on its side pressed against the asphalt roadway. The trailer lay halfway on top of Charlotte's car, *upside down*! It had landed dead-square on the right half of the automobile, traversing the vehicle from front to back. The driver's side wasn't damaged too badly. However, the impact had shattered all the glass and buckled all the doors.

Passers-by pulled Ralph free, but Charlotte was trapped in the torn and mangled metal which hung inches from her head. She was hysterical.

The lieutenant of Rescue 1 called for the highway hookup. This is a term we use for a block that allows us to use the "Jaws," the extending rams and the "O" cutter simultaneously. One firefighter began cutting the door posts and crimping the roof. The lieutenant and another firefighter used the Hurst tool to pry open Charlotte's door.

Next, they laid the "Jaws" on the hood of the car and attached chains to it, wrapping one chain around the steering wheel and the other over the hood and under the car to the axle. With the "Jaws" in an open position, they began to close them slowly. This pulled the steering wheel away from Charlotte. The rescuers' work completed, they moved out of the way so the paramedics could backboard Charlotte and place a collar on her neck. They inserted an IV of D5W, a sucrose solution, as a precaution.

Slowly, the paramedics pulled Charlotte from her car, as she cried out "thanks" to her rescuers and lifesavers. After stabilizing her, the medics took off for Francis Scott Key Hospital. She would be released later that day. It was a miracle that she lived through that accident. Only the hand of an angel or God Himself kept that truck from crushing her.

Ralph suffered only minor cuts, and he, too, was released that day. Shaking their heads, the rescuers went back into service and waited for another call. Every time that crew sees a tractor trailer, images of the "miracle on I-95" come vividly to mind.

———

Beating the odds and surviving a near fatal accident is only one kind of miracle. Another is surviving the rescue when a damaged building or vehicle cannot be stabilized.

Sarah lived all of her 60 years in the same Southwest Baltimore house where her mother had been raised. Everyone in the neighborhood liked Sarah. Every morning at sunrise she walked her dog. When she returned to her house, her husband, Ron, was at the door to kiss her good-bye and leave for his business five miles away. Sarah would then brew another pot of coffee and wash her breakfast dishes, enjoying the view from the kitchen window as the neighborhood came to life.

One morning, a block away up the inclined street, the driver of a utility truck returned home. He turned off the ignition, stepped from the vehicle and stretched. What a long, dull night, he thought as he went into his house. Bed was a welcome sight.

Two teenagers stood a few houses away and watched him close the door. Then they shot over to his truck, hoping for a joy ride. They knew the driver kept his keys in the truck. But not this day! Frustrated, they climbed back out of the vehicle and slammed the doors. The slam jolted the truck. Slowly, the large mass of metal began rolling backwards . . . right toward Sarah's house. They realized what was happening and ran off.

Sarah sang as she washed the dishes. Her kitchen, at the rear of the house faced a back yard, with a hill protruding up the end of it. As she sang, she glanced up. The truck was steaming backwards down the hill, straight for her; she was mesmerized by it. It crossed the yard and descended on her before she could cry out.

Crash! It slammed into her house, pushing the wall, sink, cabinets, table and Sarah back against the opposite wall. She screamed in disbelief as ceiling and walls rained down upon her with a thundering roar. Finally, the unbearable noise stopped.

Several units were already on the scene when Rescue 1 arrived. The destruction was so total, it seemed as though a missile had torn through the center of the house. Even more surrealistic was seeing the rear end of a truck protruding from the pile of rubble where the first floor had been. I couldn't believe the house was still standing.

A senior officer on location met Captain Goodwin to tell him that neighbors believed Sarah was trapped inside. After conferring about the stability of the remaining structure, we entered the wreckage. The upper floor seemed to rest on top of the truck. Debris covered everything. Just then, a low moan escaped from the rubble. Sarah was alive!

The Squad climbed over broken glass, sharply split boards and chunks of plaster to try to find her. "I see her!" yelled the captain. "She's over here."

He pointed to the area of the kitchen sink. Sarah was pressed between the sink and cabinets on the back wall and the truck in front. There was no way to reach her unless something could be moved. But what? We had to be extremely careful. If we moved the truck first, there was a chance that the second floor would collapse not only on Sarah but all of us. Moving any of the walls inside to reach her might also cause the structure to cave in. Breaking through the wall behind Sarah's back was too risky.

The only option was to slowly and carefully remove each piece of debris. The Squad members cautiously climbed into the strewn wreckage to form a human chain. Inch by inch, piece by piece, we passed fragments of the shattered house outside. The captain talked to Sarah, trying to reassure her of her safety. After about 20 minutes of intense effort, we were able to gingerly slide the refrigerator back, allowing Sarah to collapse slowly next to the sink.

A long, wooden backboard was eased over to us and we placed Sarah's bruised and battered body onto it. The firefighters outside pulled it to them as our patient emerged into daylight. She was free. Listening to the creaking, moaning sounds of what was left of the house, we moved back outside. Next, we assisted in rigging the truck to be pulled away from the building. With a long, deep groan, it lessened its resistance and broke free. The second floor swayed but didn't collapse. The building inspector had been called.

Meanwhile, paramedics worked on stabilizing Sarah. Amazingly, she had suffered little other than bruises and great anxiety. The medics were, however, having some trouble getting her pulse down (a somewhat normal reaction under the circumstances!). After some advanced life support (ALS), they took her to the hospital.

This was a rescue I will never forget. The victim was so near, yet we couldn't rescue her any faster. Had Sarah been cut or bleeding, she might have bled to death. I thanked God for letting her live.

There are tight spots and even tighter spots. Although this next rescue happened in February, had it happened at Christmas time, it probably would have made the newspapers.

In a northeastern port city like Baltimore, February is usually the coldest month of the year. The freezing temperatures make firefighting more hazardous than usual. Water spray from the nozzle can transform a fireman into a human icicle almost instantly. Wind-chill temperatures can plummet into the sub-zero range.

Under such conditions, firefighters earnestly pray that their services will not be needed until the weather warms. On this particular night, we were blessed with a fairly quiet evening. There were a few elevator calls and only a minor auto accident. The heating system in the fire station was hard at work and we had just finished a meal. In fact, we were watching a video movie in the lounge when the call came in.

Only moments earlier, police cars had screeched up McHenry Street chasing Jed Jensen, a small-framed white man, known as a troublemaker. Neighbors spotted him trying to break into a nearby house and called the police with a good description; Jed, in spite of the chilling temperature, was wearing only a lightweight pair of pants and sneakers. Within minutes, police found him climbing a fire escape to a set of rowhouses. They chased him on foot, pursuing the agile young man across the rooftops. Suddenly Jed disappeared! They were flabbergasted.

Downstairs in their second floor bedroom, Mable and Ed Murray were reading a ghost story to their two visiting grandchildren. When they heard the police sirens, they paused to look out the window wondering what brought the police to the area. After a few minutes of speculation, they went back to reading.

While grandma read, grandpa made scary sounds to increase the drama of the story. The children weren't scared and looked inquiringly at grandpa. Suddenly, a brushing and scratching sound came from behind the wall. Eyes made contact, and the kids sprang into grandma's lap. Grandpa carefully approached the closed-in fireplace in the wall and listened intently.

"Help! Help! I'm stuck in the fireplace!" came a voice. Grandpa couldn't believe his ears. He stepped closer. After a doubtful look at grandma and the kids, and wondering for a moment if he was being taped by *Candid Camera,* he inhaled and asked, "Is someone there?" The voice answered, "Yes. I'm stuck in your fireplace." Grandpa suddenly realized that this man might be the reason why the police were in the neighborhood. Running to the window, he called out to the police below. Grandma ran downstairs to let the officers in.

By radio, the police informed those on the roof that the suspect appeared to be trapped in the chimney. Scouring the roof, they found an uncovered chimney pipe hole. As they shined a flashlight inside, they could see Jed, the neighborhood troublemaker, sheepishly looking up at them. His arms were above his head. Several of the officers on the roof came over to look at the "victim," only to return smiling.

The rescue assignment consisted of Rescue 1, a ladder truck, an engine company and an ambulance. It looked like mayhem when we arrived. The engine and truck were already on the scene and police squad cars were parked everywhere, their rotating blue lights dancing on the walls and streets.

Lieutenant "Hoot" Gibson, the officer on Rescue 1, grabbed a handlight to assess the situation. As the rest of us approached, he turned with a smile on his face, "He's a good ways down there. Get some hand tools and a rope. Meet me on the second floor."

There were several dangers in trying to reach the would-be cat burglar. If he fell further, his chest might be compressed and prevent him from breathing. If we cut through the wall we might easily cut through him. And the temperatures were so low that he could suffer from exposure if the rescue took more than a couple hours. We retrieved the tools and advanced upstairs.

When we entered the bedroom, numerous firefighters and police were trying to find the exact location of Jed. We could hear him calling through the wall. Awestruck, the grandchildren watched every move of the uniformed strangers in their bedroom.

Despite the seriousness of the moment, I found myself struggling to contain a smile. Lieutenant Gibson came over to us and asked, "Does anyone have a Santa's cap?" The look on his face told us immediately that if we had said "yes" he would have used it.

Cautiously, we began to probe the wall with tools, searching for a weak spot. Suddenly, someone yelled from the roof for Lieutenant Gibson to come up. He hurried up to the rooftop. Moments later, the lieutenant called for us to bring up the rope. Jed's upstretched arms afforded a unique rescue opportunity. Jed could use his hands to grasp a rope and we would pull him out of the chimney, if we could move quickly before his hands numbed.

The truck company raised their aerial ladder to the front of the house about three feet above the roof line. Jed grabbed the rope for dear life as we formed a line. Then, with great effort, police and firefighters pulled slowly. Inch by inch he was raised until he cleared the edge of the chimney. Bruised and torn, and a few nerves shattered, Jed collapsed on the roof. A medic checked him out. He would recover. Jed's only comment was that it sure felt good to breathe deeply.

When he caught his breath, we secured him in a Stokes basket and slowly lowered him down the ladder to the waiting crowd and the police. As the medics put him in the back of the ambulance, police questioned him left and right until the medic told them, "No further questions until we reach the hospital."

When we finally finished securing our equipment on the wagon, the lieutenant thanked us for a job well done adding, "I just wish I'd had a Santa cap."

———

Some rescue calls are so unusual that they would defy the imagination of the best Hollywood writers. Because of the Squad's versatility, it is called upon to extricate human beings from the most unusual predicaments (when all other efforts have failed).

Some of these calls take us in very private places, such as the bathroom.

"I'm going up to wash, hon," Bessy told her husband. She waddled up the stairs to the second floor, pausing at the top to catch her breath.

Because of her very large size, she avoided climbing in and out of the bathtub for fear of slipping. Instead, she stripped and used a washcloth to sponge bathe while standing on a rug in front of the sink.

On this particular evening, she was stricken with a virus. As she attempted to towel off, she doubled over with cramps and diarrhea. Her skin still wet, she darted to the toilet. As she sat on the seat, her wet buttocks slid on the smooth surface and she found herself wedged between the toilet and the nearby wall.

That's when we were called.

Her elderly husband met the teams from Rescue 1 and an ambo unit on the porch. Before we reached the top of the steps we caught the odor. There was no mistaking what we smelled.

The woman wasn't hurt — just stuck! And, she had been splattered with her own excrement!

The paramedics examined her as best they could. She was obviously mortified, but her vital signs were healthy and she had not suffered any apparent injuries. The medics quickly turned the job over to us and retreated. We unsuccessfully attempted to pull her out. Then we oiled down her body to slide her out, but this, too, failed. The officer finally told one of the men to shut off the water to the house and flush the pipes.

Next, we removed the bolts from the toilet and moved the entire unit. We smiled at the lady through our paper masks as we assisted her in getting up. The medics wrapped her up and checked her out again. We put our things back together and went back in service.

In a rowhouse on the northeast side of the city, a young man prepared for his evening shower. He turned on the faucets and set out his towels and pajamas. Then he stepped into the tub and adjusted the water until it was just right. Cupping the soap, he began to lather himself. The soap slipped from his hands and danced around the tub. The young man bent over, soap running into his eyes, and blindly fished around the tub for the missing bar. Unfortunately, his foot found it before his hand and he became airborne, his feet pointing toward the ceiling as he splashed down into the tub on his stomach. He lay silent for a moment, stunned. Then he realized something was wrong.

He couldn't move his foot. His toe had found the drain and was stuck!

"Babe!" he screamed to his wife, "Call 911!"

It was a pitiful sight. The young man looked up at us trying desperately to maintain his dignity.

"My big toe's stuck, man! I can't get it out! And don't laugh!"

Although we are professionals, we had a hard time resisting the compulsion to howl. Bob Wagner, who was acting lieutenant on our shift, turned to the man's wife and, with a perfectly stone-like face, said, "Ma'am, would you happen to have any dishwashing liquid?"

She looked puzzled, but went to the kitchen to retrieve it. Bob bent over the tub and squeezed a generous amount of the liquid around the big toe. He knelt down and began to massage the stuck appendage. The young man watched the entire procedure from between his legs. His wife stood open-mouthed, struck silent by embarrassment and bewilderment.

Bob began wiggling the toe back and forth while sliding it up and down. With one tug he pulled hard and out popped the swollen toe.

"Thank you! Thank you!," the young man babbled. As we left, I looked at Bob and said, "There's just one thing I don't understand about this whole incident."

"What's that?" he asked.

"Why'd they call the fire department . . . when they could have called a toe truck?"

What is a typical night on Rescue 1? There is no such thing; each night is different from every other night. We do invariably become involved in the type of action that draws the interest of TV news crews and filmmakers. Not too long ago, a movie crew arranged to ride with us for two nights. We looked forward to it with a curious combination of personal pride and resistance. For some reason, they went to Boston instead and thus missed one of Rescue 1's busiest nights.

One by one that night, the members of the evening shift reported to the firehouse. Everyone on the Rescue Squad arrived by 4:30 p.m. In the kitchen, several men prepared a large roast beef for the evening meal. As it cooked, the smells stretched out the minutes into what seemed like days. We salivated hungrily but dinner would not be ready until 7:00 p.m.

At 6:45 p.m., just as our roast was pulled from the oven, a call came in for a vacant dwelling fire on Washington Boulevard. Because it wasn't our first-alarm district, Rescue 1 didn't respond; however, we monitored the call on our portable radio, anticipating that the next call would be for us. The fire began to spread to the two adjoining houses. The battalion chief called for a second alarm. That was us!

Most of the companies were already there when we arrived, their ladders positioned around the dwellings. We took our tools to the rear and climbed up to the roof of a side house. Entering a broken window we opened sections of the wall structure to check for smoke and fire extension.

Satisfied that there was only minor smoke damage, we retreated to the rear roof to assist with the handlines. Controlling the fire was difficult because of what we call the fire load — endless mounds of trash and old junk which filled the vacant house.

The fire extended out from the house on the right. Companies shifted their lines to halt the advancing wave of orange flames. The humid air held the smoke low, making it necessary for us to use masks.

Finally, after almost two hours of battling the persistent blaze, the enemy was defeated. A few firefighters received cuts and sprains, but all in all, we were in good condition. Our empty stomachs reminded us that we had not eaten. We returned to the station and cleaned up.

Our bellies could be heard echoing as we walked into the kitchen at 9:30 p.m. The roast beef we had so longed to savor was still waiting! Some of us ate our feast without reheating it! Feeling full and satisfied, we cleaned up the kitchen and sat back to watch the 11 o'clock TV news. For those who did not have watch duty, it was bedtime.

At 12:30 a.m., Rescue 1 was special-called on a firebox on the west side of town to help open a roof. The battalion chief met us and sent us to scope out the situation and report back.

We climbed up a 35-foot ladder onto the roof of the dwelling next door, quickly noticing that the roof structure was concave with several large holes already appearing.

We attempted to cut through the roof to assess the damage, but the saw's pull-cord broke off while starting it. So we manually pulled away sections of the roof using pike holes and axes. For any would-be body builder, this is back-busting work, even if you're not in full gear. A handline was brought up the ladder to hit hot spots and other areas as we pulled them open.

It took some persistence, a mountain of muscle, and an ocean of faith that the roof would not collapse under us, but within an hour, the fire was finally out. While standing on the roof waiting to get the okay to return to quarters, we felt the exhaustion of the night catch up with us. Every muscle in our backs screamed for rest. Had we closed our eyes, we would have fallen asleep standing up!

I can't remember the drive back to the station. It was as if we put the unit on "automatic pilot." We made sure that our equipment was ready for another run, then crashed into our bunks falling right to sleep. But only for a short time.

At 3:20 a.m., we turned out for an accident at Interstate 95 and Caton

Avenue. The call came in for Rescue 1 to assist Medic 9. When we arrived on the scene, there appeared to be only one vehicle involved. Both City and State Police, were busy directing interstate traffic and investigating the accident.

Wayne was on Medic 9. He came over to us shaking his head. "We think they're both trapped under the car. They're dead. We need you to get them out."

I could tell Wayne had been affected by what he saw. We approached the car from the rear. The two bodies of a young black couple lay motionless on the ground in distorted postures. Their extensive physical injuries were obvious. Already, the white chalk outlined their final resting place.

Looking under the back of the auto, it appeared that the young woman's foot was somehow pulled up and under the axle. Her husband wasn't trapped. We put the car in neutral and several of us pushed forward slowly, while Bob and the Captain Goodwin squatted and watched the progress. The woman's foot limply plopped on the ground, freeing her lifeless body. We stood back and listened to the conversations as the medical examiner bagged the bodies and hauled them away to his office downtown.

Thirty feet away sat a car with five elderly people. They were upset and rightly so. The investigators told us that their car had a flat and they were having difficulty fixing it. The young couple pulled over and got out of their car to assist the older people.

Seemingly out of nowhere, a car came speeding down I-95 and struck the couple, hurling them into and under the back of their own vehicle. It happened so fast that no one saw who or what did it. The killer got away. The woman's shoe was found on Caton Avenue, which ran under that section of I-95.

As we scanned the area a final time, I noticed a baby seat in the back of the couple's car. My stomach ached as I thought of the baby that was now an orphan. While walking away, I noticed their license plate. Around it was the slogan, "Smile — God loves you!"

We returned to the station at 4:30 a.m. It had been a long, debilitating evening. Maybe it would have made great "copy" or screen footage for some up-and-coming producer. But for us in the world of reality, it was another night we would rather not remember.

Most, but not all, calls are of a serious nature. Amusing incidents surely helped to relieve the stress we so frequently felt.

A fire call had come in from a senior citizen's apartment house. Very quickly, the first-alarm units extinguished the bulk of the fire although enormous amounts of thick smoke extended not only to the fire floor but to several stories above. Second-alarm units were sent separately to assist in the evacuation of these floors. Rescue 1 was assigned one floor. Fred was on duty.

Arriving on the floor, Rescue 1 personnel must have looked and sounded like Darth Vader with the hissing and exhaling of air from their air masks. They proceeded down the smoke-filled hallway, knocking on doors to evacuate any remaining residents.

A weak cry of help escaped from one apartment. Fred's pulse jumped. His breathing intensified. "Someone's in there!" he cried.

Using his Halligan tool, he popped the door open. A frail, little old lady cowered near the floor, coughing convulsively and groping to find her way out of her smoke-laden apartment.

Fred crouched next to her and tried to reassure her that she would be outside very soon. Then he did something he would soon regret. He took off his facemask. Pushing it toward her face, they entered the hallway.

Her gasping and coughing stopped somewhat as the cool, fresh air from the air mask flooded her hot, sooty face. Fred, on the other hand, was now coughing heavily. So heavily, that he reached to take the mask away from the lady to get some fresh air for himself.

As the poet once said, "Hell hath no fury like a woman scorned," and as far as she was concerned, he was taking back his gift of life. I guarantee that poor Fred had never been in a situation like this before. She would *not* give back his air mask!

Coughing and gagging, Fred tried to pry the mask from the lady, who sucked up the air quickly. She wouldn't consider sharing it! Each time he tried she would beat him away. Desperate now, he grabbed her and told her to follow his example and crawl on her hands and knees, close to the floor. Slowly, at a snail's pace, they proceeded into the darkened tunnel of the hallway.

By now, other firefighters had reached the crawling duo and assisted them to the stairwell. After reaching the lobby area, Fred reached for the mask, but the lady slapped him. The other firefighters reassured her that it was okay to take it off. Reluctantly, she did. As she was led away to be checked over by the medics, she turned and gave Fred a sweet, innocent smile. As for Fred, all he was heard to say was, "Hummmph!"

Fred had another encounter with an air mask and a senior citizen. This time, he had a helper, Charlie Huber. The call came in for a building fire in North Baltimore. When the second alarm was sounded, Rescue 1 automatically responded.

It was a 20-story apartment building. The fire was on the fourth floor, but smoke had penetrated the defenses of the fire-resistive building and climbed up its shafts, stairwells and vents. Additional units were called to help with evacuation, as the fire jumped quickly to a fourth alarm. Hundreds of terrified residents flooded the stairwells seeking relief from the overpowering plumes of smoke as fire alarms blared in the background.

Chaos filled the lobby as firefighters dodged residents and on-lookers to reach the battle zone. Women sobbed and men stood staring, hopelessly lost in frantic thoughts about destroyed belongings. Their homes were under siege.

Fred and Charlie went up to the sixteenth floor to check for occupants, smoke penetration and fire spread. They found mists of smoke hanging like fog in the long hallway. By bending over, they could see fairly well. They proceeded down the passageway, checking the doors to all the apartments. At the next-to-the-last door they found a tiny, 70-year-old man huddled near his living room window.

As they rushed over to him, Charlie took off his facemask and held it up to the gentlemen. At first the man seemed frightened of the mask, but he put it on and soon grew accustomed to the cool air. Valiantly, Fred told Charlie that he would take off his air pack and put the whole unit on the man. Charlie gave the thumbs-up sign.

Fred struggled to get the bulky unit off as Charlie watched, all the while feeding the man fresh air. They explained the operation of the mask to the elderly man, who responded, "Okeedokee."

They placed the oxygen unit on the old man's back and positioned the facemask, then they helped him up. They proceeded out into the hallway, where the deafening bell from the apartment building's alarm system was still clanking. The old man, hunched over from the weight of the 40-pound air unit, nevertheless walked surely as they descended single file down the stairwell to the lobby. They kept a firm grip on the old man who walked between them. The last thing they wanted was to have him wander off at one of the landings and become lost in the dense smoke.

Finally, they arrived at the safety of the first floor.

Charlie let go of the old man to talk with the medics while Fred stayed with him and waited for Charlie to come back. The old man was still wearing the air unit. Suddenly, someone called for Fred to check out a patient who had just passed out across the lobby. He let go of the man and darted across the floor.

For a minute the old man remained standing, a bent-over figure with a heavy air pack on his back and a facemask covering his identity. Then, he stiffened and fell backwards down to the floor.

Those who witnessed it couldn't help but laugh. It looked comical. However, medics ran right over to assist him. He mumbled that he was okay and to remove that darned contraption.

Meanwhile, Fred and Charlie whistled and looked up and around, while mingling with the other firefighters and the crowd.

———————

Another embarrassing moment came early one morning in the winter of 1989. It was about 3:00 a.m. I was on Rescue 1 preparing to return from a fire on the West Side. The fire was easily under control, but we had worked feverishly.

As we prepared to return to the station, the radio blared out a report of another building fire — an old downtown furniture store. Since it was in our first-alarm district, we were dispatched to the scene. Minutes later, Engine 7 bellowed out over the airways, "Engine 7, Urgent! We have a four-story building, heavy fire and smoke showing!"

In the back of the rescue, still wearing our turnout gear, Bob Wagner and I scrambled to put our air packs on as our adrenalin pumped madly. We strained to see out the rear windows where a distinctive glow filled the sky, indicating a big fire!

We jumped out and approached Lieutenant Bob Scarpati, our detailed officer. "Quick! Get a line off Engine 7," he shouted over the noise of the trucks. We hurried to Engine 7 where their pump operator passed us a 2-1/2-inch hoseline. We pulled off what we needed and waited for water. Fire billowed over our heads as dark smoke enveloped us. Water takes a few seconds to travel down a 150-foot hoseline. In the heat of the moment, it seemed to take forever. Finally, the water filled our hoseline.

With our air packs on our backs but without air masks, we tried to enter the first floor of the old furniture building. We were pushed back by the smoke. We put on our masks and again began our advance. Crouching low enough to crawl, we entered the fire building again. Instantly, we were swallowed up by a mass of hot smoke and gases.

A smokey black void makes you feel uncertain, even though you try not to think about it. It's like groping in blindness. You can't see a thing; but you know there is something ahead of you. Then you make out a familiar sight. The orange glow of the fire ahead is waiting for you.

Charlie Huber and Lieutenant Scarpati had taken tools and gone to assist another company in an area opposite ours, and help them with the heavy hoselines. Other companies moved in as the second and third alarms sounded. The inferno was taking its toll. We finally advanced enough to launch an attack at the seat of the fire, which enveloped most of the first floor. Finally the fire slowed its advance and began to quiet. At last, we were winning.

With our work done, we took a well-deserved break. Lethargically, we moved to the fresh air outside. Just then someone yelled, "There's people on the third floor. They may be vagrants. Get some men up there to search!"

Bob and I and several other firefighters scrambled up the ladders. We found old mattresses and makeshift beds cluttering the third floor, but we found no people.

The panic over, we returned to the first floor and met with Lieutenant Scarpati and Charlie. As firefighters and investigators probed through the building and rubble, we headed to the basement to search for the fire's possible cause and to check on hot spots and fire extension.

As we moved through the debris, Lieutenant Scarpati cried out, "We've got a victim!"

We hustled to where he knelt over the body of an elderly man. Bob felt for a pulse. None. I lifted him from under his arms and Bob lifted his legs. Straining under the weight of our equipment, we pulled and tugged the man's body up the set of 14 steps toward the landing. We called for help. Other firefighters darted over. What happened next was beyond belief. As we struggled to the top stair, a firefighter walked over and calmly said, "We already know he's there. FIB (Fire Investigation Bureau) wants to leave him there so they can get pictures and mark him. You've got to put him back." Exhausted, we began to protest — the fire had been hot, but now our temperatures began to rise.

At that point, a captain came over and barked, "Put the body back, *right* where you found it. Now!"

We carried the body down the narrow basement steps back to where it lay earlier. Eventually, we got the body as close to the same position as we had found it. Throughout the rest of the evening we were known as the Rescue Squad that saved dead people.

Rescue work is often as sad as it is exciting, rewarding, and frustrating. Sometimes you feel as though you have lost someone you knew or loved.

I remember one rescue in particular of a young girl and her shiny red Mercedes convertible. It had sparkled like a ruby in the bright sunshine. Maria Coslo's father stood on the steps with his arm around his daughter, bursting with pride. He had given his baby what she wanted for her eighteenth birthday. It would also serve as a graduation present. Maria couldn't believe her eyes. He handed her the keys. She grabbed them in one hand and her boyfriend Mark's hand in the other. The young graduate jumped in the driver's seat and laid her head back, laughing with excitement.

"Start it up," Mark said, "and hear how it sounds. Let's take it for a spin." Maria obliged. She revved the engine. Mom and Dad waved and yelled "Be careful!" as the duo took off for a test drive.

The firefighters of Rescue 1 had already been on duty for about five hours that night. The evening had been rather dull. They had responded to a stuck elevator in the public housing high rise and a minor accident. Bob Wagner and Charlie Huber chatted and tried to put the new lieutenant, Mitchell Fisher, at ease. He was still fairly new in the Fire Department. Fisher had only a little over five years on the job. He came to Rescue 1 from Truck 5 on the East Side. With them also sat a detailed firefighter from another company.

Back in the Mercedes, Maria and Mark drove through town, went to dinner, and went to a movie before they decided to ride around. Once in awhile someone behind them at a light would have to blow their horn to stop them from kissing so they could move on! They were in a teenager's heaven.

At a light on Perring Parkway Maria revved the engine. The light changed to green. Maria left rubber on the road as she sped off so fast that their heads whipped back. She laughed hard until she saw the blue police light behind her and heard his siren.

Panic struck her. She was overwhelmed with fear of disappointing her family. If she could escape the police, she thought they would never know. She accelerated. Mark encouraged her as he kept looking back at the police. They turned a corner and thought they lost him. But when she wound up back on Perring Parkway, there he was again. She floored the gas pedal, not noticing the approaching curve. Her new car was thrown into the guardrail, sending it up on two wheels and riding there until the excessive speed forced the vehicle off the road. As it flew sideways, the car was hurled into a bridge abutment, causing it to flip over several times and land on its roof.

The call came in to the watch desk for Rescue 1 to respond to Perring Parkway as a non-emergency for a vehicular accident. This was very unusual. Lieutenant Fisher was understandably excited; this was one of his first runs on a completely unique apparatus. Rescue 1 took off at a quick, steady pace without lights or siren.

As the rescue team pulled up to the accident, the red and blue rotating police lights cast an eerie glow of emergency. Something was wrong. No sirens. No shouting. The silence was deafening. Slowly, the intersection of Perring and Northern Parkways was backing up as rubberneckers choked the roadway.

The engine company had already put two floodlights on the accident site, bathing it in artificial daylight. The men from the Squad surveyed the horrid scene as they dismounted from their vehicle. The car lay on its roof. Both doors had been wedged into the ground after they flew open on impact. The damage, lighting and dirt on the Mercedes made it impossible to tell the true color of the car.

The officer in charge approached Rescue 1. "It's no emergency. Both the man and woman are dead. We just can't get them out. The coroner is on the way. So its your show." The three regular members of the rescue team checked out the site and related information to each other as to how to get the couple out. One would climb, one would stoop and search, and one would poke his head in to get a clear look at how badly the vehicle was crushed.

Because the lieutenant was fairly new, he relied on Bob and Charlie. Between them, there was plenty of skill. First they had to stabilize the vehicle and lift it a few feet off the ground, which would allow them to reach the victims. Lieutenant Fisher and men from other companies assisted in bringing over the cribbing, while Bob and Charlie, with the assistance of Lieutenant Fisher, set up the air bags. The cribbing was placed at convenient locations to lift the vehicle. As it was raised slowly by the air bags, the cribbing was shoved under the car.

Once the car was raised the lieutenant used the Hurst tool to "pop" the hinges on the doors to allow their removal. The "O" cutter was then placed in service to cut the convertible top assembly. Now Bob and the lieutenant along with Charlie scooted under and inside the passenger compartment. There, the Squad discovered the accident's true horror.

The girl and her companion had been thrown violently about inside the car. Her head had struck the rear view mirror, which detached and now protruded grotesquely from her forehead. She then became caught up in the convertible assembly. Carefully, they were able to pass her out to the waiting firefighters, her body covered with blood.

The boyfriend had been caught up in the soft rooftop. He had, however, suffered a worse fate. During the tossing, his forehead had caved in. Blood drenched his body. The open head wound spewed brain matter throughout the car. The rescuers worked in a cramped space as they cut the soft rooftop to remove his body. Bob pulled on the young man's leg and his foot flopped in different directions. Lieutenant Fisher related that the foot had the consistency of a "bag of water." Eventually the young man was freed and his body was passed out from the vehicle. The firefighters climbed out of the auto and straightened up. They noticed that the detailed firefighter was standing away from them, extremely nauseated.

The bodies of the two teens were placed in the waiting coroner's van and transported to the city morgue on Penn Street. The lieutenant, Charlie and Bob gathered up their equipment with the help of some firefighters and laid them all in a row. They used a 1-1/2-inch hoseline to wash off the tools. Next the hoseman washed away the blood and brain matter from the vehicle, the road and the bridge. At last they were finished.

The ordeal seemed endless. Everyone fought back feelings of dread and revulsion. Finally, with everything put away and readied for the next call, the crew of Rescue 1 headed home. "Do you always get runs like this?" Lieutenant Fisher asked, wiping his forehead. It was a question which, one day, he would be able to answer for himself.

Elevators. The average person would not believe how many elevators get stuck in Baltimore City each year! High rises, low rises, freight. Overall, they have an excellent safety record, but . . . Rescue 1 has the tools to get anyone out of an elevator. One is a screwdriver-like tool with a flat end. Sticking out of the end is a little tit that, when inserted into a small hole in an elevator door, will trip a mechanism that will allow the door to slide open. Other tools include the elevator drop key and the hook. The elevator drop key is a tool with a different amount of swiveled plates on its end that will operate the same as the screwdriver tool. The hook is a long pole that is used to push on the elevator pulley wheel to release it and open the door. This tool is used from the floor above. Elevator doors differ so we are required to carry an assortment of tools.

Some elevators jam with no one on board. When opened some reveal hysterical passengers, so traumatized from their claustrophobia that they cannot stand up and walk out. Finally, there are the quiet ones. They don't move, talk, or breathe.

The pièce de résistance occurred about three years ago on a quiet Easter morning in a public high rise on the West Side. All units sat at rest in their bays. There seemed to be peace throughout the city. Little chatter emitted from the base stations and mobile radios. At the station, everyone had congregated in the kitchen to eat lunch. You could tell it was Easter from the plateful of hard-boiled eggs in a kaleidoscope of colors and designs. Someone slipped a colored raw egg into the pile. Hysterics broke out when an unsuspecting firefighter cracked it against the table and yolk flew all over him.

As we enjoyed our eggs, Rescue 1 received a call for a stuck elevator with people on board. We dropped our lunches and took off for the poles, sliding down them like a string of beads. As each man shot to his position on the Mack rescue unit, the station doors opened and we burst into the tranquil day.

A West Side engine and truck met us at the scene. One fighter proceeded into the high rise. We ascended in the other elevator to the third floor.

Using an elevator key, Bob Wagner tried to open the jammed doors. After five unsuccessful attempts, we decided to unjam the pulley from the floor above. The engine and truck men waited in front of the elevator doors on the third floor.

At the fourth floor, Bob tried again to open the doors with the key. Success! We pulled the inner doors to their maximum and climbed in on top of the disabled car. We wedged a pole under the roller wheel to the door assembly and pulled up on the wheel. The tug paid off. We could hear the doors opening below. Then we turned the power off to the car, so it wouldn't jam again until it was repaired.

What we saw was unbelievable. In the crack between the car and the shaft wall we counted heads: one, five, eight, 11, 15, 18 and finally 23 people exiting the elevator plus one 10-speed bike! Twenty-three people in an elevator that is supposed to hold 10.

Some workers do not care about guidelines and procedures and cause problems for those who try to do a good job. They enjoy bending the rules. They usually get away with it . . . at least for a while. Then there are those that make an innocent mistake, and everyone knows about it.

Another elevator call. So what! No hurry . . . unless you're the one stuck. But who do you call for a rescue if the rescuer is trapped?

It was early evening on the West Side when three people got stuck in a passenger elevator car on the tenth floor of a high rise on West Saratoga Street. Immediately, an engine, truck and rescue company were dispatched to the scene.

The lieutenant of the rescue told the other two companies they could stay down on the first floor and if needed he would call. The doors of the working elevator opened. The three Squad members entered carrying the elevator tools. One by one, they moved to the back of the car as the doors closed behind them. Each man had his assigned tool at his side. They felt the car begin its slow ascent to the tenth floor.

The car made a stop at the fourth floor to allow two more people to climb on board. The same happened on the fifth, where three more people entered. The car rose two more stories and suddenly stopped. A look of dread swept over the rescuers' faces.

The officer lifted his portable radio to his mouth and called communications. There was no answer. He tried again. Still no answer. The radio picked up other transmissions and they could hear the business of the fire department going on around them. However, their transmissions weren't getting out because of the interference or dead spot.

Meanwhile, on the first floor, the other two fire companies watched the floor indicator lights above the elevators as the Rescue Squad was being lifted to the tenth floor. They saw the elevator stop at the fourth floor, then the fifth floor. When it stopped on the seventh floor, they assumed someone was getting on there also.

The elevator still had not moved. The civilian passengers obviously knew what had happened. The elevator had been stuck before. The officer of the truck company on the first floor finally picked up his radio after what seemed like minutes, "Truck 13 to Rescue 1." He repeated it four or five times. There was no answer. They're stuck, he thought to himself. He took his company and went for the steps. As they trudged up the stairway, he kept trying his portable radio.

On calls such as this, the driver of the rescue stays with the wagon outside. The driver heard the companies trying to contact Rescue 1 and became concerned. He hopped from the cab and went inside. The officer of the engine company told him that the indicator lights had not moved. One car was stuck on the tenth and the other with the rescue crew was on the seventh. Both men suppressed their amusement.

Inside the elevator car, the air was getting stuffy and the civilians were getting agitated. "I thought you said they was gonna get us offa here, man?" one frightened passenger blurted out. The lieutenant said calmly from the back of the crowd, "They will get us off. Just keep your cool. It won't be long." Even though he knew it would be in vain, the officer again picked up his radio and tried calling. Still no answer.

Meanwhile, the rescue driver retrieved the portapower unit from the Squad. He and an engine man carried the cumbersome unit, a mini "Jaws of Life," up the steps. Arriving at the seventh floor they saw the truck company men standing idly by the elevator cars. Their officer had confirmed that the car was indeed stuck.

The driver had a truck man take his Halligan tool and pry open the outer door a little. He took the duckbill-shaped jaws of the portapower unit and jammed them between the doors. "Now!" He told a man to start pumping the handle. It pushed hydraulic fluid to the jaws which slowly began to open. As the jaws opened, the doors were painstakingly moved slightly apart. Then with one quick jolt, the doors popped open. He laid the mini jaws down and pushed on a release mechanism on the inner doors, and they, too, slowly opened. There stood eight relieved people. The civilians rushed off without a word of thanks.

The Squad's crew naturally received a good razing. But they knew it was coming from the moment they got stuck. They gathered up their equipment and walked up to the tenth floor to release the occupants of the other elevator. The truck man went with them.

They used the elevator keys to get the car open. Ironically, the car was empty. It had been a false alarm.

———————

Sooner or later, every rescue team has a cache of favorite can-you-top-this stories that are traded more feverishly than baseball cards in a middle school locker room. This next story is one of my favorites.

One thing that has always fascinated me about the old, wild west is a roundup. Gathering all those animals in one area could not have been an easy task. It took skill and a special talent to even want to do it. It was also hard work. Who would have ever thought that a modern day fire department would become involved in a real life roundup?

A popular rock music group came to the Baltimore Civic Center for one evening. The Civic Center is located only a block from the station. As we sat on the wall out front, we marveled at the different types of people the concert attracted! The plain Janes, the over-doers with glitter and gold, the under-doers with bikini tops and ragged jeans, and the totally strange. People-watching is an interesting hobby.

A trailer loaded with squealing pigs pulled up to the curb on Howard Street. The driver planned to see the concert while on his way home with his cargo. So he secured his vehicle, and took off for the arena, while the pigs finally settled down after their bumpy ride.

The downtown area of the city quieted after the people entered the Civic Center. Once in a while, a car or truck would ride by on Lombard Street and the driver would blow his horn or wave.

When the concert was over fans spilled out on the streets. Suddenly, people came running around the corner, laughing and carrying on. Nothing abnormal for a rock concert crowd. Right? Wrong! They were being chased by a small herd of pigs. A prankster from the concert opened the doors of the trailer and the "dirty swine" took off.

We watched from the wall in hysterics. Someone decided to post a bulletin on the station intercom. Communications called back asking if they had heard our message correctly. The officer reassured them. That's when the officer decided to put us out of service to assist in rounding up the pigs.

Someone yelled "Yahoo! Let's get 'em boys!" and off we went. Our noses led us to the trailer. Doug Wagerman was nominated gateman. He would open and close the gate to the trailer as the pigs were put back in. Everyone else would help to round up the pigs. We tried grabbing them around the body, the head, the neck, a leg, the tail. Nothing seemed to work very well. Most often we landed on our knees, our rears or our faces.

The owner of the trailer returned to his empty truck, and was very upset. He screamed at everyone before he realized we were trying to help him. Once he calmed down, he showed us the proper way to catch pigs: grab them by their back legs, lift them, and walk them to the gate like wheelbarrows.

One by one, we walked the pigs down the city street and back to the trailer as Doug opened and slammed shut the gate.

Eventually all the pigs were retrieved. The owner thanked us and left. Slowly, the concert-goers dispersed into the night and the street returned to normal. As we sat back on the wall, someone summed it all up: "Who said this job isn't exciting!"

6 Captains

The organizational structure of the fire service is absolute. One person is responsible for decisions at every step of the way. In an emergency where someone's life depends on an immediate decision, and where teams and pieces of equipment are used in a coordinated manner, there is never a time-wasting doubt or argument as to who is in charge.

At the top of the organization is the chief of the Baltimore Fire Department who commands 42 engine (hose) companies, 22 truck (ladder) companies, six aerial towers, 18 medic units, one rescue squad and dozens of miscellaneous units, such as fireboats. Under him are several deputy chiefs, each overseeing a section of the city. Under the deputy chiefs are the battalion chiefs, responsible for several companies. And under each battalion chief are the captains.

Like the captain of a ship, each fire captain is responsible for the men and equipment on his apparatus. Each captain oversees three lieutenants, who act in his place on the other three shifts. Officers work two days and two nights on duty, and four days off. Firefighters work two days and two nights on duty, and two days off.

The captain is always in charge, day or night, on or off shift. He answers for the actions of all the men in his company. Like a battleship, a truck or engine company is only as organized, responsive and effective as is its captain.

Technically, a fireman must have more than five years of duty in the fire service and pass a complex written examination to become a captain. In reality, he also needs a hefty dose of vision, intelligence, leadership, and excellent human relations and communications skills. You cannot test for all these qualities, but they are what make or break a fire team. Such are the qualities of Bill Goodwin.

Captain William Goodwin walked down the line-up, shaking hands with each of the men. Young, intelligent, and dedicated, he became captain in just eight years, a prodigious feat in any department. Now he was assigned seven men. He gave each man a stern smile, but his nervousness was impossible to hide. The veterans in the department saw a rookie who didn't know all that was involved in firefighting. How was he going to lead *them*! Still, they agreed to give him a chance.

Goodwin went upstairs to familiarize himself with the new station while the men downstairs went about their chores on the apparatus floor. He checked the files, drawers, closets, bunk room and even the pool table. Next, he familiarized himself with the boiler room and equipment in the storage area of the basement. His stomach flip-flopped every time a call came over for another company. Goodwin was almost dreading his first run as a new captain. He knew he was responsible not only for his own life, but for the lives of his men.

BEEP! BEEP! The communications desk called out an address and company numbers. Goodwin's company was called.

"Let's go!" the man on watch duty shouted, throwing the gong.

The pump operator approached the new captain as they ran out the door. "Didn't they say children trapped?"

"Yeah," Goodwin said, his stomach knotting, "they sure did."

In the fire service, when we hear the words "children trapped," we are suddenly transformed. Our feet can't move fast enough, the apparatus seems excruciatingly slow, and the water in the hoses seems to take forever to spurt out the nozzle. We go to extremes, sometimes taking incredible risks, to aid children.

It was a hazy, hot and humid day in 1984, a typical Baltimore summer day. Two children played in the back bedroom of a North Baltimore rowhouse, while their mother went next door for a cup of coffee with a neighbor.

The eight-year-old girl turned to her younger sister and asked, "Have you ever smoked a cigarette?" The six-year-old girl shook her head. The eight-year-old passed her sister the cigarette, but the little girl panicked and dropped it on the mattress. The girls turned their attention to other things, and minutes later, the mattress ignited.

As the firemen neared the address, Goodwin spotted black smoke billowing over the rooftops. No, he thought, not on my first run! Why couldn't it have been a false alarm! The two men in the jump seats were already donning their air masks. The first arriving engine company called in: "We have fire and smoke showing . . . people say two children are trapped in the back!"

"Take us to the rear," Goodwin ordered. "We'll get a line to the back." The pumper grabbed a hydrant half a block away. The hose connections were made with breakneck speed. The rookie captain and a firefighter, both in full protective gear, grabbed a 1-1/2-inch line and moved toward the doomed house.

A truck company had also answered the call. Two of their men laddered the small addition in the rear of the house, called a "summer kitchen" in Baltimore, which has an angled roof at the first floor.

Goodwin looked over and saw the ladder momentarily unmanned, as firefighters struggled to get hoses to the back of the house. Without a second thought, he ascended the ladder onto the roof of the summer kitchen, followed by the firefighter. They struggled with the water-filled hoseline as they climbed. Flames arched irregularly from the windows. As both men approached what they were told was the girls' window, the firefighter leaned on one knee positioning the hose as Goodwin bent over behind him. The firefighter turned the nozzle on, spurting cool water into the flames. Instantly the water became superheated steam.

As if by a miracle, a break in the smoke and steam revealed what could have been a body lying about 10 feet inside on the charred floor.

"Keep me covered with that," Bill yelled to the firefighter. "I'm going to try to go in there and get them out." The firefighter looked through his water-spotted mask at the captain as if he were crazy.

"Just keep me wet," Goodwin ordered. He slipped into the thick cloud.

Other firefighters massed below as truck men opened the roof to draw out the fire, heat, smoke, steam and deadly gases from the house. Another contingent readied a hose to aid the captain and his partner. Neighbors held back the hysterical mother and watched the men in yellow suits combat the raging fire.

The heavy blanket of smoke hung down from the ceiling only inches above the floor. The flames spiraled and arched trying to get outside. Stepping through the blazing window, Bill Goodwin entered another world — a world of darkness and deadly heat. He inched along the floor on his stomach in what he desperately hoped was the direction of the body. Heat seared the exposed skin around his neck and facemask. His breathing intensified as he groped through the dark. The cool hose stream provided his only comfort.

A foot! A surge of hope. Bill pulled the limp body toward him and began crawling back, unsure of his direction but following the stream of water. Then he crouched, pulling the unconscious child to his chest, and dashed into the stream. The water pounded mercilessly against them. It was like pushing against a 200-pound fullback. Finally he reached the window. He leaned out and handed the child to the firefighter with the hose. Truck men scrambled to help.

Before the firefighter could speak, Goodwin disappeared once again into the smoke and flames. Again he crept across the floor. The roof had been opened somewhat, allowing some of the smoke to escape. A chunk of debris fell, grazing him. As he turned to avoid it, he saw her.

The young girl's body was sooted and steaming. Most of her clothing had been hardened by soot burns. He touched her. She wasn't breathing! Disregarding his own safety, he ripped off his mask and held it to her face. He tried pumping air into her heated lungs. Nothing! Goodwin lifted her, blowing air into her while compressing her chest, and made a mad dash for the window. His chest was heaving from the searing air and smoke. The water blasted against them. He couldn't breathe. At last, he reached the window!

Firefighters grabbed the body as Goodwin staggered and collapsed over the edge of the opening. Pulling himself onto the roof of the summer kitchen, he turned in time to see the floor inside disappear in a shower of sparks and flames, plunging to the first floor below.

The eight-year-old died from extensive burns. The six-year-old suffered second and third degree burns over 10 percent of her body and died three days later.

The rookie captain received a meritorious conduct award and later was named "Firefighter of the Year" by a local community group. Goodwin's courage earned him the respect of his men. If you ask the men at his station, they'll tell you he was baptized by fire!

Sometimes one of your own company returns as a captain. Then it becomes a little like Old Home Week.

At Steadman Station, the shift welcomed the new squad captain, Joe Brocato. Having served as a firefighter on the wagon five years earlier, Joe was excited to be back at Rescue 1. Our previous captain, Bill Goodwin, had been promoted to battalion chief. We appreciated seeing Captain Goodwin's inspiring enthusiasm carried over to our new captain. Joe looked forward to working with us as a captain and couldn't wait until his first working rescue. This night he would work with Bob Wagner, Doug Wagerman and myself. We were enjoying the evening talking about the goings on of the company, sharing stories and catching up on our personal lives. We were all proud of Joe. He had done well for himself.

As we sat around the office "chewing the fat," a few miles away, a bus filled with senior citizens and women from a Baptist church in the northwest sector traveled home from an evening at a sister church. The bus slowed as it prepared to leave off one of its members.

Several blocks behind them, Elaine Martin wiped the tears from her eyes.

She and her mom had been arguing again. Home was all she could think of as she drove northward in her new Chrysler LeBaron on Park Heights Avenue.

At the same time, Evasar Smith was driving his conversion van home from Lexington Market. He hurried down side streets until he found the main street. He let his foot off the brake at the traffic light and turned north on Park Heights Avenue. The three vehicles converged at the corner.

"There it is!" the elderly woman called out to the driver, "That's my stop." He moved the bus into the far right lane. Elaine and Evasar also moved from the left to the right lane. What no one knew was that the bus brake lights were not working. Evasar and Elaine were preoccupied with the recent events of the day. Evasar, in a hurry, pulled ahead of Elaine. He then reached down and over to his radio to change the station. His eyes shot over quickly to the digital station display. He didn't see the bus come to a stop.

Elaine's eyes were swollen with tears. As Evasar's car passed her, she reached for a Kleenex. Dabbing her eyes, a red glow just up ahead caught her attention. Quickly she tried to focus, but all she saw was the back of a van.

The large bus stopped. Evasar slammed into its back, crushing the front end of the van. His seat belt saved him from kissing the rear of the bus.

Elaine's auto, still carrying temporary tags, careened into the end of Evasar's van. Without her seat belt, the violent impact sent Elaine sailing. Her legs propelled forward as her body weight cast her downward below the dashboard, her legs then veered upward. Her legs were pinned under the dash. Finally, her chest pounded into the steering wheel and her head flew forward, jerking her neck. She was then flung backwards into the seat in a very awkward position.

The bus driver felt the two thuds double-bumping the large vehicle. Women screamed. He jumped off the bus and ran to the rear. He couldn't believe what he saw. How to get help? There, across the street and a half-block away, stood a fire station. He ran over and banged on the door.

Instantly six firefighters, dividing into pairs, dashed over to render assistance to the bus, the van, and the car. Meanwhile, the officer on duty called for medic units. One of the firefighters yelled from the LeBaron, "Captain, you'd better call for the rescue, too! She's pinned in here!"

Six miles away, the alert tone came in at Steadman Station for a vehicular accident in the 4200 block of Park Heights Avenue. Joe called out, "Let's go!" and leaped from his chair in the office to the brass pole. Close behind, we each slid to the apparatus floor. There we mounted Rescue 1 and took off. I drove.

As we raced northwest to the accident scene, talk was monitored by the captain. Our estimated time of arrival (ETA) was eight to 10 minutes. While I drove, I could almost feel the heartbeat of the rig accelerating. Joe turned to me and we looked at each other when we heard another medic unit being dispatched to the accident.

Hundreds of people gathered at the site to watch. Aerial Tower 122's men had their hands full. An engine company was also on the scene, their charged hose laying along the area in case of fire.

Our immediate problem was the automobile. AT 122's officer conveyed the events to Joe as we got out of our vehicle. We hustled over to survey the damage and determine our plan of action.

Evasar stood near his van talking with an EMT. He seemed to be okay. Everyone on the bus was all right, we were told, save a few that were shaken up. We focused our attention on Elaine's Chrysler. She was bleeding and hurt. We had to get her out fast.

I ran to the wagon to retrieve the generator for the "highway hookup." Bob and Doug grabbed their connections as I passed the hose to them. Then we ran back to the crashed vehicle and Elaine.

With all the connections hooked up, I started the generator. Seeing a live victim trapped, in unfathomable pain, and bleeding externally and perhaps internally, we felt the adrenalin surge through our bodies. Like the "Incredible Hulk," what we saw propelled us to peak strength, agility and even wit.

Captain Joe and Bob, closest to the car, looked inside to identify exactly where Elaine was pinned. Joe called for the "O" cutter on the passenger side. Doug worked with him. Bob and I were on Elaine's side. Bob took the extending ram and tried to push the dash up and out of the way. But he couldn't get a bite on the door frame. Bob told me to take the "Jaws" and pinch the door frame to hold it there to give him something to push against. He lined up the ram and turned the handle. Slowly it began to push the dash out of the way.

Simultaneously, Doug and Joe cut the door posts and crimped the roof near the end. One by one, they made their slices as I ran to the windshield. With an axe, I carefully jabbed the pick end into the bottom of the windshield, to allow us to eventually pull it out away from the roof. The captain and Doug passed the "O" cutter to me as I made the crimp-cut and cut the door post on my side. Then we all gave a push and laid the roof over backwards, exposing the entire inside of the LeBaron.

The medics brought over a long backboard which we laid behind Elaine's head and along the back seat and exposed roof. At last, Bob freed Elaine's legs and we slid her up onto the board, freeing her from the wreckage.

What happened then never happened before in my career. Nor had anyone else there experienced it. The large crowd that had continued to swell throughout the incident began to cheer and clap. Here and there we could hear a hearty "All right!" It gave me a warm feeling to know that there was unanimous concern for the victim and support for us at our work, more than just the curiosity for a good side show. We even noticed a little smile on Elaine's face, despite her extreme pain.

We transferred Elaine to the medic's stretcher next to the car. The medics adjusted the neck collar, strapped her down, and hurried her to the waiting ambulance. As they worked her up with telemetry, they conversed with Sinai Hospital's Trauma Center.

Captain Brocato came over and thanked us. He said he felt better now that he had his first full working rescue as a captain. As we talked, a man from the bus came over to tell us that some women were complaining of injuries. Joe asked me to check on them, because I had been a paramedic.

Entering the bus, I was amazed by the number of elderly women in white dresses. I called out, "Is anyone hurt?" A few hands shot up. I went down the aisle and checked each one — a total of nine. They seemed fine, just disturbed by the accident. I told them we would call an ambulance to come so that the medics could check everyone thoroughly. That reassured them.

Joe called a medic unit. The nine women checked out as normal and agreed to see their own physicians for any further complications or concerns. With that we loaded our equipment back on Rescue 1. We felt pleased with our performance as a new team and with the outcome of our first rescue. We were deeply grateful for the cheering section. Joe's career as captain was off and running with the highest possible welcome.

The pressure on a captain is constant and intensifies when you know you must earn the confidence and loyalty of your men.

On the other hand, the men worry each time they are assigned a new officer, especially a captain. The captain usually sets polices in the company. A persnickety lieutenant can generate acid indigestion, but a distempered captain can give you bleeding ulcers!

About 10 years ago, a new captain came to Rescue 1. We had heard stories about him, some a reflection of truth, some the result of kitchen conjecture, and some the product of downright paranoia. It was rumored that the new captain was a Major League *perfectionist* who was long on detail and short on patience and humor. That wasn't all he was short on. He stood in the 5-foot 4-inch range. Maybe shorter. As we heard things about him from other people, we worried about how well he would take to a crew of clowns and practical jokers.

But when I learned who he was, I felt relieved. I knew him from school and liked him. Trying to convince some of the guys that the new captain was a good leader was like persuading a kid that a tonsillectomy under anesthesia wouldn't hurt. When the new captain arrived, he called the men of Rescue 1 into the office where he gave them a pep talk and said he would work with them if they would work with him. He seemed, they said afterward, like a nice guy after all.

Bob Wagner loves a good practical joke. Charlie Huber loves a good practical joke. Even respectable Augie Stern does. All three decided to find out how much fun this new captain was.

Bob found a small stool. Running down to the wagon on the first floor, he opened the officer's door and set the stool down on the floor next to the door. There was no mistaking his intent — it would serve as a step stool for the short captain to climb up into the wagon. The three men howled as they imagined the captain climbing up on the stool. Then they wondered whether they had not made an imprudent mistake. Finally, Bob decided to remove it. But before he could retrieve it, a call came in. They swallowed hard as they slid down the poles and headed for the rescue wagon. The captain came running over. It was too late to hide the stool as Charlie climbed up front and waited for the captain to climb in. He closed his eyes. The captain came up to the open squad door and stopped. He looked down at the stool. A small smile brushed his face. He stepped up on it and sat down. "Let's go!" he shouted. The rescue vehicle roared out the door.

During the incident and returning, the captain said nothing. Charlie wondered if they would "have a talk" when they got back to quarters, or worse, a line-up! Bob and Augie shook their heads in the back of the vehicle. Charlie eased the wagon up on the ramp and slowly backed it into the station. The members dismounted and gathered together to walk up the steps to the watch desk. Where was the captain?

The trio turned around and saw the officer still sitting in his seat. Thinking the worst was to come, they pictured him stewing in his seat and getting ready to lambaste them. Finally, Bob mustered the courage to ask what was wrong. His nerves shot, he approached the captain. "Are you getting out, Cap'n?" he inquired. With the coolness of an ice cube, the captain replied, "I can't get out until someone puts my stool back!" He broke out into a smile, breaking the tension. The trio and the captain burst into laughter. Bob ran over to get the stool and put it at the base of the officer's door. The captain descended carefully, making sure to use the stool — so thoughtfully placed there for him. From that day forward, they knew where they stood with the captain. And he knew where he stood with them . . . on a pede-stool!

Captains often display a courage rarely seen in other lines of work. A good captain would never ask his men to do something he would not do. In many cases, captains do things *no one* else would do.

Twelve-year-old Joey was 80 pounds of pure orneriness. He and his friends were hanging out together on a lazy, listless summer day, searching for something to do. As they walked restlessly along the quiet street, one of the boys looked up.

A massive high-voltage tower rose above them. They noticed how the tower seemed to rise forever, stretching into the sky. Miles and miles of identical towers lined up behind it and seemed to run to infinity, all connected by thick cables.

The boys saw the unspoken dare in each others eyes. "Okay, who's gonna climb to the top?" one inquired. The stage was set. The baseball bat they carried became the deciding factor, they all crossed hands in a game of elimination. Joey "won."

"Piece of cake," he blurted out as he stared the other boys down, and began his ascent. Quaking inwardly, he climbed past the "DANGER" placard on the bottom post and continued upward.

Neighbors and children gathered around the base of the tower, calling out to the arriving fire units. Joey lay motionless on a strut brace, 45 feet above the ground, just inches below the power line, which officials estimated carried 30,000 volts. Joey was semi-conscious. His clothing was scorched, and wisps of smoke rose from his body.

The Fire Department contacted the electric company to cut the power, but the company said there would be a delay because of the area affected. As the crowd stood waiting, Joey attempted to get up, but the arcing electricity struck him down repeatedly. People cried out as they watched, and firefighters yelled for him to remain still. Again and again he tried, only to be pierced by the intense current.

The captain of the truck company couldn't just watch anymore. He ordered his men to position the truck at the base of the tower. They slowly raised the aerial ladder and rotated it into position. The ladder began stretching to the brace where Joey rested.

No one could understand how he could still be alive! Even as the ladder rose toward him, Joey tried to stand. Again and again, he was knocked down. Each jolt drained more life from the boy's tortured body. Technically, the officer thought, he should be dead! His mother cried out for him, as his dad grabbed her.

A power company official finally arrived. "The power's off," she said, "but we can only keep it off for half an hour. You've got to get him down now!"

The captain grabbed a lifebelt and ascended the ladder. The tillerman had a tough job — to keep the tip of the ladder away from the tower, but close enough to reach Joey. A firefighter followed the captain.

The crowd watched silently. Joey's mother and father tightened their grips on each other. The captain froze as he saw Joey attempt to rise again. "NO!" he screamed, "STAY STILL!" He was close enough to hear Joey's low moaning. As he neared the tip of the ladder, the captain put on his lifebelt and hooked it on the last rung. He then put on his thick electrician's gloves.

The captain stretched toward the brace and put his hands on Joey. The child was unconscious now and didn't move, but he was breathing! The captain gave the men on the ground a "thumbs up" sign, and the growing crowd roared. Slowly and carefully, he lifted the smoking body into his arms.

Once back on the ground, the medics took over and in minutes transported the boy, still unconscious with second and third degree burns and internal injuries, to the hospital. As Joey's mother and father followed their son their eyes met the captain's. No words were necessary to convey their gratitude. The captain nodded, picked up the baseball bat, and flung it away from the tower.

Like the men he commands, the captain's work places him in constant danger. One spectacular Baltimore fire claimed one truck and very nearly one dedicated captain among its casualties.

The Downtown Truck Company proudly polished its new white and orange fire truck, caressing and cleaning it as if it were a prized trophy. The men stood back, admiring the flawless vehicle, then returned to their chores, anticipating a run. The gleaming truck sat, silently awaiting its fateful voyage. It came sooner than expected.

Across town, Captain Martin Catterton arrived for his shift at Truck Company 6 in South Baltimore and began checking his men and apparatus. Outside, Firefighter Adam Watkowski stepped out of his car and headed into the station house.

Meanwhile, downtown, a man in his forties got off the bus on his way to work. He took his first few steps on the sidewalk and stopped to sniff what he thought was smoke. His blood ran cold as he looked up at the Hochschild Kohn Department Store building next to him. The grand old building was being restored. But gigantic flames rolled out of the upper stories. Immediately, he ran across the street to a firebox and pulled the alarm for the Fire Department. The men on shiny new Truck 16 could barely contain their excitement. One of their first calls on the new truck, and it was a *big* one. They were anxious to see how well this truck operated "under fire." Their destination: Lexington at Eutaw

Street.

The new truck arrived at the narrow, crowded street and put down its jacks. The crew began the laborious task of hooking up the ladder pipe assembly, then turned on the hydraulic lift. The aerial ladder rose from its bed as hoselines were attached and charged, and the nozzle sprang to life. Instantly it sprayed gallons of water into the flames.

As Truck 6's Adam Watkowski entered the fire station across town, his relief man told him to hurry up. "A second alarm is coming in. It's the Hochschild Kohn building!" "Let's go!" Captain Catterton shouted, as he and Watkowski jumped on board and Truck 6 rolled out the door. They pulled up on Lexington, just off Howard, a half block from Truck 16. Catterton took one look at the size of the fire and called for the ladder pipe assembly.

The old building was quickly being devoured by flames which were advancing to every floor. The battalion chief didn't wait to call for help. The fire load was enormous and already the first firefighters were swarming about, setting up hoses, master streams, and deluge systems. The chief quickly asked for the sixth alarm, and turned the fire over to the deputy chief.

The captain stood nearby, proud at the power of Trucks 6 and 16 and, like everyone else, overwhelmed at the awesome magnitude of the fire and the difficulty that the six alarms had in trying to contain it.

Both crews stood in Lexington Street by the trucks as the water spewed forth. They felt helpless, but this was a "bail-in" job. It was far too dangerous to send in men. Almost every floor was engulfed in flames. The deputy chief, sensing the urgency of the situation, asked for more alarms. The tenth alarm was sounded. By now the building was "totally involved," which means consumed with fire on all floors. The deputy chief decided to move the two truck companies off Lexington Street due to the possible danger of the building collapsing. The driver and tillerman of Truck 16 rushed to their prized apparatus. The driver jumped in the front seat and the tillerman made his way to the rear seat. Meanwhile, Firefighter Watkowski and Captain Catterton prepared to move Truck 6 out of harm's way.

Without warning, a brick fell from the burning structure striking Catterton on his helmet and knocking him out cold. Its force sent him reeling forward. Watkowski saw it happen and lunged, catching the captain as he fell.

Suddenly, someone began yelling and pointing skyward. A large section of the upper wall had broken loose and was hurtling down at Trucks 6 and 16 and their crews. There was no place to run.

Watkowski reacted instinctively. He pushed the still-unconscious captain to the ground, covering him with his own body. The mass of falling concrete and brick, smoking from the extreme heat, exploded on the apparatus and men. Watkowski felt the meteors of bricks and masonry pound his legs and helmet. A thick cloud of dust and ash mushroomed above the battered firefighters and their equipment.

The men from Truck 16 never knew what hit them. The force of the impact threw the driver out of the truck and onto the street. The tillerman was trapped in the tiller cab. Knocked unconscious, he lay limp in the crushed seat. The new fire truck was destroyed — crushed, mangled, and flattened.

The force of the explosion burst out the huge windows of the Hecht Company Department Store across the street. A huge cloud of dust, dirt and smoke billowed throughout Lexington Street. As it slowly began to clear, firefighters began searching the rubble for the men of the two companies.

Captain Catterton regained consciousness to find Watkowski on top of him. The darkness of the huge pile of bricks, glass and rubble covered them. Slowly, they pushed off the hot debris and broke through the mass of destruction. Their turnout gear smoked from the heated bricks. As Watkowski made his way out, a hoseline sprayed water onto his face. He still isn't sure if it was from an abandoned hoseline or from a company spraying them down. Just yards away, firefighters were busily extricating the tillerman from the tiller cab. He was unconscious. Other medic units were called in, and the driver and tillerman were rushed to a nearby hospital. Watkowski and the captain went on fighting the fire. Eventually it was brought under control.

The building was a total loss. Truck 16's driver was treated and released. The tillerman, who commented that he felt as if he had been run over by a tank, was hospitalized for a few days. Captain Catterton and Watkowski were treated for aches and bruises, and walked out of the hospital several hours later wearing neck braces. Watkowski's major complaint was a severe headache. Other than that, they were fine.

Truck 16, however, wasn't so lucky. It sat flattened and scarred, mourned by the men in its company.

When Captain Catterton saw Truck 6, pocked and charred by hot falling bricks, he shook his head.

"If I had a gun," the officer said dryly, "I would shoot it."

Watkowski received a Meritorious Conduct Award. His heroic, selfless actions had brought him close to death, but he had upheld the highest tradition of Fire Departments the world over.

7 Days Best Forgotten

Rookies everywhere take a beating — in boot camps, newsrooms, locker rooms and fire stations. It's part of the conditioning process. If a rookie can take the skepticism, criticism and relentless kidding of his peers, he's ready for the rigors of high-pressure teamwork. We all went through it and survived, although for most of us, those are days best forgotten.

A new Fire Academy graduate cringes to think he might be "written up" on lateness charges. He dreads the inevitable razzing by the men in the station. And he senses that being late is the wrong way to get to know his battalion chief. Surrounded by seasoned veterans with stories a city block long, the rookie soon feels inferior. If he is caught sleeping on watch, he feels as if he has a bellyful of bad fish. Living ones! I know, it happened to me after only four months on the job.

After graduation from the Fire Academy in 1972 and due to a mix-up on my first assignment at Engine 1, I was transferred to Engine 23 on Saratoga Street. A double house, it boasted two fire units (Engines 23 and 15), Ambulance 1 and the deputy chief of the First Division. Although it was a busy station, the men were so nice that you would even let one marry your sister. They treated me like an old friend and made me feel at home. So, it was not surprising that I did the usual thing a rookie does, I fell for their firehouse humor. Hey, I was only 23 — fresh meat to a gang of seasoned firefighters.

I was told to familiarize myself with the pumper. Knowing where to find each piece of equipment in more than 10 compartments on the apparatus is critical on the fireground. After I memorized every piece, my officer and a few men quizzed me. I did fairly well until they asked me where the five-gallon can of *dehydrated* water was! And the sky hook! I thought they were items of Fire

Department jargon. I was wrong and too green to admit it.

Maybe I was a little gullible, but up until then, I was *never* late for work. Then the fateful day came. At this time, I lived alone in a small, small rowhouse in South Baltimore on Race Street. The night before, I had been out partying with the guys. We were girl-watching and having a good time. I used to drink occasionally. Knowing I had to go to work the next day, I called it a night around 1:00 a.m. and when I turned in I set my alarm clock for 4:45 a.m.

All of a sudden, I awoke with a start, knowing I should be up doing something important. But I didn't know what it was, what time it was, or even *where* I was. I kept rubbing my eyes, trying to recognize the source of a strange repetitive banging sound. Feeling the knot grow in my gut, I looked around the bedroom and at the ceiling. Suddenly I realized that the sun was pouring in the windows. I focused foggily on my watch . . . 7:35 a.m. My shift started at 7:00 a.m. "Oh, No!" I screamed. The banging noise grew louder and I realized that someone was pounding violently on my front door. I staggered over to the bedroom window. To my surprise, a fire engine sat out front! I pulled the curtains apart and saw firefighters waving for me to come downstairs and open the door.

With the speed of a cue ball, I shot downstairs and opened the door. There stood an officer from Engine 26, stationed just five blocks away. The lieutenant boldly asked, "Are you Firefighter Hall?" I swallowed, "Yes."

"You're late!" he barked. "Call your company officer right away and get to work."

"Yes sir!" I turned and ran back upstairs, jumping into my pants as I heard the diesel pulling away. As I grabbed my shirt, someone else pounded at my door. I ran to the window again. A Baltimore City police car sat out front! "Do they always do this if you're late?" I wondered, struggling with the buttons.

I leaped down the stairs and flung open the door. As I tucked my shirt in, the officer said, "Are you Firefighter Hall of Engine 23?" Obediently, I responded, "Yes, I am." "Call your company officer right away." He turned away coolly and departed. Was this really happening? Was it a bad dream — or was it bad beer?

My nerves twanged like an out-of-tune guitar. I'd never been in real trouble before and I didn't like the feeling. I went to the telephone next to my bed, and discovered that I had somehow knocked it out of its cradle during the night. I looked at the alarm clock and saw that it had stopped during the evening. It showed 2:26 a.m.

I grabbed a banana for breakfast and lunch and darted out the door, leaving my German Shepherd "Champ" still waiting for his pat on the head. The early morning sunlight raked my eyes. I stopped at the red lights, looked both ways and then sped through them.

Finally arriving, I pulled into the only parking space left. The man I was to relieve walked past me in disgust. I entered the station at 7:50 a.m. The men exchanged knowing glances that said, "Boy, are you in for it." Some vocalized their thoughts: "What a load. Just four months and late already." One guy even called me a "banker" — the worst!

I stiffened and headed for the office to report to my unit officer. I explained my true but fishy-sounding story, while earnestly praying for pity. He nodded sympathetically. Then put his hands flat on his desk, stood, and said he had no choice but to put me on charges. I felt like he had just sentenced me to five years in the penitentiary! He inhaled and handed me the charge papers to sign, which I did rapidly, before he could exhale, hoping he would drop it at that. But then he explained the penalty. I would be reprimanded by my battalion chief. "No, not him," I thought. Chief Charles Loughlin was from the old school, tough as rhino skin and sharp as tiger teeth. He chewed up rookies like me for breakfast.

Chief Loughlin came around later that afternoon. I felt like a 10-year-old who'd smashed his dad's windshield with a hard ball. He called me into the office, looked me over and snorted. "You know why I've got to rip you?" As I tried to respond, my voice jumped an octave in spite of my best efforts. "Yes sir," I squeaked. "I was 50 minutes late." His next utterance was one for which he was best known. He simply said, "Nyehhhh." Then he turned and went back out to his vehicle and disappeared into the city confusion. Thus I learned that Chief Loughlin had a heart of gold. Many of the guys liked him so much, they called him a prince.

I had to stay an extra 50 minutes to make up for the lost time. Never again have I been put on charges for being late, thanks largely to the efforts of my fellow firefighters and police, and my champion fire-wife who boots me out of bed if I don't get up on time.

Another "best forgotten" rookie incident happened six months after I graduated from the Fire Academy. As my probationary period on Engine 23 on West Saratoga Street ended, I was detailed to the "dreaded" ambulance. Ambulance 1 was an old four-speed SWAB box unit on a Ford truck chassis. I had never driven a stick-shift vehicle until I joined the Fire Department.

When day-shift rolled around it was my turn to drive Ambulance 1 while the regular man, who had first-aid training, attended to the patients.

It was the practice of the department at that time for the regularly-assigned ambulance man (a firefighter trained in first aid) to drive the vehicle to the hospital while the detailed firefighter stayed in the back with the patient! Except in my case. . . . When I was a youngster I couldn't cut a worm in half to bait my fishing line because I turned green at the sight of blood. Now I was to attend to people bleeding and sick?

I couldn't even swallow my coffee. Just then, the "veteran" on Medic 1, Lou Jordan, came to my aid. A young man well versed in first aid, Lou helped initiate the Emergency Medical Technician Program in the Baltimore City Fire Department. He and a handful of others went up to New Jersey to learn the program and return as instructors to teach other firefighters.

He took me down to the ambulance and we reviewed the many pieces of equipment on board. I sat in the driver's seat and for a moment felt a surge of pride at the prestige that went with the job. Then, I worried that I might screw up and do more harm than good. My biggest fear was driving a stick shift. To practice I drove the bulky piece of fire apparatus on deserted streets in the early evening or one Sundays, but to figure out how to maneuver through the streets during rush hour made me quiver.

Lou tried to reassure me and calm me down, while I tried to convince him that it had worked. As he kept explaining how the ambulance worked, I kept praying, "Please Lord. Don't let us get any calls!"

But at 9:30 a.m., a call came in. I turned off the hose which I was using to wash the unit, while Lou answered the phone. At the time, ambo calls were given over the telephone. I jumped in the seat and quickly refamiliarized myself with the controls and lights, but it all seemed to blend together. Lou climbed in the passenger seat and gave the address . . . Harford Road and Lanvale Street.

Harford Road and Lanvale Street! Panic struck me. I felt reasonably sure I could drive the ambulance but I didn't know the city. I was raised in Locust Point in South Baltimore and like most Baltimoreans only knew my section of town. I had studied department maps and knew how to get to major streets and hospitals but for some reason, my mind went blank.

I started the engine, turned on the radio and lights, and sat there. Lou asked, "Are you okay, Bill?" "I'm fine, Lou. But which way do we go?" He looked baffled. "Pull out of the firehouse and turn left." I could tell he was becoming frustrated. And rightly so! I thrust the shift in first gear and we jerked out the door.

My confidence began to return a few blocks later. The sound of the siren pumped me up, and the authority I felt as every vehicle pulled out of my way was exhilarating. Only once did I grind a gear.

The address was one of a long row of houses. I pulled the ambulance up to the curb, turned the siren off, and kept the lights on so people would see we were

132

on a call. As we exited the unit, Lou stopped in his tracks. "Hall! What's that smell?," he inquired with a turned-up nose. "It smells like something burning," I said. "Is that coming from the ambulance?" "I don't know. I'll check." I hurried over to the unit. As Lou went in the house to check on our call, I could find nothing wrong. After several minutes, he came out and said it was a false call. Then we both checked out the engine for the source of the now powerful burnt smell.

"Hey, Bill. Come here." Lou called. He was leaning over the driver's side looking down at the floor. I hunched over his shoulders and leaned in. "Don't you believe in releasing the parking brake when you drive?" Suddenly I wished I were back in the Coast Guard. He saw the pain on my face and smiled. "We'll let it stand here for a few minutes to cool down," he said. "Then *I'll* drive it back." Another call came over the radio as he finished the sentence. Lou took the driver's seat and released the parking brake. I climbed in the passenger seat and answered the radio as we took off.

A veteran firefighter will do anything to make a rookie feel at home. Charlie Huber came to the Rescue Squad from the Fire Academy. He hoped for an engine company, but was satisfied that the Squad would at least bring him a lot of excitement. How right he was.. . .

One by one, the guys welcomed Charlie to the company. Then he met Captain Meushaw. The gruff, burly old fire captain came out of his office on the second floor and asked, "Where's the new boy?" Augie Stern, the "old man" of the Squad, proudly presented Charlie to the captain. Charlie noticed, as the captain walked away, that the captain had a limp in his right leg. Augie saw Charlie staring and whispered to him, "See that limp?" Charlie nodded. "Well," Augie continued, "it gives him a lot of pain sometimes. It's the responsibility of the new man in the company to help him into the wagon." Augie could barely contain his laughter. "So if you're on watch and we get a run, turn the company out and run over to the pole hole. When the captain slides down the pole, catch him before he hits and carry him over to the Squad. That way, if his leg is hurting, he won't have to hit the floor."

"No problem," Charlie agreed.

The call came near the end of Charlie's watch. He "threw the gong" and the men slid down the pole. "The captain!" Charlie cried anxiously. Looking up faithfully, like a new puppy, he eagerly awaited his cargo at the base of the pole the captain used.

The captain curled his legs around the brass pole and began his descent. The men watched in delight as the rookie snatched the captain in his arms and began to carry him to his seat. "What the . . . get this guy away from me! What're you doing, boy?" the captain roared. The men convulsed in laughter.

Knowing he had been had, Charlie lowered the captain and went to put on his own turnout gear. He returned, red-faced, and joined the others for his first call. Between bursts of laughter, the men again welcomed him to the company, and as Captain Meushaw climbed aboard the unit he mumbled something about the "new boy."

Part of the problem with being a rookie is that you do stupid things! Some are harmless, like letting the veteran firefighters convince you that you're stupid; others, although innocently intended, can have drastic, even deadly, results.

A young medic named Joe and a seasoned firefighter named Roy were assigned to Medic 4. They got along fairly well, except that whenever young Joe made a mistake, Roy would mutter, "Well, Stupid!" For obvious reasons, he was not a confidence builder for Joe. On this particular night, Joe fulfilled Roy's expectations.

While transporting their patient to the hospital, Medic 4 received a call for an attempted suicide. Wasting no time, they delivered their patient to the emergency room of a city hospital and headed northwest. Roy drove. At 46, he already had 25 years of service. He longed for the day when he would make first acting lieutenant and he wouldn't have to ride the ambo anymore.

Joe, however, was still considered a rookie, at least by the old-timers. Although he was 28, he had only been in the department three years. Moreover, he had one fault: he was too cocky.

As they reached in the ambo for the stretcher and med kit, they glanced up at the location of their call — a public housing high rise, which the police had nicknamed the "O.K. Corral" because of the many shootings there. The summer before, five people had been shot in cold blood in one week.

They road silently to the ninth floor in the urine-stained elevator. They knocked at the door and a woman reluctantly let them in. "He's in there," she said, pointing to the bedroom.

They spotted a trail of blood on the floor leading down the hallway. A young man, about 18 years old, sat sobbing on a bed. The smell of alcohol on him reeked havoc with the odors of the apartment. Joe asked what was wrong. The young fellow held up his wrists revealing superficial cuts from what appeared to be a blunt instrument. Joe examined the cuts which were minor and probably would not require stitches.

Joe became irritated as he stood in a stuffy, confining apartment with its unpleasant odors facing a sobbing drunk who wanted to kill himself with an emery board! The thought of flying through the streets with lights and siren on for *this* made him blurt out, "That scratch ain't gonna kill you, for crying out loud! If you wanted to kill yourself, why didn't you jump out of the window or something?" He turned away from the man and began filling out his report, while he talked with Roy.

Their conversation was interrupted by a rustle behind them. They turned just in time to see the man leap out the ninth-floor window. Spellbound for several seconds, Joe picked up his radio and called for the police, reporting that he had a suicide victim.

When Joe and Roy came out of the bedroom, the woman who did not know about her brother's suicide, asked if they were going to take her brother to the hospital. Silently, Joe led her and the family downstairs and outside to the young man's body.

After letters of complaint and a series of investigations, Joe and Roy were found not to have been negligent. The young man wanted to kill himself, and nothing anyone could have done would have prevented it.

———————

Although it is rare, even veterans in the fire service can become lax and suffer from "rookie-itis" — a kind of rookie vision disability. They overlook what is right in front of them.

Midnight frost covered the city. Everyone had turned up their heat except those who could not pay their electric bills. To keep warm, these people turned on their gas ovens. A young woman walked into her bedroom to check on her boyfriend. They had been up most of the evening, drinking and partying, using candles for light because she couldn't pay the electric bill. What she did not realize was her boyfriend had a history of seizure activity in which drinking and failing to take proper medication bring on seizures.

When she left the room to make coffee, he suffered a grand mal seizure. She was unaware of what happened, as was the other couple at the apartment.

Carrying the cup of coffee she hoped would wake him up, the young woman walked into the bedroom, dodging the beaded curtains that hung in the doorway. Seeing him lying there with foam around his mouth, his eyes lackluster, she screamed.

Dropping the coffee to the floor, she ran to get the other couple. "He's dead, Eve," the man said, feeling his cold body.

Paramedics Onizuku and Trikali responded to the early morning call for a possible DOA (dead-on-arrival). The whole time they were en route, Trikali complained about how dirty the other shift had left the ambo. They arrived at the rowhouse to find a woman in the doorway screaming, "Hurry up! I don't know what's wrong. I think he might be dead!" "Man, this place is cold," thought Onizuku. "It must be barely 50 degrees in here."

The other couple pointed to the bedroom. The victim lay in bed, stone cold and still. As Trikali wrote on his pad, Onizuku examined the man. Dried drool covered his face. His eyes were dull and his skin was cold. "He's dead," Onizuku said, not bothering to take vital signs.

The woman broke down sobbing. Her friends tried consoling her but to no avail. Trikali, with his pad in hand, began asking questions. As they talked, Onizuku repacked his med kit. A man passed by. Onizuku glanced up at him and thought to himself, "Boy, he sure looks familiar." The large man walked into the living room where the others were consoling the woman. The woman looked up at him and passed out. Trikali turned and saw the "dead" man standing before them, drool still on his face. "What's happenin', mama?" he asked.

Trikali and Onizuku babbled an excuse. The woman regained consciousness and starting cursing, demanding they leave.

A complaint was filed with the Fire Department and an investigation followed. Both paramedics were reprimanded and took a loss of 15 vacation days each. I have never heard of another incident like this in Baltimore. It's a lesson. Don't let yourself get too comfortable at what you do, or you may get "Rookie-itis," something you definitely could regret.

When I served with Engine 23 in a double house on Saratoga Street, we were assigned two rookies from the Fire Academy. One went to Engine 23, the other to Engine 15.

The new man at Engine 15 reported to his company officer, who introduced him to all the men on the shift. Later, he showed him Engine 15 and its equipment, where he would be riding, and what would be expected of him. Then the young man assisted the others in the housework of the station.

As they cleaned, he became more relaxed and thought to himself that this was not going to be so tough. In fact, he became almost too relaxed. On his first watch-desk duty, as he nodded off to sleep, he was jarred by the officer on duty who called him to attention. He bolted upright not daring to blink until his relief man came. His stomach was in knots.

After watch, he went upstairs to the kitchen to eat lunch, only to find that the lunch didn't agree with him. It seemed his nerves won the battle of the butterflies. He took off for the bathroom, just in time. There he sat motionless for 15 minutes, afraid to get up. "Murphy's Law" applies to simple human functions. Every time you go to the bathroom, the chance of getting a call increases proportionally to the amount of bathroom calls you need to make.

The call came in. The old gong was thrown and the firefighters dashed for the brass poles. Drivers revved the engines as they prepared to leap out to the streets. Meanwhile, where was the new boy?

Engine 23 had departed. The officer of Engine 15 blew the horns and rang the bell. Finally they saw him sliding down the pole. He jumped onto the back step of 15 and they headed east on Saratoga Street.

But what was hanging from his backside? Yes! A long stream of toilet paper trailed like a kite tail from the back of the rookie's pants! Meanwhile, he kept leaning over, trying to keep them from falling down! He didn't want to get in trouble by being late and in his haste, had not completely finished his endeavor when he took off for the wagon. His obvious embarrassment gave us a much-needed laugh for that day — and for several months afterward.

8 Crimes of Passion

When pent-up emotions overheat, tempers explode and violence destroys in seconds what a lifetime has built. Guns, knives, fists, or fire — each takes their toll. Because of the savage force exerted in such crimes, the injuries are usually grim if not fatal.

Crimes of passion fall into two categories: those motivated by love, or the loss of it; and those motivated by excessive pride, or the loss of it. The most serious injuries are from guns; and most of these involve disputes between lovers, spouses, family or friends. Even if the victim survives, the emotional damage is permanent.

Shortly after I joined the ambulance service, I encountered one of the most gruesome incidents of my career. My partner that night, Ken Young, had seen a *lot* of action as he had served on the medic unit for about five years.

The night was exhausting. We answered call after call for six hours. We responded to shootings, stabbings, a hanging, one childbirth and a few unrelated cases. Most of the calls involved domestic fights. All of our skills and equipment were being tested that night. We rarely made it back to our bay before receiving the next call.

A call came in for a shooting at an address just off McHenry and Carey Streets. We answered it. When we arrived, the street was crowded by a squadron of police cars. Neighbors jammed the sidewalks. From the house we could hear wailing. "Bad sign," Ken sighed. He reached for the clipboard as I grabbed the med box. We ran through the wave of people into the small rowhouse, pushing police out of the way to get up to the second floor. We passed one officer on the stairs who looked at the med kit and said, "You won't need that!" In a small, poorly lit room we found the first body, a 16-year-old girl. She rested in a sitting position on the floor leaning against a sofa. Her head drooped toward the floor. Ken squatted next to her to examine a small caliber bullet hole on the left side of her head above her ear. Almost immediately, he stood, exhaled and went to the kitchen. I stooped in front of her to check her vital signs. Ken said, "I don't think you need to do that." I looked flabbergasted. We always took vitals on all patients. Then he pointed to the other side of her head. On the right side was a hole about the size of a half-dollar. Protruding from it was brain matter. "Oh!" I said. I got up and, holding in my stomach, followed him to the hallway leading to the kitchen area. As we went into the hall, we found the body of a 17-year-old boy. He had bullet holes on both sides of his head.

In the kitchen, an older woman stood near the oven with her hands on her face covering her grief. She sobbed uncontrollably. A female police detective held her while asking questions about her dead son and his girlfriend. Rescuers attempted to piece together what had happened. It seemed that although the young couple were to be married, their relationship had been stormy. They argued continuously. The son was so jealous of his girlfriend that whenever she looked in the direction of another man, he would drag her to a private area and beat her. His mother begged him to seek help but he refused, becoming so angry that even she became afraid of him.

On this evening, the young couple had argued violently in the living room, while the mother cried helplessly in the kitchen. Neighbors on both sides could clearly hear their accusations and rising voices. Several times the distraught mother went into the room to plead for them to stop. The boy accused his fiance of being unfaithful to him with a delivery boy who had recently delivered groceries. She denied everything but he slapped her, splitting her lip and drawing blood.

Witnessing this, the mother decided she had to do something and went to telephone the Police Department. As she picked up the receiver, she heard a booming gunshot from the living room. She ran through the doorway as her son put a pistol to his head and pulled the trigger. She screamed in shock as his body dropped limp to the floor. Hearing the gunshots, neighbors rushed through the door to find the homicide-suicide before them. They consoled the mother, while someone called the police.

Ken pronounced the teens dead at the scene, completing the necessary reports and giving the detectives a copy. The Medical Examiner's office would take over from here. We gathered up our equipment and headed for the ambo. The small home was enshrouded in death — hopeless, pitiful, gruesome, senseless, stomach-twisting death. I couldn't wait to get outside to breathe fresh air. It had been my first homicide call in the ambulance service. Now I knew what veteran firefighters meant: when you see death at its worst, all you can do is turn your head, take a deep breath and climb back in your unit to wait for the next call.

———————

Mother's Day — a special time to demonstrate appreciation and affection to the woman who bore and cared for her children. It's a day to do something special for her as well as to share love and precious moments, contemplate the important things in life, and create memories.

But Mother's Day in 1983 was different. Jim Blake and I were working Medic 1. It was a gorgeous day and I hated having to be on duty instead of spending the time with my wife and mom. It goes with the job — one of the things that people forget when they squabble over taxes, fire fees and municipal budgets.

It was a typical Sunday morning, slow. So slow in fact that we were able to get lunch and eat it in one sitting. After that we joined others to watch a movie on TV. A call came in for Medic 1 at 12:30 p.m. — a reported shooting in a low-income high rise. Jim handled the ambo with ease as we broke through the holiday inner-harbor traffic.

Police were already on the scene, running along the fenced balcony on the seventh floor with their guns drawn.

By the time we got off the elevator at the seventh floor with our equipment and stretcher, the action was over. One police officer stood at the door, grimly looking into the apartment. Between two other officers stood a young black woman, handcuffed. Desperation and remorse filled her face. Behind her stood a police woman hand-in-hand with two small children, three and four years old. They kept their eyes on their mom in disbelief.

We were pointed to the bedroom. Lying on a bed, face down and naked, was the lifeless body of a young, black man. As we examined him, we noted a bullet hole in his forehead which exited the back of his head and a hole that had bled profusely from the right side of his neck. They were small holes but they did their job of emptying life from this body.

What had happened to ruin this meaningful day? The young couple had an argument about sex. The battle grew out of hand as the live-in boyfriend began to beat the woman. The children watched fearfully as the man pulled the telephone out of the wall and hit the woman on the head with it. Then he straddled her pounding her head and face.

She broke away and ran to the nightstand. Yanking open the drawer, she pulled out a pistol and fired two shots at point-blank range. The startled man lunged toward her in a final attempt to inflict pain, but collapsed across the bed which crashed to the floor under his weight.

The children stood mesmerized. The mother stood in disbelief, looking at the dead man, as she dropped the gun to the floor. She walked over to her next-door neighbor's and asked her to call the police. Then she went back to her children and held them tightly.

After we pronounced the man dead, I wrote up the ambulance report while listening to the conversation between the police and the young mother. When the policewoman told the mother that her children would have to be put in a foster home, tears welled up in her eyes and etched lines down her cheeks. As she was taken away, the children screamed and cried, "Mommy! Mommy! Come back! Don't leave us!"

I found myself fighting back my own tears. Her action had come in self-defense in an intense moment. One side-effect: homeless, parentless, innocent children. Caught up in this crisis, they would suffer the most.

One of the Baltimore Fire Department's most gruesome calls occurred on a wintery night in the early 1980s. Two engines and a truck company on the West Side responded to a report of smoke in the area of a West Side shopping center. At first, no one could find any sign of a fire.

Then Truck 13 spotted smoke and flames cascading out of a tiny rowhouse. Several firefighters entered the house as Truck 13 turned its ladders to the structure. A firefighter entered the second floor and groped blindly in the thick smoke. He stumbled, waving his arms, and fell onto a bed. As he fell, he felt two bodies. His scream, although muffled by his air mask, was heard all the way downstairs. Two fellow firefighters ran to help him as he carried a twisted body down the steps to the first floor.

The smoke was thick even on the first floor. The two men began cardiopulmonary resuscitation, but fell back as they caught a glimpse of the disfigured body beneath them. The woman had no face. Where her face had once been was now a gaping cavity. The officer came down the steps, "Forget the man up there," he said. "He . . . he doesn't have a face either."

When the fire was brought under control, arson investigators arrived on the scene. Neighbors stood off at a distance, stunned. The newly married couple seemed very happy.

Later, the investigation explained the horrid circumstances. As the couple slept that evening, the woman's ex-boyfriend entered their home with a sledgehammer. He quietly approached the bed and bludgeoned their heads, hitting each one of them in the face repeatedly. He continued battering them mercilessly, until they were mutilated beyond recognition. To cover his crime, he set the bed on fire and fled.

The next morning, police and fire investigators arrested him. It was a crime he would have years to think about and one that left its mark on the whole neighborhood and several fire companies.

———————

Knives are as deadly as guns and, like guns, are most often turned against loved ones. One evening a call came over the radio: "Respond to . . . Springhill Avenue for an injured person. Acknowledge Medic 1." We raced through the streets in the "gut bucket," a slang term used by firefighters for ambos. We encountered the usual drivers who wouldn't pull over; drivers who pulled over into the open lane; drivers who panicked and stopped dead in front of us; and drivers who looked at us wide-eyed as they roared through the intersection in front of us.

Several people had gathered on the front porch of the rowhouse. Inside, a young white man sat in the middle of the floor, rocking back and forth and crying.

"Excuse me," I asked, "but are you the patient?"

"NO!" he sobbed, "She's in there." He pointed a shaking finger at the kitchen. We walked to the doorway and stopped. I immediately grabbed my portable radio.

"Medic 1," I said, "dispatch the police to this location for an apparent homicide."

I took the vitals of the young woman lying on the floor, although it wasn't necessary. A butcher knife was embedded in the center of her chest so deeply that only the 6-inch handle was visible. A small trail of blood ran down to a congealed pool on the linoleum floor. The police arrived shortly and took the young man away. The couple had been having a lovers' quarrel and he went berserk. His anger had won the argument, and she had lost . . . everything.

———————

Crimes of passion often involve an assortment of weapons. Woman may be the weaker sex, but when enraged she will fight with whatever is handy.

Wayne and I on Medic 1 were called to the west side of town for an injured man. A young black woman led us upstairs and pointed to a back bedroom where a young black man sat on the edge of the bed, fully dressed. We asked him what was wrong. He didn't respond, but stood up and began to undo his pants. "Whoa!" Wayne cried. "We just want to know what's wrong!" "I'm showing you what's wrong," he said, grimacing. He dropped his underwear. Wayne and I could hardly speak. I swallowed hard and cleared my throat. "How did this happen?" I asked.

He nodded in the direction of the girl. "We had an argument while we were in bed. She got mad and did this with her fingernails." She obviously had *large* fingernails. She had reached under his scrotum and sunk her nails into it. With a forceful tug, she pulled forward, ripping open the sack completely. The testicles were fully exposed.

We notified the police and bandaged the exposed appendage. He insisted on pulling up his pants before we helped him to the ambo.

According to the hospital staff, the couple left five hours later, arm in arm.

Pride and prejudice cause many senseless crimes. One late night Bubby Johnson and his gang finished their last round of drinks. The small-statured young man gulped his drink quickly, his face showing his enjoyment. He and his friends gave the bartender a hard time, cursing and gesturing, as they left the building.

This area of Baltimore has always seen eruptions of racial tension between blacks and whites. But recently, problems had accelerated and several incidents had been precipitated by both sides. Police knew of the explosive potential of certain people who filled the late-night streets. Such was Bubby Johnson.

Bubby never liked blacks. Whenever he had the chance to put one down, he did so. His body bore the marks of some of those acts, but it didn't change him. In fact, he proudly displayed his scars in the bars, even embellishing the tales to make himself look bigger.

As the gang left the bar, they headed toward their motorcycles. On the corner two black men were waiting for the bus. "Hey!" Bubby called to them, "What'cha waiting for? A free bus? All you people ever want is something for free!"

The two black men ignored him. "I said what'cha doing, man?" Bubby slurred his speech as he became more demanding. "You think you're gonna ignore me? No way! I'll show you two."

Bubby left the gang and approached the two men. The tallest man declared, "Hey, man. We don't want no trouble. Why don't you just leave us alone?"

Bubby looked back at his companions who urged him on. He continued standing, face to face, with the taller black man. Sneering and spitting alcohol fumes into his face, Bubby clenched his fist and fired it at the tall man putting his whole body into the roundhouse swing. The man dodged him, which threw

Bubby off balance. The smaller black man drew a switchblade from his jacket. He flicked the 6-inch blade open and thrust it into the staggering Bubby. The blade flashed three times in the abdomen and chest. Eyes grew large as the few bystanders realized they had just witnessed an attempted murder. The two black men melted into the night as Bubby fell to the ground. His gang hurried to his aid. One returned to the bar and told the bartender to call 911.

As police arrived on the scene, blacks and whites gathered around the corner, some exchanged racial remarks. Everyone was, however, cautious not to precipitate another act of violence.

By the time we arrived, most of the crowd had left, not wanting to be identified or involved. Bubby lay on the cool concrete with three holes in his body bleeding the life out of him. A young girl, probably 14 or 15 years old, huddled over him, sobbing and crying out something about blacks.

As we worked on Bubby with our backs to the street, I sensed something warm behind me. I turned around to see that the automobile parked next to us was totally engulfed in flames. Someone had put an incendiary in the vehicle as they left the scene.

We lifted Bubby and moved him about 20 feet away at the side of the building, in case the gasoline tank exploded. Using my portable radio, I called for an engine company to respond, as we continued to work on our patient.

Within a few minutes, Engine 47 pulled up and sent torrents of water into the burning car. Meanwhile, Bubby had lost consciousness. We placed him on our stretcher and put him in the ambulance. In the cool, air-conditioned medic unit, we hooked up the advanced life support and sped off to University Hospital.

Bubby Johnson died three days later from internal injuries. The two black men were never found. To this day, racial tension persists in that area of the city, taking its toll on both sides.

Hopkins walked out of the cold air into the bar and up to the counter. He demanded a shot of whiskey. The bartender obliged. He gulped it down effortlessly. "Give me another!" he demanded, and the bartender hesitantly poured another. Hopkins walked over to an old, dusty jukebox at the end of the bar and dropped a quarter into the slot. The beat boomed out of the crackly speaker.

"I'm taking this baby home with me tonight," he said coldly, patting the jukebox, "and ain't nobody gonna stop me!"

"Well, son," the bartender calmly replied, "I don't think you're gonna take anything out of here tonight."

Hopkins, a tall, lanky black man, turned around, ready for violence, only to face a double-barreled shotgun pointing at his nose.

"Now, I suggest you go vent yourself somewhere else," the bartender continued.

"You'll pay for this, man," Hopkins said, retreating. "You'll pay for this! I swear!" He left the bar, shaking his fist.

Customers cheered. Smiling, the bartender put his shotgun away under the bar.

Later that night a soft, quiet snow began to fall. At 2:30 a.m. after the bar had been closed for half an hour, Hopkins left his nearby home and headed for the darkened bar. He had a .357 Magnum pistol tucked inside his jacket.

Wayne and I felt like yo-yos. Every time we sank into the bunk we got another call. We were just turning in again when the dispatcher's too-familiar voice called us: "Medic 1 . . . respond to . . . Street for a shooting. Police are on the scene. Use extreme caution . . . shooting still in progress!" We looked at each other grimly.

Blasts of gunfire filled the air as we approached the scene. Police had barricaded the surrounding streets which prevented us from getting close to the incident . . . luckily!

A police major walked over. "You guy's don't have a patient yet," he said. "Two officers were wounded initially, but they have both been taken to the hospital."

"What happened?" I inquired.

"The bartender was killed," he said, pointing to the bar, which was now crawling with plain-clothes detectives. "Something about an argument over a jukebox. Guy's name is Timothy Hopkins. He shot the bartender, wheeled the jukebox out the door and over to his house up there," he said, pointing up the street toward the shooting. He continued, "We sent two of our men to his house. He blasted both of them when he opened the door. One seriously." He shook his head. "We got a Signal 13.. . . Officer needs help. Now, the guy is holding his own family hostage, three kids and his wife. We're evacuating the neighbors." The major left, walking slowly through the fresh snow.

We never did transport a patient that evening. Hopkins let his family go about 4:30 a.m. He emerged from his house, rifle over his head in what appeared to be a gesture of submission. Suddenly, he began firing wildly at the police. From the distance, we heard the sounds of gunshots, then silence.

Timothy Hopkins lay dead on the sidewalk, blood pouring from several wounds.

The Police Department would not let us near the body to pronounce him dead. A coroner had been summoned and would take care of the situation. The last item they put in the police vehicle was a jukebox, police evidence, now silent forever.

Josiah Epps and Malcolm Bey had a long-standing feud. The two lived next door to each other on the east side of Baltimore. One morning Epps and Bey came to blows over a parking spot in front of their houses. As it ended in a draw, Bey yelled at Epps that he would burn his house down!

Later that afternoon, as Epps slept in a chair in his kitchen, Bey made a Molotov cocktail. He walked out the door to Epps' house, his hand clutching the bottle of gasoline. "Epps!" he screamed, "This is what I think of you!" He banged on the door, then the window. No answer. Bey threw the homemade bomb through the window. When Epps woke up he found his house in flames. "Now Bey's done it!" he thought. He ran to his gun cabinet and grabbed his 30.06, loaded it and pointed it at the door.

The East Side fire company responded, and within minutes hands were adjusting couplings, turning knobs and pulling heavy firehoses. The firefighters raced up to the front door and pounded on it. No reply. One of the firefighters began to break it down.

Epps cocked the gun and aimed through the thickening smoke. With a burst of sunlight and a spray of water, the door finally opened. Epps fired twice. The firefighter on the nozzle was blown backwards into his comrades, knocking all three of them down the steps. The pump operator screamed into the radio for help. The men scrambled about, helping the wounded firefighter, pulling him away from the flames.

Epps, realizing what he had just done, raised the rifle to his mouth, pushed it in until he gagged, and pulled the trigger.

Bey was found guilty of arson, attempted murder, and second-degree murder. The firefighter who was shot is now pensioned because of his injuries. He has a permanent pin in his shoulder and a colostomy. He was only 33 years old.

9 Under the Influence

The majority of calls to the Fire Department have little to do with fighting fires. Many are for accidents or crimes resulting from the abuse of alcohol or illegal drugs. Substance abuse is responsible for eight out of 10 crimes and over half of the nation's accidental deaths. The drunken driver who kills an innocent person generates universal outrage.

In the early 1980s, Wayne and I responded to a call on the west side of the city that was to receive much publicity. The Warren family had just returned to Baltimore from a large reunion at Atlantic City, New Jersey. Family members from up and down the East Coast had attended. The matriarch of the clan, the energetic and popular Delores Warren, was still a good looking woman, appearing to be much younger than her 81 years. Delores was pleased that so many relatives had attended. With the long weekend over, their charter bus slid easily through the evening streets.

Not far away, a bartender urged a difficult customer to finish his drink and go home. He refused to serve him any more liquor. Dismayed, the man fumbled through his pockets and searched for his keys. Shouting in slurred excitement when he found them, he held up the keys for all to see. The patrons cheered and clapped. He bowed and almost fell head over heels. Straightening himself, he pointed to the exit door and swayed across the floor, departing in an air of triumph.

Meanwhile, the charter bus pulled up alongside the curb, its air brakes hissing. On the opposite side of the street stood a welcoming committee of family members who could not attend the out-of-town reunion. Delores and the bus load of family members gathered at the curb to cross the street. They chattered away and waved to the family on the other side, waiting for the light evening traffic to pass.

The street seemed clear of automobiles when Delores, leading the other Warren family members, stepped off the curb with her small suitcase. The family members across the street began to cheer as she crossed.

No one saw the drunken man's car heading toward Delores because he had forgotten to turn on his headlights. The car slammed into Delores' body, hurling her 20 feet ahead before running over her. The car slowed only long enough for someone to get the license number. The driver, sufficiently sobered, realized what he had done and burned rubber as he drove away.

Delores' limp body lay crumpled in the street, unmoving. The family stood in disbelief. Finally, someone screamed. It broke the trance. People ran to Delores and tried to help her. A neighbor ran into his house to call 911.

Wayne and I were only minutes away. The area was a madhouse. Police cars, a fire truck, and even a reporter were already there. As we pulled to a stop, the medical lieutenant parked behind us. I was driving, so Wayne ran to the victim while I retrieved the stretcher and other equipment. The lieutenant assisted us in assessing the patient. Police tried to console and restrain family members and friends. Another medic unit was called to assist a woman who had passed out.

We looked at Delores and inwardly shook our heads. She was not breathing and needed immediate CPR. We enlisted two firefighters. The flailed chest would not matter. I inserted the EOA and had the lieutenant pump air while Wayne and I set up the IV line and, using the portable radio, called University Hospital for consultation. We advised them of the non-existent vital signs, the flailed chest, and two crushed legs and pelvis. We were told to apply medical anti-shock trousers (MAST) — a special set of pants that inflate and push much-needed blood up into the heart. We began drug therapy and bandaging, ending up with backboarding, hurrying at breakneck speed to package our patient. The lieutenant and two firefighters got in back with us and another firefighter drove to the hospital with lights and siren.

We burst through the doors two minutes ahead of our estimated time of arrival (ETA), finding the trauma team still setting up. After transferring her over to the emergency room (ER) personnel, we waited and watched. Respiratory therapy tubed her, blood was taken to be cross-matched, and the team leader called "CLEAR" for the fifth time, as Delores' body jumped from the electrical charge that shot through her. More IVs were set up and her stomach was tapped. Blood poured into the container, somewhat relieving the internal bleeding.

The EKG still showed defibrillation, and again, the team leader called, "CLEAR!" The rhythm stopped and started again but this time it was a straight line. "OK! That's it. Call it at 1:42 a.m." That was the time of death for Delores

Warren.

We could hear the cries and screams of anguish from the family members who waited in the ER waiting room, when the doctor told them the bad news. It was a moment of heart-wrenching pain. An active grandmother, involved with her family and not ready for death, was snuffed out by a drunken driver. Her family, full of love and appreciation, did not have reason to say "Goodbye." Many people think medics are above "feeling human." Far from the truth. We feel the same compassion and sorrow. Once in a while, we cry, reach for, or even hold a hand.

The driver turned out to be a well-to-do state official with prior drunk driving convictions. When the police found him he was pulling up in front of his house, headlights still off. I believe he only received a three-year term. Delores was sentenced to eternity.

———————

Sometimes accidents seem particularly unbelievable.

It was 3:00 a.m. as Bill Beam pulled his 18-wheeler along the curb. He jumped out of the cab to awaken the dispatcher of the trucking firm. Groggily, the dispatcher showed Bill which door to back in his trailer. "You'll have to block the whole street when you do it," he said.

He was right! Even then, it was going to be tight. Bill revved the engine. He had the rig three-quarters in position when he saw the flash of light.

Matt Hicks sped toward him — mad, drunk and half-awake. He had had an argument with his drinking buddies and had left in a big hurry. Hicks only wanted to get home. He roared around the corner in his pickup truck and didn't see the tractor trailer.

Bill watched in disbelief as the pickup truck plowed into him. THUD! The explosive sound of glass and metal ripped through the silence of the early morning. Bill jumped from the rig and looked in horror at the twisted metal.

The pickup had run right under the belly of the truck and the entire front of the cab was gone. He thought the driver was decapitated, seeing the river of blood that flowed from the bottom of the passenger door.

When Rescue 1 arrived, a man from the engine company ran over to us and cried, "He's still alive!" We ran to the pickup to find Matt lying on the front seat. Someone had put a turnout coat over him. Captain Bill Goodwin called for the Hurst tool and equipment. A Halligan tool jabbed inside the door and gave us the access to insert the "Jaws." We spread them slowly, moving the door somewhat.

To our surprise, the victim's hands emerged and began waving frantically.

Matt tried to get out, but he couldn't move. The door finally popped as we pried it away. What we saw was repulsive. His skull was split open from the occipital area to the forehead. Blood rushed out.

The medics took over, quickly bandaging his head and placing a Philadelphia collar on his neck. The rest was done by backboard. They rushed him to the ambo and worked him up on the ALS. Finished with their initial work, they raced him to the Shock Trauma Center downtown. As we put our equipment away, we surveyed the truck. It looked like a scene from a movie. Only our patient wasn't a stunt man. He would probably never heal completely, mentally or physically.

Many times a drunk driver takes several victims. Carrying a load of steel beams, the tractor rig slowly moved northbound on Hanover Street toward I-95 heading to Pennsylvania. Its driver was tired but alert to the traffic around him on this busy Sunday evening. Ahead of him, he could see the middle branch of the Patapsco River, the Hanover Street Bridge and the Baltimore skyline. Just past the bridge was the on-ramp to I-95. From that point, it would be smooth sailing all the way north. The red flags on the overhanging beams flapped in the evening breeze as the truck headed north.

In Brooklyn, three teens sat in the front seat of their Pontiac convertible. The girl sat between the two older teenage boys. As their radio blared hard rock music, they passed around cans of beer. Then they decided to head home. They swerved around several vehicles as they sped north on Hanover Street. They laughed and talked as the wind blew through their hair. They felt weightless, invincible, free.

Meanwhile, the trailer neared the drawbridge. Ahead, the road bends slightly but in a way requiring careful navigation. Signs, lights and markers also warn drivers to slow down as the road changes from one-way to two-way traffic on the bridge.

The tractor driver saw brake lights ahead and started to slow down. He thought he saw a road crew working on his side of the bridge. There were a few cars ahead of him but not many. He eased up and relaxed back in his seat, waiting for the word to go.

The teens sped past Harbor Hospital and approached the slight bend in the road. The teen, at the wheel, passed a beer to the other boy and then turned his attention back to the road. Suddenly his eyes swelled with fright. The red flags seemed only inches away from his car. There was no room to move, no room to swerve. Instantaneously, he knew they were going to hit. He screamed and threw his hands up. The other boy stopped kissing the girl long enough to realize what was happening.

The girl turned her head to see why they were screaming. The steel beams plunged through the glass windshield and caught her head at the neck. The beams tore her head from her body and cast it in the back seat as they continued to grind through the vehicle, tearing into flesh and metal. The boys were crushed against their seats. Their car finally stopped moving but the mangled metal continued to groan.

Rescue 1, not yet back to quarters from its last run, was dispatched with an engine, truck and ambulance. The lights and siren went back on as they drove past the station, waving to other firefighters sitting on the firehouse wall outside. While responding, they heard the first arriving unit call for more medics.

Bridge traffic northbound had been halted by the police and southbound traffic was severely restricted. As they headed south, the squad weaved around cars and trucks. As they approached the accident, they could see the steel-carrying rig. Where was the other vehicle?

It was there . . . but not there. It looked as if the trunk of the car had a mouth on the end and that it had opened up and began digesting the front end of the Pontiac. The vehicle was crushed in up to the dashboard and there were three bodies inside.

The officer jumped out, followed by the two firefighters in the back. The driver went directly to the on-board generator. He started it and flipped the switches for the floodlights. In a moment, the scene was basking in almost-daylight. He, too, then ran to the rig.

As a lieutenant from the truck company advised them, they toured the carnage. Medics said that the boy on the passenger side was still alive, but he was pinned by the metal beams. The driver was crushed to death and the girl was obviously dead.

The officer of Rescue 1 talked with his driver as the firefighters joined in. It looked like a football huddle. While the medics inserted an IV in the victim, Rescue 1 sprang into action. The driver moved the apparatus down from the accident and backed up within 30 feet of the wreck. He put the power take-off on and placed the two ground-jacks down. As he did this, the firefighters took off a back-plate on the rear step of the squad to reveal the 10-ton winch. They pulled out enough wire cable to reach the wreck and then some more. The driver grabbed a wire rope sling and U-bolts. Together they connected the sling to each side of the axle of the car and then to the end of the winch's wire cable. The officer gave the thumbs-up sign to let the driver know to start pulling the car.

As a medic monitored the teen that was alive, the car began to groan. Metal ground against metal creating a crunching sound. The dead bodies bobbed in the front seat uncontrollably. The teenager started moaning loudly as the steel beams began to move. The medic created a faster drip with the Ringer's lactate IV solution. The metal was finally moved enough so the boy could breathe more freely. The oxygen flow was raised. Bandaging quickly, the medic knew he was running out of time. The boy's pulse rate was rapidly starting to slow.

The squad now had the "Jaws" out working on the crushed door. It had to be opened first so they could use the ram tool to push back the dashboard that was pressing against his body. There was very little room to work in. Soon it opened. Medics slid a backboard in and under the patient. The rescuers secured him with straps and collars and he was on his way to the trauma center.

The two remaining victims had already been pronounced DOA. Firefighters took their time removing the bodies, so no one would get hurt. A brave firefighter carried the girl's head, wrapped in a blanket, over to the coroners' vehicle to go with her body. The boy at the hospital died from massive internal bleeding the next morning.

The engine company washed down the blood from the incident as Rescue 1 put away their equipment. They took a moment to survey the accident scene. Incredible. One minute three young people with long lives ahead of them. The next, nothingness and families that would live a lifetime with an empty place in their hearts. It seemed so senseless.

The driver of the truck was so shaken by the accident that a medic unit took him to University Hospital for counseling. The accident wasn't his fault, but the memory of it would victimize him for the rest of his life.

———————

A heart-rending incident happened when I was a paramedic. The call came in for a possible DOA just off Washington Boulevard on Nanticoke Street. We were told that police were already on the scene.

Most calls for DOAs come in the early morning hours when people wake up to find the bodies of loved ones or friends who died in their sleep or in the night. After we examine the corpses we can officially pronounce them dead. It is unpleasant. Relatives stand and stare at you. Some scream. Some shout. Some try to beat you up as they lash out at their grief.

It took four minutes to arrive on location. A police car was parked out front. The street was peaceful; a few heads peeked out of nearby doors. The police officer got out of his vehicle and strolled over as we gathered up our equipment. "You won't be needing any of that," he said. "It's a young guy. He's dead, for sure." Nevertheless, by protocol, we still had to examine the body.

It was a typical rowhouse with a formstone front, wooden steps, and a storm door. This one was mid-way in the long block of look-alikes. In the doorway of the next house, an elderly woman with a five-year-old girl watched us carefully as we approached the house. Concern covered their faces, and the little girl looked as if she had been crying.

The firefighter held the door open for the policeman and me, and followed us in. We didn't have to go far. Our patient, a white man of 25, lay sideways on the living room sofa. His long and stringy hair appeared not to have been recently washed. He sported ragged jeans and a black leather jacket with studded stars all over it. Around his wrists and neck were heavy gold-colored chains. A 6-inch pocket knife was hooked to his belt and a 10-inch knife blade was slid down into his left boot.

The young man looked as if he had been sitting straight up and had keeled over on the couch. I went around him to search for a cause of death. By the time I reached his head, it was obvious. He had been sniffing gold spray paint in a plastic bag. Beneath his right side lay the can of spray paint. Dumb, dumb, dumb was the only thing I could think. How could a grown man do something so stupid!

He had no vital signs. In fact, rigor mortis was starting to set in. As I filled out my report, I told my driver to take the equipment back to the ambo. I stared at the DOA. His eyes had been sealed shut by the dry paint. It looked like a scene from *Goldfinger*. The plastic bag was partially stuck to his nose and mouth.

I finished my report and tore off a copy for the policeman. We stood there talking about the man: why does anyone jeopardize their life for a "high," especially one that lasts for so short a time?

The policeman asked me to tell the man's mother who was next door. "She's got his daughter over there. The kid is the one that found him this morning. She told her grandmother she got up to watch cartoons and couldn't wake her daddy up."

"The people I saw when I came in?" I inquired. "Yes, it's sad. She's a beautiful little girl," he announced.

The family still stood at the door. I sensed the little girl already knew what I was about to say. The closer I came, the more she began to sob. When I went inside, she was crying her heart out.

I told the mother as she cradled her grandchild. My heart began to break in two as I watched the little girl. Her only security was a grandmother's lap. Her daddy would never be there for her again. His lust for a fix had snuffed the life out of him. She cried out through the tears, "Daddy, Daddy. I want my daddy. Please let me get my daddy." My chest began convulsing as I swallowed my own sobs. I had to leave.

As I walked away, I felt enraged by this man whose utter stupidity left an orphan in the world. He had a beautiful little girl who loved him dearly. But his love for a fix was even greater than his love for his daughter. I turned to my driver and said, "Let's get out of here. The coroner will take care of him." We went back in service.

———

Cigarettes and a combination of alcohol and cigarettes cause their share of fires and death.

Steadman Station sits across the street from a major hotel in downtown Baltimore. It's a modern concrete structure that is kept in fair shape.

Late one night, a man staying on the hotel's eighth floor fell asleep after "drinking and partying" most of the evening. He "went out like a light." The cigarette in his hand lazily dropped to the floor as he rolled over, nestled comfortably under the covers. Soon a smoldering fire broke out.

The heat in the room began to rise as the smoke thickened. Waking with a start, the man realized what was happening and ran for the door, gasping for air. When he opened the door, fresh air from the hallway poured into the room. The air fanned the fire and the room flashed over as fire engulfed it. Flames licked out to the ceiling of the hallway. They touched the solder on the sprinkler head near the door. Water poured down in a cooling shower. Too late! The room was in flames. Heat continued to build across the large glass window until it burst out to the street below. Now flames lapped at the walls outside, threatening other rooms.

The surge in the water pipes from the open sprinkler head generated a water-flow alarm, which activated a call to the Fire Department. The signal came in to fire communications. The officer-in-charge transmitted the information to the dispatcher who, in turn, relayed it to the responding companies in their order of dispatch.

Bunk room, bay, and hall lights came on, and the house speakers told us where we were going. Although as we pulled out the bay doors, it was obvious where we were heading. We looked up and saw the flames reaching out of the eighth floor. Because of the hazard to life, the battalion chief immediately called for a second alarm.

The water tower set up operations almost directly in front of the row of windows that lined up with the fire. Slowly it was raised as an engine company supplied hoselines to its pipe. The members of other companies ran inside and began evacuating rooms.

After dropping the high-rise pack on the seventh floor, Engine 15 proceeded to the eighth floor with Truck 2. Heavy smoke filled the hallway.

The hotel manager, a 28-year-old black man, was very obese. When the alarm in the hotel went off, he checked the annunciator panel and ran to the eighth floor. He ran up the steps, not the elevator. People he worked with said he was a stickler about fire safety; he would never take an elevator in the event of a fire.

His large size impeded his movement as he climbed the stairs, huffing and puffing. Running down the smoke-filled hallway, he banged on doors to warn the sleeping occupants and evacuate the building. Holding a towel up to his face, he continued banging until a pain shot across his chest. As he closed his eyes, he could hear the sirens from across the street.

Personnel from Engine 15 bumped into him as they crawled in the hallway. "We've got a man down!" the officer screamed through his mask into the portable radio.

The battalion chief had us set up across the street from the fire in a parking lot next to the station. On Ambo 1, we had a good view of the overall operations. As we monitored the radio chatter, we heard the call for a man down. Before the officer was finished, we had the stretcher and equipment on the way to the front of the building.

The firefighters had used the fire service key on the elevator to bring the patient down. We met them in the lobby. As they administered CPR, we checked for vital signs. Nothing! "Let's get him in the ambo. We can hook him up to the monitor!" I yelled.

Several firefighters helped us carry him across the street, stepping over hoselines as we went. A man came up and identified himself as a doctor. In sequence, we began to perform life-saving techniques. Defibrillation, sodium bicarbonate, IV-D5W, epinephrine, more defibrillation. Nothing showed on the monitor.

The doctor asked for an intracardiac needle to inject sodium bicarbonate into the heart. When I told him we didn't carry that type of needle, he said he couldn't believe it. He tried with a regular needle on a sodium bicarbonate syringe. It didn't work. "Continue CPR," he said, "and let the emergency room know we're coming in!"

Because of the size of the victim, we had to call another company to help us remove him from the ambo. Otherwise one of us might have been hurt lifting him. The hospital crew went to work to save him.

Meanwhile, the water tower and Engine 15 worked to put out the fire while other companies checked the floors and rooms for possible hot spots or smoke and water damage.

The manager never regained consciousness. The newspaper called him a hero. They were right. Had he not alarmed so many people, the fire could have claimed many more lives. Many of the rescued patrons sent flowers and cards to his family, thanking them for his bravery. He left a wife and two children behind.

Compulsions, whether to alcohol or cigarettes, can have horrible consequences.

Like a remote-control dune buggy, the ambulance swerved through the streets. The firefighter drove and the medic rode shotgun because of a shortage of paramedics in the department.

An elderly gentleman lived on the fifteenth floor of a high-rise apartment building. He had smoked cigarettes since he was nine years old and the habit had taken its toll on his body, which convulsed with the hack of emphysema. Although his wife had nagged him about his smoking, he refused to stop. He kept a supply of smokes in hiding places around the apartment. "You keep smoking them things and you're gonna kill yourself," she called out each time she found a pack. His uniform response was, "You've got to die from something."

Even as breathing became more difficult, he insisted on his cigarettes. But after some time he depended on fresh oxygen to survive. Tubes ran to his nose, connecting him to the tank that held the breath of life. When he went on oxygen he had to stop smoking because of the presence of the highly flammable oxygen tank. Now he was in painful nicotine withdrawal. Anything his wife said caused a verbal eruption from her husband.

Needing a break from the emotional stress of their arguments, the elderly woman visited a nearby neighbor down the hall.

The old man listened briefly for the sound of her receding footsteps, then gathered his breathing equipment and slowly moved across the apartment. His shaking hand searched frantically behind a kitchen cabinet and came to rest on a fresh pack of Lucky Strikes hidden a long time ago for a nicotine emergency such as this. The old man looked briefly at the pack thinking, "These are a man's cigarettes."

Most children and certainly nearly all adults know what happens when you mix oxygen and an open flame. But there are times when the most intelligent people succumb to passion or addiction.

Dragging all of his life sustaining breathing equipment in one hand and the pack of cigarettes in the other, he laboriously made his way back to the sofa. Along the way he stopped for a breath of oxygen. When he reached the sofa, he was exhausted. His wrinkled hands shook as he pulled a cigarette from the pack.

Automatically he readjusted the oxygen flow valve with his other hand. Then he put the cigarette between his lips, took a match from the pack and struck the graphite.

Just then, the man's wife returned to the apartment. As she opened the door, she saw her husband strike the match. In a second, a ball of fire enveloped his head. He yelled as his fingers tore frantically at the nasal tubes to remove them. His wife screamed and instinctively ran toward him. Grabbing the afghan from the back of the sofa, she threw it around his head. Then she yanked off the tubing and flung it across the floor. Like a rattlesnake, it hissed as the flame came out of it. She turned off the tank and ran to her husband who was still wrapped like a mummy in the afghan and was vigorously patting his face and head.

When the ambulance arrived, the medics were amazed that all he suffered was a bad "sunburn" and singed hair. The engine company arrived first and stabilized the oxygen bottle. The old man's nerves were "fried." To make things worse, once inside the ambo he was captive to his wife's incessant lecturing. "You see! I told you that those cigarettes were going to be the death of you."

When most people think of death caused by drugs, they think of dealer-buyer gun battles and street wars. But most deaths from hard drugs occur silently in lonely rooms.

The three-year-old girl carefully descended the steps of the apartment. The locked door shut behind her, so that she could not get back in. She cried as she told a neighbor that she couldn't wake up her mommy.

Engine 38 and Medic 1 took the call for a lockout. We found the little girl sobbing, clutching her neighbor's hand as firefighters took an extension ladder off the engine and raised it to the second floor. From the ladder, Firefighter Brian LaHatte entered the window and came down the steps to let us all in.

The look on his face told us this was a devastating call. Holding a one-year-old baby with a bottle in his arms, he nodded, "Their mom's up there in the kitchen." He paused, looking to the neighbor. "Ma'am," he said, "I think you'd better keep the kids down here."

We went upstairs. The body of the young woman lay crouched in the corner, leaning against the refrigerator. When we went to move her, we saw the small-bore needle lodged in her arm. On the kitchen table was the paraphernalia. Small amounts of heroin could be seen in bottle caps. An already empty syringe sat next to it.

In that one week, medic units had responded to several heroin deaths. Another bad batch had come up the I-95 corridor from Washington, D.C. I will never forget the look in that poor little girl's eyes — she and children like her are the silent victims of the drug trade.

Baltimore, like most major cities, wrestles with heavy drug trafficking and gang-like "drug wars." One day, in a high rise on the east side of town, a small calico cat looked up with a start at a closed door. Suddenly the door was thrown open. The cat leaped from the bed and hid beneath it, watching silently as the shooting took place.

City police responded to the public housing complex for the third shooting that week. Cruisers lined the street below. Other officers patrolled the area for suspects. A large crowd gathered on the street and in the long, concrete hallway. The activity could be watched through the heavy chain-link fencing that acted as an outside wall.

Police officers, with guns drawn, charged into the apartment. One body lay on the living room floor. An officer felt for a pulse. "Get an ambulance here! Quick!" Another officer went into the back, where he found another body on a bedroom floor.

We had heard reports that some of the Los Angeles gangs were moving into the Baltimore-Washington area because of its potentially lucrative drug trade. But to move in successfully, they would have to wipe out their competition. They seemed to be doing it fairly well. Execution-style murders had increased.

Paramedic Mark Hofmann and Firefighter Dennis Williams served on Medic 1 that busy evening. At 9:00 p.m., the call came in for a shooting at 200 North Aisquith Street, third floor. They acknowledged the run and left. Police officers met them and discussed the two victims as they proceeded to the elevator and began their ascent to the third floor. They had to push people out of the way to get off the elevator and reach the apartment.

The medics knew they had a gruesome job ahead of them when they entered the living room. On the floor before them lay a young, black man about 20 years old, breathing very shallowly. The abdominal region of his shirt was saturated with blood. Mark knelt next to him and checked his pulse rate — about 50-60 beats per minute. Blood pressure — 94/60.

As Mark took his scissors and snipped the buttons on the man's shirt, the shirt flew open and organs jutted out of his body. Thinking quickly, Mark took an IV bag, which is sterile on the inside, cut it open and laid it over the exposed organs. Dennis handed him strips of tape. They slowly rolled him to the side to reveal holes in his back where he had taken the blast of a shotgun. They bandaged the injury. Nervously, Mark asked the cops, "How's the other one?" "Don't worry about him," they said. "He's dead for sure." Dennis, in the meantime, set up an IV of Ringer's lactate for Mark. Working feverishly, the paramedic inserted a number-14 catheter needle for volume flow. Oxygen was set at 10 liters with a non-rebreather mask. They loaded the man on a stretcher once he was stabilized.

They then went into the bedroom. Another young man lay sprawled on a bed with his head blown off. Blood splattered the walls like spray paint. All that was left of his head was a small part of the right side of the skull. Suddenly, a police officer behind them yelled. They turned to see the cat eating part of the brain matter on the floor.

Mark and Dennis ran back to the living patient and rushed him toward the elevator and the ambulance. Once on board, Mark consulted with Johns Hopkins Hospital's Trauma Center, sending an EKG which showed a bradycardia, or slow heartbeat. The doctor on the line advised rushing the patient to the hospital without any other intervention. They agreed. Dennis and Mark stayed in the back of the unit while a firefighter from an engine company drove the ambo to Johns Hopkins with a two- to three-minute estimated time of arrival (ETA).

They arrived at the center in two minutes and wheeled their patient to the trauma unit. After transferring him to the hospital gurney, they watched as skilled surgeons and nurses dove into their work as if they saw this carnage every day. If ever there was trauma, this was it. Mark and Dennis began their ritual of completing paperwork and cleaning equipment.

Police arrived at the hospital to check the status of the victim. Mark and Dennis asked them about the circumstances leading to the man's demise.

A gang from Los Angeles had moved into this part of Baltimore to build a drug trade. Apparently the two victims had dealt in "the hard stuff" and got in the gang's way. The gang sent a hit man to the apartment who broke in the door, apparently startling the two occupants. The killer went to one bedroom where he found the first victim in bed. When he raised his gun to shoot, the other man ran out of his bedroom in an effort to get away. The hit man put a sawed-off shotgun to the first victim's chin and pulled the trigger, blasting the head off its shoulders. As he finished, he turned to catch the second man running through the apartment into the living room and fired directly into his back. After this, he casually walked away, leaving the weapon, without any fingerprints, at the scene. Everyone heard the blasts but no one saw anything or anyone.

Mark and Dennis related the story back at the station. Dennis' mistake was telling us about the cat. All evening and for almost the entire shift, he had to tolerate anonymous "meows" throughout the firehouse. It was our way of trying to help him overcome the horror he had witnessed. Mark did put it behind him, but events like this one affect us all, sometimes in ways other people do not understand.

As far as we know, the man shot in the back is alive. We wonder what he is doing with his life? Hopefully, he has found a better line of work.

10 Ups, Downs and Rebounds

"What's the hardest part of being a firefighter?" kids often ask. It is not the grueling labor, long shifts, interrupted sleep or constant danger — all of which take their toll. The hardest part is coping with the emotional "ups and downs."

The physical adjustments are difficult — work sites that take you to a rooftop 150 feet up in heavy winds, or to a stuffy, dark parking garage 30 feet underground; one minute teetering at the top of a 100-foot ladder as you battle scorching flames, and then crawling into the icy coffin-like spaces of a collapsed building.

But, the emotional adjustments are harder. Firefighting is a lot like being a surfer, who spends hours or days waiting for the big ride, wading through the little stuff, being battered by the surf *just* to experience the thrill of riding the big one. When it arrives, he cheers and rides it as long as he can.

When you rescue a family from a fire or breathe life back into a drowned teenager, you experience a unique emotional high. Just the opposite occurs when all your efforts are in vain. It's like crashing on rocks or being pounded mercilessly into the gritty sand under the surf when you see the monitor line go flat, and the life of a broken or burned body in your arms slip away forever.

Many firefighters suffer burn out; it seems inevitable for anyone with a conscience, a memory and a heart. After almost 20 years, I still find these jagged peaks and valleys as difficult to accept as on my first day on the job.

When I think of soaring feelings of highs and lows, aircraft accidents come to mind. One minute, the pilot is master of his craft; the next, he is grounded. These sudden and final "falls from grace" are haunting. When they involve others, the grim picture is etched indelibly.

One cold winter morning in Baltimore, the male pilot and the female emergency medical technician (EMT) breathed simultaneous sighs of relief as the "Medivac" helicopter touched down safely on the roof of the city hospital heliport. The fog had almost grounded them at the scene of an automobile/tractor-trailer accident in the mountainous western part of the state. Their patient stabilized, they had endured the worst part of the trip, landing the large craft on the "X" atop the high rise. After registering their patient, they departed the operating area on the fourth floor to gather supplies to replenish their med kits.

Then they returned to the top floor of the multi-level garage where their white metal "nurse of the air" stood waiting another run. After the flight check, the blade turned and began its revolutions. The chopper rose slowly and then darted northwest in the thickening fog to its base.

Air Traffic Control at Baltimore-Washington International Airport came over the radio: "Helicopter 2, we have you on radar in heavy fog. Use caution on your flight path. You are clear for run."

"Roger, BWI," the pilot responded. That was the last communication heard from Helicopter 2. The radar operator confirmed that the aircraft had disappeared from the screen somewhere in the west end of the city. It was about 4:00 a.m.; the City Police were notified.

An intense search began and extended statewide, all the way to Frederick, Maryland, the origin of the flight. A caller from Baltimore City said she heard a helicopter during the night that sounded like it was "right over" her house. The search was narrowed to a small park on the West Side. Finally, a police cruiser called in and reported spotting the wreckage on a hillside in the park.

Fire units and police vehicles arrived within minutes. Rescue 1, responding on the first alarm, arrived to see state and city police cars stretched along the street flanking the park. In the distance were the white and yellow markings of the air ambulance.

We pushed our way through the crowd, climbing the steep, soggy ground. What carnage: trunks, limbs, branches, pieces of steel and fiberglass were strewn everywhere. In the midst of the wreckage lay the beaten and ravaged shell of Helicopter 2 with its two victims.

The pilot, compressed under the weight of the main rotor, was folded in half in his seat like a wallet, his back completely crushed. The EMT's face had been smashed into a tree.

We fought back feelings of revulsion and anger as we labored to free the two bodies. It was a vicious death for two courageous people.

After cutting and removing pieces of twisted metal, our faces and hands burning in the icy winter cold, we freed the two bodies. Watching our footing on the slippery hillside, we carried them carefully to the waiting morgue wagon. Our only consolation was that their deaths had come swiftly.

———————

Another aircraft incident occurred on the south end of the city. On its way to New York, a single engine airplane with two men and a woman suddenly lost altitude and headed toward the Potee Street bridge.

"Mayday . . . mayday!" the pilot sputtered into his radio. "I'm losing altitude and approaching a populated area — unable to maintain control of aircraft!" He gave his coordinates. There was no time for more talk. His hands worked feverishly, but the dials and gauges were unresponsive.

On the bridge, passengers noticed the erratic course of the plane and speculated on its collision course. Some stopped their cars short of its approach.

The pilot miraculously twisted his craft to port side to avoid a hospital looming ahead. In one last effort, he pulled his stick forward and barely skirted the bridge, only to crash nose-down on a small island bridge on the other side. The plane toppled, and lay upside down.

Everyone survived. Civilians ran over to the accident site. A door popped open, and the two passengers crawled from the wreckage, bleeding and sobbing.

But the pilot was suspended upside down, jammed into his seat by the twisted equipment. The crushed-in door trapped him and he banged on it for assistance. No one could believe he survived the crash, but no one could free him, either.

Sirens wailed in the distance. A spark ignited in the rear of the plane, and flames shot up. Black smoke streamed from holes in the tail as the fire inched toward the front of the plane.

The pilot screamed and pounded furiously at the door. Several people tried to reach him, but were driven back by the intense heat. As the flames assaulted the small cockpit, the pilot's screams became the agonizing, high-pitched wails of torture. Onlookers could do nothing but listen as his fading cries blended in with the approaching sirens.

When the fire was finally extinguished, passers-by stood in disbelief as firemen and rescue workers removed his charred body. Might they have saved him if they had thought more quickly or had more courage? These unwilling witnesses had experienced the helplessness, guilt and heart-wrenching pain that firefighters feel over and over.

One of the ups I remember best was an incident involving a young baker's helper who got a "rise" out of his work. Although the incident was humorous, it could have been deadly.

A doughnut company, four blocks from the station, baked doughnuts throughout the night. Its fresh doughnuts were a favorite of the local firefighters. John Carter, the baker's helper, assisted preparing the assorted pastries, then cleaned up.

When the baker asked John to take out the old dough, John gathered up the scraps and threw them in a vat, which he then took to the dumpster.

After several minutes, the baker realized John had not returned. He went out to the dock and looked around, but didn't see him. He called, but John did not give an answer. Finally, he went back inside thinking John had left.

Meanwhile, Engine 23 was on its "doughnut run." One of the advantages of working near the bakery was that the "castaways" and "day-olds" found a welcome home at the station. Companies took turns rescuing day-olds on the way back from a run.

Returning from a false alarm, Engine 23 pulled up to the bake shop dock. Suddenly, the tired men heard a strange, muffled noise. They looked around, but saw no one. As they marched up the steps in unison, they again heard the sound. Once more, they stopped and listened.

"Help! Help!" came a faint cry. The firefighters examined the grounds before narrowing their search to the area of the dumpster. What they saw when they looked inside was unbelievable!

In the middle of the smelly container stood a young man stuck in dough up to his neck! The dough had been rising for some time. Incapable of moving his arms to escape, and close to suffocation, the young man had tilted his head back to breathe. Dough splatters grew like fat leeches on his face and hair. It looked like a scene from the *Twilight Zone* or a movie about slimy space aliens.

Medic 1 was called for a medical evaluation and possible transport. Engine 23 placed ropes around John and slowly pulled him free, leaving his shoes deep in the dough. The owner, coming out to see the source of the commotion, was surprised to find John.

Although his vital signs were normal, Medic 1 took John to the hospital to be examined. Firefighters nicknamed him the "Pillsbury Doughboy."

Window washers face dangerous working conditions every day of the week. By the time they have washed their way to the bottom of a high rise, it is time to return to the top. There is the constant threat of a fatal fall.

The year was 1983. Sam and LeVar were window washers. Arriving at the McCormick Spice Building in the Inner Harbor, they set up their equipment as business went on around them. Sam and LeVar had worked together as a team for several years. Their routine was second nature. After they unloaded the van, Sam moved it around to the McCormick parking lot as LeVar went up to the top of the building to ready the lines on the scaffolding. Sam joined him later on the roof with their accessories and they tied the lines that would lower the scaffolding.

Far below them, five well-to-do women entered McCormick's for a tour and tea. After their tour, they were guided to the famous Tea Room where they chatted with the friendly hostess and gazed out the huge picture window enjoying a seagull's view of the busy harbor.

LeVar climbed over the edge of the roof to the scaffolding and stood reaching for the tools which Sam handed down to him. Sam stretched for the tools. What LeVar didn't notice was that he was slipping away from Sam. A faint noise caused Sam to glance to his left. He realized then that a knot in one of the lines was slipping! The safety line around LeVar was stretched up to the roof level. Sam reached for it as the knot passed clear. Sam yelled for LeVar to grab the line as the scaffolding's right side swung out from LeVar's feet, leaving him dangling eight stories above the cold, hard concrete.

On the street, a man returning from lunch saw LeVar dangling dangerously and ran to tell a police officer. The officer called for the Fire Department to respond and a medic unit to stand by.

Wayne and I were enjoying our halcyon years together as an ambo team. We received the call while returning to the station from Maryland General Hospital. We didn't know what the incident was about, only that it was a standby situation.

Sam held onto the rope with all his strength. Slowly the energy seeped from his arms. He knew he could not hang on much longer, yet alone lift LeVar to the roof. LeVar hung precariously by the strands of rope. Fear consumed him. He, too, knew death was imminent. Tears lined Sam's cheeks. He cried out for his friend to hang on. The rope began to inch downward, leaving burns on Sam's hands. Sam called upon an inner strength he wanted so desperately but knew he didn't have. The final inches of rope passed through Sam's hands. LeVar's face, still hoping, turned cold blue as he plummeted to the ground below.

Meanwhile, the five women chatted happily while enjoying hot tea and cookies and the view of the bay. As they talked, LeVar dropped before their eyes. Cups and saucers flew. Two women went into hysterics and one fainted.

The large letter "C" in the McCormick sign caught LeVar's body as it hurled earthward, and cast him the rest of the way to the ground. LeVar lay on the hard concrete sidewalk. Almost lifeless, his face seemed to search for the man on the roof who peered, in a stupor, over the edge.

Engine 2 brought Sam down from the roof by the time we arrived. Their captain apprised us of the situation as we ran from the wagon. One man almost dead in the street, one man in apparent shock. Sam stood before us, wrapped in a blanket, unable to speak. Wayne looked at Sam's hands and asked the engine company to wrap them with bandages.

I examined LeVar. Unbelievably, he still had a pulse. We began ALS workup on him. His blood pressure was almost nonexistent. An untold number of bones were broken throughout his body. An open fracture of the tib-fib lay wide open while a pool of blood began to gel around it.

Wayne started an IV line. We put the MAST trousers on him and pumped them up. His blood pressure rose very little and his pulse began to slow. A cervical collar and backboard, along with splinting, came next. Once in the ambo, we put a cardio-pak monitor system on him and communicated with the hospital. Because of the trauma, we took him to the trauma center at University Hospital.

All attempts to save LeVar's life failed. Within one hour he died from massive internal injuries, a fractured neck, and multiple fractures throughout his body. Sam was counseled for hours as doctors and nurses treated his bleeding hands and shock. He was released later that night.

As we drove by the sight of the incident later that day we were amazed that LeVar had lived as long as he had.

Frank Kelly was one of the finest firefighters I've ever met, and also one of the shortest. Standing a few inches over five feet, he was constantly teased about his diminutive stature. One thing every firefighter learns quickly is that you can't let anyone know they can "get to you" about anything. Frank Kelly certainly didn't. He took the ribbing like a champ.

One night during the summer of 1984, Frank and I responded to an ambo call for a seizure. We arrived at a rowhouse with a huge cement porch, which was swarming with about 30 people who were drinking and arguing. We glanced at each other and approached cautiously. I pulled myself up as tall as I could. Next to Frank, I must have looked like a giant. We needed all the height we could get.

The patient lay in the midst of this chaos between two women. Each argued vehemently as the "patient," looked up at them in confusion. I tried to calm the women, but the more insistent I was, the louder they became. Suddenly the two women began to fight, throwing punches at each other right over the patient's head! Frank and I stepped back, just in time. A chair flew between us and broke on the concrete. The crowd joined in the fracas. I looked for the patient, but he had wisely crawled away. Someone cracked a bottle over someone's head and he crumbled to the ground.

I looked around for Frank, but he was gone. I yelled, "Let's get out of here!" and jumped off the porch, running for the ambo. When I reached the medic unit, Frank wasn't there. I radioed for police backup and waited. I began to fear that he had been knocked out in the brawl. Suddenly from the middle of the muddle, Frank emerged on all fours, unscathed. We waved frantically at a passing police cruiser for assistance, but it kept going. Not his district. When a cavalry of police cars finally arrived, we patched up a few victims and took them to the hospital.

Later, at the firehouse, Frank Kelly relayed the exciting details of his escape. "I didn't waste any time," he said proudly. "When they started swinging I dropped down and ran right between their legs." "Well, Frank," I said, "that couldn't have been too hard!" He grinned sheepishly as the firehouse exploded into laughter.

Unfortunately, Frank would have to endure another fall. I was a paramedic on Medic 1 during one of the hottest summers in Baltimore's history. The early part of the night shift had been predictably busy. En route to a West Side hospital my driver, firefighter Dan Davis, called back to me that a firebox had been called out for a fire just a few blocks from Engine 38's station. I flipped the dial of my portable radio to the fire channel and eavesdropped or "watergated," as Baltimoreans describe it.

I heard Engine 38's call for a second alarm. "We have a two-story warehouse — heavy fire and smoke showing!" We hurried our non-emergency patient to the hospital and proceeded to the fireground to serve as a standby ambulance.

The second alarm units arrived as we did. With precision, they set up their engines and ladders to assist the exhausted first alarm companies and advanced on the fire which had all but consumed the building.

Just as the men from Engine 38 and Truck 2 climbed a fire escape with their equipment, balls of fire rolled out of the shattered windows directly over their heads. The fire escape began to vibrate erratically, as smoke seeped from the mortar joints.

Without warning, the fire escape jolted, shaking the seven men on it. One was Frank Kelly. Frank grabbed for the railing, but was struck by loose bricks falling from the parapet. He lost his balance, and fell over the rail of the trembling fire escape. Before the men could reach him he tumbled to the sidewalk. The firefighters cringed, hearing the thud as his body hit the concrete two stories below.

We scrambled from the ambo and raced to Frank, pushing other firefighters out of the way. We removed as much gear as possible, but access to his body was difficult. His bulky turnout pants had absorbed a lot of water, and they seemed to weigh a ton.

Finally, we got his vital signs. They were stable, but his blood pressure was low. We put a collar around his neck and stabilized him. I gave him an IV solution of Ringer's lactate, and we placed him on a backboard. His eyes fluttered as he began to regain consciousness. He slowly realized what had happened, screamed out in pain and fortunately passed out again.

Once in the ambo, his blood pressure plummeted. Suspecting internal injury, we put medical anti-shock trousers (MAST) on Frank and pumped them up, forcing the blood to his heart where it was desperately needed. The hospital seemed an eternity away. I watched Frank's face, praying that what we were doing would save him. In one quick motion we pulled Frank's stretcher from the ambo and rolled it to the emergency room where doctors and nurses took over. Our job finished, we could only watch, and wait.

Frank was punctured with needles, catheters, and intubation tubes. A nurse rounded the corner with a portable X-ray machine. The team worked quickly, and precisely. They told us he suffered a punctured lung, as well as fractures. His fate was uncertain. We waited.

Finally, the doctor, soaked with perspiration, walked over to us. When he removed his mask, we noticed he was smiling. "It's gonna be okay," he said. "We sent the grim reaper home."

Frank Kelly has recovered and now lives on his pension, although it took the City two years to persuade him to retire. His left leg still causes him to limp, but, he says, it's a small price to pay for being alive.

———————

Physical ups and downs take their toll, too. It is an unexpected part of the job, and one never discussed at the Fire Academy — how your body rebels against constant fatigue.

I can't help but smile every time I think of this incident. At the time, I lived in Glen Burnie, a suburban area south of Baltimore City. I was going on day shift. When I went to bed the night before, I knew I had to get up early.

We had just had our third daughter, Holly. Holly suffered from colic. Colic is rough on parents as well as the baby. Emily was 13 months old, and Amy was a precocious four-year old. It was a handful. I was not only a firefighter, but worked a part-time job, went to college two nights a week and sold Amway. Carol and I were exhausted and we fell asleep instantly.

Several hours later, I awoke with a start. "I've got to get to work," I thought. Hastily, I dressed. When I came back to the bedroom, Carol lazily rolled over and asked what I was doing. I told her I was dressing for work. "It's 2:00 in the morning, Bill. Come back to bed." I felt like a dope, but I was glad to crawl back in bed, even if I was already dressed. This happened two more times that night. Carol was perturbed. The babies were finally sleeping but I was waking her up. Each time I came back to bed, I would pass out. At 5:30 a.m. it was time to get up. The alarm clock rang and rang. I thought it was the telephone. I stretched my arm out and picked up the receiver. "Hello, hello." I didn't get an answer. The ringing continued. "What's going on?" I said. "It's the clock, Bill. Turn the clock off before you wake up the kids," Carol moaned.

I hung up the phone, turned the clock off, and laid still unable to lift my body from the bed. "Come on and get up, Bill. I want to go back to sleep!"

"Okay, okay." I went to get up and, boom! I went flat on the floor. My left leg was asleep. I felt as if I was dragging a boulder around. Each time I tried to stand up, I fell down. I tried and tried until I heard Carol's laughter.

All she could see, as she lay in bed facing me, was this appearing and disappearing body flopping up and down next to the bed. "What's the matter with you?" I inquired.

"You look so funny popping up and down. What's going on?" Carol giggled. "My leg's asleep. I can't stand up!"

After a few minutes, the leg stopped tingling and I gathered myself together and was ready to go to work.

I had another leg incident while being assigned to Engine 23. I had been in the Department for two years and was no longer a rookie. Now, I was in on the jokes and took the jokes. It was a good feeling to be accepted.

On this particular night, pranks were in the air. We had to watch out or we might be the brunt of a joke. The pranks continued until 3:00 a.m., before we settled down for the night. Around 5:00 a.m., the bells on the watch desk started ticking off a firebox. The man on watch counted the holes in the tape. It was a downtown firebox. Everyone in the house was called. He threw the gong. The lights came on, as we tossed covers off and our feet aimed for our boots and found them. All but one person . . . me.

My leg flopped to the floor. "No," I cried out. Some men were already sliding the pole. I sat on the edge of my bed and used both hands to lift my leg into the boot. Once it was in, my other leg went in easily. I stood up and tried to advance to the pole, but my leg wouldn't move. I knew I had to get to the wagon on the first floor, but my leg dragged behind me as if someone was holding it. I must have looked like Quasimodo from *The Hunchback of Notre Dame.*

Sliding a pole with one leg isn't easy, especially when you're upset. By the time I climbed on the back step of Engine 23, the tingling hit me. It was the weirdest sensation to have a leg waking up as you hang onto a truck, flying through the city streets. "What took you so long?" the captain asked. I told him, "I really didn't have a leg to stand on."

———————

Rescue 1 returned to the station one night to find several of the men in the kitchen sharing a good story. The Squad had a good one to tell. They had been evacuating occupants on the upper floor of a senior citizens complex, running down the smoky fourteenth-floor hallway and pounding on doors to alert the occupants. If a door would not open, they broke in and searched the rooms. Afterwards they printed an "X" on the door with chalk to let others know the room had been checked.

When they came to room 1415, where an elderly gentleman lived, they pounded and pounded on the door. No response. Fearing the man was incapacitated or overcome by smoke, the lieutenant reared back and with his large booted foot, crashed in the door. It only opened halfway. As they peered inside, they saw the old man lying on his back, arms outstretched and feet pointing skyward with his walker on top of him.

He had apparently begun the agonizing walk to the door when he heard the pounding of the firefighters. He had almost reached it, only to be knocked off his feet by the eager lieutenant. Fortunately, he only received a small contusion to the forehead and, perhaps, a reluctance to answer the door when the firefighters knock.

———————

One of the funniest things I ever saw wasn't really funny, because someone could have been hurt. But it was funny after all.

It happened one beautiful spring evening when the weather was too nice to be working. The airways were quiet. We took advantage of the lull and gathered on the ramp in front of the firehouse. The weather was ideal for walking and we enjoyed people-watching.

Nearby on Eutaw Street, road crews had been resurfacing the street and working on the manhole covers on the sidewalks. It had been hot, and the road crew was glad to stop work at 6:00 p.m. The street was peaceful.

We noticed two blind men with seeing-eye dogs come across and up the street, conversing as they walked. They strolled casually through the area where the construction crews had been working. We marveled at their ease of movement, as they relied faithfully on the reactions and sight of their well-trained dogs. We were impressed at the grace and skill of the animals.

Suddenly, the lead man's dog, for some reason, moved a little to the right. The man didn't change his course and couldn't see the open hole. As the dog maneuvered around the hole, the man kept going straight. Plunk! He fell about eight feet. As we instinctively jumped up to help him, the second dog did the same thing. The second blind man fell into the hole, right on top of the first man. The two dogs stood befuddled, looking at each other and then at their masters down in the hole.

As we approached, the dogs backed up. We peered into the shaft and heard loud moaning. "Get off of me," said an agitated voice. "I will, I will. Gimme a minute!"

One of the firefighters yelled down, "Are you two okay?" They answered, "Yes."

We lowered a small ladder down the hole and the duo slowly ascended to street level. They brushed themselves off and asked for their dogs. We checked the men over. They didn't want an ambulance or to go to the hospital. They simply took their dogs and went on with their walk.

When we went back to our chairs, we sat quietly and stared at the now-covered hole. Without warning, a giggle, then a snicker and finally a belly laugh was heard. We laughed the more we thought about it. It just looked so comical. There they were, there they weren't. One of the guys suggested that the dogs had led their masters astray. Another swore he heard snickers coming from the dogs.

We were all glad they weren't hurt, but it was funny.

When Fire Lieutenant Phil Janson was a firefighter, his unit responded to a house fire at a typical Baltimore rowhouse whose brick front had been replaced by formstone. Fire seriously damaged the dwelling, and smoke and water ruined the rest.

Once the fire was under control, the elderly woman who lived there panicked. "My baby! My baby is still in there!"

The firefighters knew that at her age she couldn't have a baby. "What baby?" they asked her, thinking perhaps it was a grandchild.

Soon they discovered the baby was her cat. Phil reassured her they would find the feline. What he didn't tell her was he was sure he would find it dead.

Room by room, the hunt went on. No luck. No cat! Finally, in the last closet, the last room, they heard what sounded like a baby crying. The firefighters looked at each other and then at the door. Quickly they pulled it open.

A sooty, gray Persian cat leaped out at them. Startled, they jumped back, but the grateful cat clung to them. Phil went over to the burned-out frame window and yelled to the lady that they had found her cat, and it was alive. She clapped her hands together in glee, smiling broadly at the firefighter.

Phil nicknamed the cat "Lucky" and set her on the floor. It purred and jumped around, every now and then stopping to rub up against their wet boots. The little animal seemed to say, "Thank you, thank you, thank you!" Suddenly, she darted out the door and down the steps. Meanwhile, Engine 19, responding to another fire, drove past Phil's fire scene. As they turned the corner, the driver revved the engine to pick up speed.

The lady who owned the cat reached out to it, but it darted right past her. As she stood straight up, she saw Engine 19 approaching. The driver saw the cat, but didn't have time to stop. Engine 19 rolled right over the cat. The lady gasped in disbelief.

Phil stood frozen at the door, watching. All he could remember was opening the closet door and watching Lucky jump out after living through a fire. As they packed up their hose and equipment, the woman walked by with some friends. She sounded angry, but not at the firefighters. She was muttering something about her "darned cat."

11 Little People: Big Joys, Big Pains

Few firefighters would argue that the most stressful calls involve infants and children. On ambo duty, one type of call is "Childbirth in progress!" Medics often transport, assist and even deliver babies into this wonderful and dangerous world. If you are squeamish, I would *strongly* advise you to forego these stories.

During my years in the ambulance service, I was blessed with the privilege of delivering 24 healthy babies. Only one, three months premature, was stillborn. One other birth, I should say, was unusual.

Mike and I responded to a maternity case in a high-rise apartment building. The patient was on the eighth floor and both elevators were not working. We trudged up the stairwell with our med and obstetrics kits to find a woman lying across her bed in heavy labor.

Mike, a rookie, stood in amazement, unsure of what to do. The woman's groaning made him uneasy. A neighbor watched intently as I checked the woman's progress. I sent Mike to get sheets to give him something to do while I prepared for the delivery. I told the woman to inch down to the end of her bed and for modesty's sake draped a sheet over her. I put on my gloves, and set out the absorbent pad, scissors and syringe. Mike stood transfixed, cringing visibly each time the woman cried out.

The baby's head began to crown. Soon, we saw the head appear. It was emerging quickly, then stopped! We waited. I began to worry. Was the baby being strangled by the umbilical cord around its neck? What was holding the baby?

Something was odd. The head looked like a hairy coconut! It was without features. The contractions continued but there was still no movement. "We'll wait a few more minutes and then get her out of here," I told Mike. Nothing happened so Mike packed things up. We took her to the ambulance and consulted the hospital. I could hear the hospital staff snicker when I told them about the "featureless coconut."

An eternity seemed to pass as we drove to the hospital. The woman's screams became louder and more frequent. We rushed her into the elevator and up to the sixth floor. By this time Mike's face had turned a pasty green. Soon *he* would need oxygen.

The young doctor asked, "What'cha got?"

"I don't know!" I said.

He lifted the sheet. When he dropped the sheet, he looked at me, as perplexed as I was. "Nurse!" he called.

The nurse lifted the sheet. "Oh, Doc," she said, coolly, "That's her bag of water! It hasn't broken yet."

It was one of the most comforting, if embarrassing, explanations I had ever heard. I could tell the doctor felt the same.

After leaving the hospital, Mike and I broke out in nervous laughter. I had been standing between the woman's legs, in a direct line of fire! If the bag had broken, I would have been drenched. The rookie complimented me. "That's the first time I've helped to deliver a baby!"

"Mike," I said, "That's the first time I've helped to deliver a coconut!"

When Paramedic Mark Hofmann and I worked together, we had a few out-of-the-ordinary experiences.

This childbirth incident was fairly normal, from our point of view. At about 8:00 a.m., we received a call for an obstetrics case at an East Side high rise. We pushed through the morning rush-hour traffic which is fierce along the Inner Harbor at this time in the morning. Cars moved bumper-to-bumper.

As usual, the elevator was dirty and slow. But, eventually it took us up to the fourth floor. We knocked on the door and waited for a response. We knocked again. No answer. We had become concerned when the door finally opened and a frightened toddler looked up at us, her dark eyes speaking words she lacked. In the background we heard a woman's voice ask us to come in. We maneuvered around the tot and headed in the direction of the voice. In a small bedroom, a young woman, covered with blankets, lay on a mattress on a concrete floor. These were her only bedroom furnishings.

She cradled a ball of covers in her arms. "I've had my baby," she stated. "How long ago did you have the child, ma'am?" "Oh, about an hour ago. I believe that was when I looked at the clock," she said. Mark couldn't help but retort, "Why did you wait to call for an ambulance?" Softly she replied, "I don't have a phone and I was waiting for someone to come who was suppose to call for me."

As Mark questioned her, he checked out the baby, a healthy, round little boy. The stretcher filled the narrow hallway, so we had to maneuver it carefully to bring it into the woman's room.

Her vital signs were stable so we decided to place her on the stretcher as soon as possible. "Have you passed the placenta?" Mark inquired. "No, not yet," she answered. During a normal delivery, the placenta is expelled within 20 minutes. The birth had been well over an hour ago and there was no sign of the placenta. We passed the woman a pad to put on to stop any bleeding while we maneuvered her onto the stretcher. The baby, meanwhile, decided to let out a few hallelujahs.

Mark placed a small cotton stretch cap on the child's head to make him an official member of planet earth. He handed the baby back to his mother who cuddled up with him in her arms. We pulled the blanket up over both of them and proceeded to the elevator. A neighbor took the little girl aside. Once off the smelly elevator car, we lifted mother and baby into the warmth of the unit. Mark climbed in with them and I went to the front cab. Mark radioed the hospital that the placenta had not been expelled but that the baby was fine.

Once at the hospital, we moved our patient to a bed with stirrups. As we gathered up our gear, our patient was grilled by personnel asking the same questions. She answered calmly, as they proceeded to examine her and the baby.

Suddenly the delivery area filled with doctors and nurses rushing in and out of another room. We moved back, pulling our gear out of the way. Inquiring about the commotion, we were told that another woman had just delivered a healthy baby before going into multiple seizures brought on by high blood pressure. They couldn't get the seizure activity to stop. It looked as if they might lose her. Outside of the room sat a crash cart — holding the tools and medicines used for a cardiac arrest. Our hearts went out to her and her family.

Meanwhile, our patient and the baby passed their first check-up.

The joy of that delivery was short-lived. Of my 24 delivery cases, none angered me more than this next one.

A 17-year-old white girl paced the streets incessantly, hoping to bring on the birth of the baby inside her. She thought that if she exerted herself and kept pushing, her labor would begin early and last only a short time. Once in awhile, she attempted to double over, to literally squeeze the baby out of her body. Knowing she was about due, she searched for a place to deliver her child. The sooner, the better, she angrily thought.

She entered a large downtown hotel and was immediately consumed by its plush red carpeting. Her eyes ogled the high ceilings and rich decor. She began to investigate the luxurious surroundings, including the bathroom. She entered the women's room on the first floor and marveled at the room's size and fine fixtures. There were 10 stalls in just this one bathroom. She relieved herself and went back out into the hallway. A cleaning woman saw her and asked if she was all right. She answered that she was fine. The woman asked, with a smile on her face, when she was due. The girl replied, "Soon!" and left the hotel, telling herself that this would be the place.

The next morning, Jeanette, one of the cleaning women, was making her hourly rounds. Her job was to check all the bathrooms open to the public. She kept them clean and restocked supplies when needed.

Her day began early. About 6:45, she entered the first floor women's room and noticed the young, very pregnant, white girl going into one of the stalls. As she continued her cleaning routine, she heard a moan once in a while. "Are you okay?" she finally called out. "I'm fine," came the answer. She thought perhaps the young woman was not feeling well. Without further concern, Jeanette left to complete her rounds.

At the station, Mark and I were busy cleaning the ambulance and the ambo bay. It was a very clear, pretty morning. At nearly 8:00 a.m., we heard a medic unit receive an OB call.

Meanwhile, Jeanette returned to the first floor women's room. She noticed that the young woman was still in the stall. She thought it unusual but continued her cleaning, polishing the fixtures until they sparkled. She then went out into the hall to the supply closet for her vacuum cleaner and began vacuuming the carpet outside the bathroom. She saw the young woman leave the bathroom. But she looked thin and was walking very slowly, holding her abdomen. Jeanette rushed to check the bathroom stall where the girl had been.

She pushed open the door to the stall and gasped. Mounds of red-tinted toilet paper lay balled-up in a mass on top of the water. Blood covered the toilet and the floor. Curiously, she peered into the paper in the toilet.

The call was so nearby that we arrived in one minute. Oddly, no one met us at the door to show us where to go.

We pushed open the large glass door and entered the hotel. A hand pointed in a direction without a word spoken. As we went down the hallway, we tried to ask employees about a mother and baby, but no one would answer . . . they just pointed.

A large security guard met us near the bathroom. "We've got what we think is a fetus in the women's toilet. We called you to verify it. The mother is in the security office. She seems fine but wants to go. The cleaning lady said she saw the girl go out of the bathroom; she then went in to clean it. She found what she thinks is a fetus. There is a lot of blood in the toilet, man. We need you to check."

I pushed the door open slowly. What a mess! Bloody water filled the commode. Blood-stained paper lay on top of it. Inside the commode, Mark and I saw what looked like an umbilical cord. As we examined it closer, we saw the placenta lying next to it. Our eyes met as we realized that there was a baby in there.

"Here, Bill," Mark said as he handed me the latex gloves. "Thanks, Mark," I responded nervously. As Mark and the security man peered over my shoulders, I slipped on the gloves and lifted up the wad of paper. There lay, not a fetus, but a perfectly beautiful, full-term baby floating motionless in the toilet water. "Get a plastic bag, Mark." I instructed. We put the messy paper in the plastic bag. Then, for a moment, we stared at the dead baby; our hearts grieved for this new little person who had not had a chance to live. "What do you think, Bill?" Mark questioned. "I think we have a possible homicide and should call the police." I said, fighting back the anger that clouded my mind.

Rage filled me as Mark called for another medic unit to attend to the mother who sat quietly in the security room. I told him I did not want to see her. Even though I no longer stared into the commode, wherever I looked I still saw the baby lying in the water. How could a woman carry a child for nine months and then drop it in a toilet and walk away?

We had to leave the baby where it was until the homicide detectives arrived. Medic 5 took the mother to University Hospital. The tall security guard asked if we wanted to get a cup of coffee in the cafeteria. We agreed but first called our dispatcher to tell him we would be delayed for questioning by the police for an undetermined amount of time.

As we sat in the cafeteria, I thought of my four healthy daughters. I had always wanted a son, too, but assumed that the Lord did not want me to have one, at least not yet. My partner, Mark, was silent, too. He and his wife had just had a healthy son. We struggled with our feelings, inwardly wanting to strike out at someone or something. The hot coffee did not help to settle my nerves. As a professional, I know I should not let my feelings get in the way of doing the best at my job, but for some reason this incident blinded me. My emotions frightened me. I longed to fight for every child who has ever been abused. I've seen dead bodies, decapitations, mangled bodies, burned corpses . . . but none has filled me with such a desire for retribution.

As I drank my coffee, I thought to myself that eventually someone would have to remove the baby from the commode. I hoped it would be a staff person from the coroner's office. I dreaded the thought of doing it but, in my heart, knew that I would if I had to. Mark's radio picked up a call for a medic unit to respond to an accident, a pregnant woman had fallen down a flight of steps. I sipped my coffee and tried to think about something else.

A police detective interrupted us. We told him what we had found. He politely thanked us and asked that we return to the bathroom. I was sure he would ask me to remove the baby. Emotional trauma overpowered me when we entered the bathroom. Innumerable police surrounded the bathroom. I wanted to turn and run.

As we entered, a detective asked us about the box with the plastic bag. He wanted to know if we had placed it there or if the mother had. We explained that we had readied it for the fetus, but when we found a newborn, we decided not to use it. The crime lab arrived and photographed the commode.

As we approached the stall, another detective told us that the crime lab photographer would remove the baby. Praise the Lord!

Mark and I stood in the background. Only the lower part of the commode was visible from under the stall. The lab man laid plastic out on the floor beneath the toilet. Trickles of water dropped on the plastic and then big drops of coagulated blood. The baby's body was laid finally on the plastic covering. "It's a boy," he called out for the report.

I was wiped out. The full impact of my desire for a son hit me. Here was a baby boy that someone had dropped in the commode. I love my daughters dearly and would not give them up for the world, but deep down inside, I (and I expect most men) would like to have a son.

Finally, I turned to Mark and said I was going to ask the police if we could go. "Sure. I'm ready," he answered. With their permission and thanks, we left the room rapidly. Mark carried the med kit and I carried our clipboard.

As we walked down the hall to leave the hotel, we were besieged by reporters and camera crews asking questions and wanting answers. I was sure they wouldn't want to hear my *real* answers which would have been hostile and derogatory. "You'll have to talk to the police," Mark and I curtly responded,

We packed up our equipment and got back in the medic unit. "Medic 1 is back in service," Mark called in. The dispatcher replied, "Okay, Medic 1 . . . "

We didn't get far. "Medic 1 . . . Medic 1." The urgency in the dispatcher's voice came through clearly. "Medic 1," Mark answered. "Medic 1 . . . respond to Pratt and Carey Streets for a seizure on the street . . . acknowledge." Mark gave the address and acknowledged the call. We were off again.

We worked up our seizure patient and gave him his priority code. Mark informed University Hospital that we were bringing in a multiple seizure patient, unconscious and unresponsive. They were ready.

We arrived minutes later with a critical patient. We burst through the emergency room doors and took our patient to the critical care area. Nurses and doctors helped us get our patient onto the hospital stretcher. They began their workup as we pulled our stretcher out of the way. Mark relayed what information he had to the ER staff.

The trauma area was filled with activity. We went to learn what had happened to the other OB patient we had heard about while responding to our previous call.

The patient was a young mother who had started labor pains and tried to negotiate the steps downstairs to call for an ambulance. As she took her first step, her husband, at the bottom, saw she looked light-headed. Before he could get to the second step, she tumbled down, end over end. He screamed out for help but no one heard. She was unconscious. He ran to the phone and dialed 911. A medic unit arrived on the scene minutes later. They treated the patient. She was placed on a long backboard and given a neck collar to immobilize her. An IV was established and the patient was watched on the cardiac monitor all the way to the hospital.

Once they arrived at University Hospital, she was put in the trauma room. An obstetrician and a pediatrician were immediately paged. The obstetrician performed a Caesarean section on the unconscious and unresponsive woman. The baby boy came out screaming. The pediatrician immediately took him to the pediatric ward upstairs.

Meanwhile, the doctors worked feverishly to save the mother. When we left she was not doing well. Her little boy, however, was born strong and healthy. I sighed and looked at Mark.

Many people pick up the phone and dial 911 for the wrong reasons. They need to be taught what are true emergencies and how to handle them. A recent rescue assignment is a case in point.

A woman ran the bath water for her seven-year-old child. As the child undressed, the mother poured bubble bath into the swirling water. "Ready to play

Moby Dick. Up we go!" the young mom said gleefully as she helped the child into the tub.

The child soon disappeared in a cloud of bubbles. The phone rang. The mother told the young child not to stand or get out of the tub while she talked on the phone. As she chatted, she listened to the tot playing in the water.

Noticing a silence, she said "Good-bye!" and ran to the bathroom. No child. The water was draining. "Oh, no! My baby! Where's my baby?"

She ran for the phone and dialed 911. "My baby! My baby's stuck down the drain!"

Rescue 1, an engine, a truck and a medic unit were dispatched to the scene. They arrived almost simultaneously. The woman met us screaming hysterically. "Calm down, now!" an officer said. "Just tell us and show us where the child is." She led them to the upstairs bathroom. "He's in there," she said sobbing. "Where?" inquired the officer. "In there! In the drainpipe!" she said, pointing at the tub.

"You mean to tell me your son is down the bathtub drain?" he said with a look of amazement on his face. "Yes," she said. "He was taking a bath while I was on the phone. When I came back in, he was gone!" She began to sob even harder again. The firefighters turned and headed back downstairs as the officer questioned her further. "Have you looked around for him?" he asked. "No. He's down the drain. That's where he is!"

"Ma'am," the officer continued, "no one, not even a small child, can be sucked down a bathtub drain. He must be around here somewhere!"

Just as he was finishing his sentence, a small boy dashed out of a bedroom and down the steps. "That's him! That's my baby. Oh, my lord!" she began crying again.

A neighbor who knew the family brought the naked young lad back into the house. "Where've you been, boy?" the mother screamed. "I'm gonna blister your hiney! You're gonna give your mama a heart attack!"

As the firefighters gathered back on their apparatus, they could still hear the lady screaming at the child.

When there is a fire, tragedy often follows. It seems to intensify when children are involved.

Christmas had passed but the Carter family kept its decorations up. It was as if to hold onto something that promised happiness. They strained not to let it go, especially as the winter chill overtook their home. One evening the father sent the three children off to bed so he could have a few moments alone with his wife. Off they went upstairs, surprising the couple who thought, "Surely they must be up to something."

The children must have been worn out because they went right to bed. As they fell off to sleep, Mr. and Mrs. Carter laid in bed talking. Before long, Mrs. Carter nodded off.

Mr. Carter, feeling chilly, turned the heat up on the kerosene heater. He went to the refrigerator for a beer. Popping the top off, he sat in an easy chair and slowly drank the cool liquid. Before long, he, too, was asleep.

The dog slowly pushed himself up from the floor and moved over near the heater. Something outside rumbled down the street, startling the animal. He jumped up to investigate. As he did, his body brushed against the heater, knocking it over. Startled, the dog cowered and ran out of the room. Kerosene slowly spilled from the container's loose cap. As it pooled around the unit, the heat from the flame reached it. In a moment, it flashed into an orange monster.

No one in the house knew what happened. They slept soundly. The fire grew and ignited the other furnishings and the Christmas decorations. Smoke enveloped the first floor and crawled up the walls as the fire headed upstairs.

Horror filled the man's eyes as he awoke to the dog's barking. He coughed and gagged, then screamed and yelled. Running to his wife, he awoke her.

"The children!" she screamed. They ran for the steps that led upstairs but were thrown back by the heat and flames. Finally, overcome by the smoke, they retreated outside. Mr. Carter banged on his neighbor's door. At last they answered and ran to call the Fire Department.

We received the call for a second-alarm dwelling fire at about 3:00 a.m. The three-story Victorian rowhouse stood proudly, a monument of days gone by. Flames devoured the wooden structure. The fire was so intense that the firefighters had trouble controlling it. They saw it advancing on them instead of them on it. Now it was a third alarm. Exposures were threatened as thick, heavy black smoke lapped around them. Because of the long, stretched-out blocks, firefighters had long hose lays. Then came the fateful cry: children trapped inside.

Third-alarm units arrived and tapped into the resources already there. The companies operating in the rear were confronted with more fire then smoke. Ice and snow on the ground created a new danger. Despite the heat the fire created, the cold air rapidly turned the spray from the hoses and the run-off from the fire building and surrounding structures into ice.

Without any warning, the second and third floors crashed in. Sparks and huge fireballs rained upward toward the evening sky. A few moments later, the firefighters in the front of the building scattered as the facade of the dwelling collapsed straight down. No one was injured.

But the children. Would they miraculously survive? Another crash inside sent the roof onto the first floor. Hope for the children vanished.

The two to three homes on either side suffered heavy smoke damage. The firefighters ventilated the roofs and at least two floors of each. The occupants were away on vacation.

The fire was declared under control around 4:30 a.m. We stood in awe of the damage. There was no front to the house, no roof, no back to the dwelling. Only sporadic beams stood, stretching from one house to the next, across the carnage.

One of the children was found, burned beyond recognition, in the rubble that sprawled across the first floor. He was five years old.

We had trouble finding the other two, when, suddenly, a chief officer exclaimed, "Oh, my God!" Heads turned as he pointed to the other two children. Up, on the third floor rafters, were draped the bodies of the remaining children.

A plan had to be devised to get them down. Great caution was needed because of their precarious position. One false move and the remaining structure could come crashing down.

Finally, ground ladders were moved in and raised, allowing men to move cautiously up to the bodies. Because of the amount of trauma, the chief asked for volunteers. Many volunteered. With that task completed, the men ascended the ladders with ropes and harnesses.

The first child was slowly lowered to the waiting stretcher. The paramedics took the seven-year-old to the waiting morgue wagon. The eight-year-old boy still lay sprawled on the charred beam. He was burned so badly that he almost blended in with it. As the firefighter stretched himself to reach around the boy, his arm bumped the child's head. Gasps came from the crowd as the boy's head came loose from his neck and tumbled to the debris below! The firefighter wavered with shock, but controlled himself. He stood motionless for a moment, then he stiffened and went about his task. At last, the remaining child was brought down.

It was a tragedy indeed. The parents were taken to the hospital for treatment for smoke inhalation and shock.

Harborplace, in the Inner Harbor, is the showcase of Baltimore. Tourists by the thousands visit each day to shop and sightsee among the stores and historic attractions. It was on a gorgeous, sunny September day that a bus from a home for handicapped children discharged the exuberant youngsters.

The children moved as a group, some on crutches, and some in wheelchairs, through the many tourists walking alongside the harbor. Boats and yachts lined the waterway, and a foreign naval vessel sat nearby in the calm water.

Julie suffered from muscular dystrophy and was retarded, but her bubbly happiness was infectious that day as she was pushed in a wheelchair by Annie, one of the older children. She smiled as she was pushed along, laughing with the other children.

The walkway along the edge of the water had a ramp for wheel chairs and the group moved toward it. The counselor, busy with several children, did not see Annie let go of the wheelchair's handles. Julie, strapped into the chair, began rolling to the water's edge. No one could stop it before it plunged into the water. The counselor turned just in time to see the wheelchair roll over the edge of the walkway. The children began screaming.

Two sailors from a nearby naval vessel dove into the dark water. Harbor Police called the Fire Department. Rescue 1 immediately responded. We had to push people out of the way to get to the water's edge. The sailors could not find her. We cast grappling hooks while Fire Department divers readied their suits. A police boat approached from across the harbor to aid in the rescue.

It was too late.

Little Julie had gone down to the muddy bottom face down, pinned by the weight of her chair. Even if she could have gotten out of the chair, her heavy leg braces would have prevented her from reaching the surface.

The crowd watched sadly as we put her little body on a stretcher and left the scene. We transported her to the city morgue.

That night, when I got home, I hugged my kids a little longer and tighter. I put them to bed and watched them for a long time as they slept until finally, I was able to fall asleep.

12 Faces of Death

Death has many faces and, as firefighters, we have seen most of them. We have also seen the different ways in which people cope with death. Some people seem surprised by the death of an affluent or influential person, but accept the death of a poor person.

One night, a few years ago, Fred Ehrlich was acting lieutenant on Rescue 1. Charles Huber was the driver as usual; Doug Wagerman and I were in the back. We were returning from an auto accident when we heard a firebox call come from the East Side. Within minutes, calls of "fire and smoke showing" poured over the airways.

We arrived at a row of homes with white marble steps threatened by smoke and flames. Visibility had been diminished. Firefighters were doing their best to try to contain the blaze but smoke began spilling from the cocklofts of homes opposite them. The chief pulled a special call. He wanted another engine and truck company. He also requested the Rescue Squad.

Earlier a 20-year-old white man was awakened by cries of "FIRE!" as he slept in the second floor bedroom. His mom was sleeping in the front bedroom and awoke to the smell of smoke. Yelling to get out, she ran for the stairs and made her way to the kitchen going out the back door, the door she used most often.

Her son heard cries, awoke and ran down the steps. He called for his mom but couldn't find her, and left the house by the front door, the door he usually used. Not knowing that his mom had escaped, he panicked. "Mom! Mom! Where are you? Mom!" he cried in a frenzy. He thought she was still inside and ran back into the house of flames looking for his mother. He couldn't bear the pain of losing her after just attending his father's funeral that morning.

Doug and I were already suited up when we arrived on location. We told Fred, as he suited up, that we would check with the battalion chief to see what orders he had for us. We were told to enter the house and bring out the body in the front room. Firefighters were going in and out now as the fire was brought under control.

Doug and I pushed the front door open but it resisted. We peeked around the door and saw the nude body of a young, white man. He was coated with third degree burns, although he had nearly made it to safety.

I ran and got a blanket and covered him completely. Carefully, we backed our way down the steps and gave him to the waiting ambo crew. The young man died needlessly, but valiantly.

As Doug and I walked back to the wagon, Fred showed genuine concern and asked, "Are you two okay? Y'all right?"

"We're okay, Fred," I said.

With that, we put up and went home.

I have seen many horrible deaths. One was most unusual. The evening before, concealed beneath an iron grate under the sidewalk, a steam valve burst open, and hot vapor spurted out at 15 psi (pounds per square inch). Fire department units quickly responded from various downtown stations and sealed off the area. The shrill whistling of the valve was deafening. Steam service workers temporarily plugged the leak.

Johnny Billet was a 35-year-old white man who lived in Baltimore County. He had worked for the Metro Steam Service for 14 years. As usual, he kissed his wife goodbye when he left for work.

Johnny's work orders were to permanently fix the leaky valve. He pulled his van up onto the sidewalk and set up orange safety cones. He waited for Steve, his partner, but Steve never showed up. The Service had a rule . . . to always work in pairs so that one man could protect the other should someone get hurt. But, John lost his patience waiting and descended into the concrete pit, alone.

He took his tools and began loosening the bolts that held the steel plate. He could hear the city coming to life above him as the early rush hour began. Trucks shook the street and echoed in the steam tunnel. John twisted the wrench. Once. Twice.

Steam began pouring out of the pipe's seam, and the whistling pierced the tunnel. Superheated steam surrounded him, blistering his skin instantly. John brought his hands up to cover his ears in an attempt to shut out the deafening noise. His eardrums began pouring blood, which ran through his fingers. The escaping steam blocked his access to the ladder, causing John to turn and run into the tunnel, searching for a way out.

He found a tunnel that led to a nearby building. His body faltered. He stumbled, holding his bleeding ears as he neared the exit. His body fluids were rapidly evaporating; his skin began to peel. He fell to his knees and crawled toward the exit light. Twenty feet from safety, he curled into a ball and was swallowed up by the swelling cloud of steam.

The call came in around 9:30 a.m. for an explosion at a hotel. As Rescue 1 approached, we heard what sounded like a teapot whistling on a hot burner. As we drew closer, we saw people holding their ears and running from the huge cloud of steam rising up from the street. The noise was so piercing we had to scream, our mouths at one another's ear, to make ourselves heard.

A man approached me, pointing to the tunnel. I turned and grabbed the Chief. We both looked at the pit, then back at each other. Nothing more needed to be said.

Metro Steam Service finally arrived. After a conference with the Chief and the realization that we could get ear plugs from a fire boat, we approached the pit. Steam rolled above us, climbing like a vine up the side of the hotel. We could see men's gloves lying in the steaming water, but no body.

Abruptly the noise stopped. The Steam Service had finally capped the main line two blocks away. Only some residual pressure seeped through the ravaged line.

An officer left the conference with the Chief and ran to us. "The Chief wants the Rescue Squad to go in and retrieve the body," he said. "Search for anyone who might've been in the immediate area."

Building personnel took us to the basement. Walls were soaked with condensation. The floor was flooded, and chunks of soggy ceiling tiles had fallen in the water.

"He's got to be in there somewhere," the superintendent said. "That's the tunnel that comes in from the outside."

"Put your masks and gloves on," the officer told us. "We don't know what it's gonna be like in there." We could feel the heat through the door's seams. He opened the door, and we felt the intense rush of hot, wet air. One by one, in full turnout gear, we entered the small passageway.

We sloshed through the hot water, stooping low to see; the steam near the ceiling was virtually impossible to penetrate. Even near the floor visibility was poor.

Doug Wagerman stopped us with his hand. His voice sounded reedy through the air mask. "I've found the body," he said.

The three of us gathered around the body. John Billet lay face down in the steaming water, his body swollen and red. We dragged him to the exit, struggling to maintain a hold on his slippery mass. Firefighters at the exit took the burden from us.

Homicide officers were on the scene, and the morgue workers were waiting for the body. The summer air felt icy as we removed our sweat-sodden turnout gear. People had gathered around the police lines to look at the body. Television crews fought for the best angle of the steaming pit.

The rescue members and I walked to the curb and swigged from a water jug. Doug, Bob Wagner and I looked at each other. No one could break the silence.

Howard McFadden had been employed by the Southern Grain Elevator for 22 years. He enjoyed his work. Over the years he had worked his way up to become Shift Supervisor. Now men worked under him. Howard was the kind of person who took his job seriously.

Today one of his men didn't show up. There was a vacancy on the feeding bin at the top of the towers. The bin held grain, which was diverted by its long chutes. A man with a long stirring pole had to churn the grain as it was released into the extension tubes.

Howard decided that he could fill in for the absent man. He went to the top floor and grasped the stirring pole and proceeded to agitate the grain as it slowly went down the chutes. For some reason the grain was moving too slowly. Howard thought it was jammed. So he climbed up on the ledge of the bin to better reach the central core. No sooner did he stir when the pole jammed. He wiggled the pole and tried his best to free it. With a final tug, Howard jerked it free, only to lose his balance. He plunged into the pool of dusty grain.

As Rescue 1 responded, our radio broadcast a call for a fire in a dwelling in the northwest section. The first unit on the scene reported the dwelling with smoke and fire showing. It appeared normal, which meant the incident could be handled with the initial assignment.

When we arrived at the grain elevator, an engine and a truck company were there with a medic unit standing by. Supervisory personnel from the Company escorted us to the elevator to take to the upper stories. Captain Bill Goodwin led the way as we went to the scene of the accident.

We were a floor below the grain hopper. We scanned the area to see the four off-chutes of the long, central core. Men stood by with ropes, tools and rescue equipment.

A battalion chief came over to explain what had happened. He pointed uneasily to a young man in the corner who had been weeping. He told us that the employee had heard the accident happen; and, when the noise of the grain elevator stopped, he continued to hear a banging sound from inside the chute. Panicking, he realized what had happened. Then, the thumping and banging stopped.

With this information we had to determine from which of the several chute cover plates the sound was last heard. Then we had to open it. By this time, the Company realized that the missing person was the shift supervisor, Howard McFadden.

We climbed what ladders we had and got onto the steel beams around the chute. The first cover plate we removed was the right one. When we took it off, Howard McFadden lay before us in a grotesque position. He was dead! The grain on which he lay gave his skin a dark gray color tone. Agony was written on his face. His asphyxiation had been excruciating. He lay in the tube, straddling the central tube with one leg, while the other leg was forced around the chute. He was caught with no where to go. Dust had robbed him of his life.

Meanwhile, the dwelling fire had begun to grow. A second alarm was sounded. The hot, humid weather was beginning to take its toll on the firemen. The fire in the old, wood-frame dwelling began to lick out of the roof and attic. They were losing the battle.

Charles Huber was sent back to the wagon for a come-along and safety harness. When he returned he told us of the second alarm. We placed the harness around the body of Howard and attached the come-along to it. Wires and ropes were hooked around beams and made steadfast. Charles worked the tool as Howard was raised up and out of the chute. Firefighter Doug Wagerman, the captain and I assisted in guiding the body around beams and ladders as Charles began to lower it to the waiting firefighters and medics below.

The paramedics were told by the police to leave the body where it was for the medical examiner to transport. Howard McFadden's body was placed in a Stokes basket and the police took pictures and checked out the scene for possible foul play. We waited.

At the fire hoselines were pulled out quickly as crashing sounds could be heard from inside the large frame house. Firefighters scattered just in time as the roof and roof supports collapsed. The fire had gotten completely out of hand.

We were "chomping at the bit" to get to the fire now that Howard McFadden had been extricated. The captain asked the battalion chief about responding, but we were told to stand fast. In another half hour the fire was declared under control. Howard McFadden's body was taken by elevator to the waiting transport vehicle by the medical examiner. We left and went back to quarters. From reports of the fire, firefighters had been on the roof when it fell in and they just made it to their ladders.

We could not help but conclude that if we had gone to the fire, we would have been on the roof, ventilating the smoke and intense heat. Possibly, Howard's death had kept us from the fire and so saved our lives.

Sometimes an apparently innocent act can be fatal. Joan and Dorothy, two middle-aged women, were finishing their Christmas shopping. Arms full of packages, they arrived at the garage where their car was parked. A convenient bench seemed like a long-lost friend, and they collapsed eagerly onto it. They handed their keys to the car attendant, who went to get it.

Joey had been a car jock for seven years at the busy downtown parking garage. It was the only job he could get with his meager education. He slid behind the wheel of the spotless Chevy and started the engine.

Joan and Dorothy waited. They were anxious to get out of the cold garage. They noticed that the other attendants were delivering cars to their customers, but theirs hadn't arrived. Joan walked to the desk to see what was causing the delay. Dorothy sat, shivering, guarding the brightly-colored packages.

Joey twisted the wheel as he wound through the maze of turns. As he approached the next-to-the-last level he put his foot on the brake at the turn and pressed. Nothing happened. His eyes widened. He pumped the brakes, but the car kept rolling, gaining momentum. Joey twisted the wheel as the car rounded a concrete column and headed onto the open entrance level.

Joan heard the screeching tires, and turned to see the car. It was heading directly at Dorothy.

Dorothy did not know what hit her. The car shoved her off the bench, pushing her head-first into the concrete wall. Her skull split in half as it was crushed between the bumper and the wall. The car rebounded from the impact, then rolled to a stop. Joey's head rested against the steering wheel. He had been knocked unconscious when his head hit the windshield.

Joan stood screaming, staring at the body of her friend lying amidst the blood-spattered Christmas packages.

When we arrived at the scene, other shoppers were gawking at the gruesome scene. We declared her dead. We covered her with a blanket and placed her in the ambulance. I radioed for an engine company to come and wash away the blood and body debris. We took Dorothy, who moments before had been planning a Christmas with her children, to the morgue.

Joe was taken to a nearby hospital for observation. He was released that day and, within a week, committed suicide.

A woman decided to end her life, and to do so in a way that caused her the least pain, and the least pain for those that loved her.

Wayne and I responded to a call for a possible DOA at a posh downtown apartment house. A security guard was waiting to admit us. He was very shaken. He opened the apartment door and led us to the living room, his face ashen.

The walls were covered with pictures of demons and grotesque monsters. Beneath the pictures were stacks of Christmas presents, neatly arranged in groups for family members and friends. It was a bizarre and chilling contrast.

We followed the guard into the bathroom.

A young, white woman in her early twenties was lying in the bathtub, naked, a pillow propped behind her back. Her skin was chalky, the unmistakable hue of death.

An IV needle was stuck in her hand and taped down around her body into the drain. We saw a small drop of blood trickle out the end of the plastic tube. She had bled herself dry.

A letter was clutched in her other hand.

The police arrived, and the guard handed the letter to one of the officers.

She had been despondent over her fiance's death four months before, and apparently could not bear the pain of living without him. She had written everyone she had known. If she owed anyone anything it was in the letters attached to their Christmas presents. She had even left a will.

An "oldie" played by a group called "Three Dog Night" says that "One" is the loneliest number. So many times we take people for granted. We feel that someone will always be there. How sad for those who have no one to turn to for help or a hug or a kind word.

One frosty, winter morning, Wayne and I were working together; he was driving, I was the attendant. The call came from a neighbor of Agnes, a little old woman who lived in a small row home on the southwest side of Baltimore. Neighbors considered Agnes a hermit. She hardly ever went out. Her shades were always down and her door never open. She had had several cats but when she stopped feeding them, they went away.

Agnes would sometimes see a kid from the neighborhood come by and she would open the door slightly. She would give the child money to go to the corner store to buy her cat food. When she continued to buy cat food after the cats left,

190

neighbors began to wonder. Agnes would never talk to anyone other than to get food. She was kind but had a sharp tongue. She would let the kids keep any change after running her errands.

But, Agnes hadn't been seen for some time. Finally, the neighbor knocked at Agnes' house. No answer. She knocked again. No answer. She tried peering in the window but the shade blocked her view. Then the neighbor tried the door handle.

Slowly she pushed the door open. But, the stench revolted her senses. She shut the door, ran down to her house and called "911."

When the police arrived they questioned the neighbor. He then cracked the door open and began to call for Agnes. He, too, was overcome by the stench. He picked up his microphone and called for an ambulance.

Wayne and I had lunch set out. I opened my bottle of Pepsi and took a drink. Before I could swallow, the alert tone went off. The watchman's voice boomed through the speakers, "Medic 1, you've got a run."

We repacked our lunches and took off. Here and there, mounds of snow dotted the sidewalks. It was indeed a chilly morning. The heater on the ambo wasn't working properly. We had to pass a towel back and forth to keep the windshield clear. When we turned the corner, we saw the police car and the neighbors huddled on the sidewalk.

The police called the one neighbor over and she related what she had told them. The officer that had opened Agnes' door gave a look of "Whew!" when he explained what had happened. Wayne and I got our paper facemasks and plastic gloves.

One step inside the door and we looked at each other. We had smelled this odor before. It was nauseating. Even in the cold air of the house, it unsettled the stomach. We went from room to room in search of Agnes. We couldn't find her. Then Wayne noticed a large mound of blankets on the kitchen floor.

We went over to investigate. We each took a corner and slowly peeled the covering back. A hand appeared. It was Agnes. She was a grotesque sight.

Her heat had run out several days ago and to compensate, Agnes had gathered several blankets and clothes into a large ball on the floor and crawled in between them to keep warm. But, the cold weather from a recent storm had lasted too long. Agnes froze to death in her own home.

We noticed sores or scars on her arms, hands and face. As we checked her body, a large rat ran from under the covers to a hole in the floor nearby.

The marks were bite marks. The closer we looked at her body, the more we realized that chunks of flesh had been ripped away from her decaying body. A finger from one hand was gone. The soft area of her cheeks left gaping holes.

Between the odor and these gruesome details, we decided to go outside in the clear light of day.

The crowd backed up, almost as if they expected us to stink. Wayne turned to the police officer in charge and said, "Call the coroner. There's nothing we can do." I filled out the ambo report and gave the officer his copy.

As we prepared to leave we agreed that if some neighbor had cared a little or showed some interest in her, this might not have happened.

We put the equipment away and finished the remainder of the report. As we sat there, we listened to the neighbors puzzling over how a thing like this could happen. Wayne started up the unit and we left.

Low income high-rise apartment buildings are all cast from one mold. To a visitor they each look like the next. Nearly 140 families reside in each of these units.

Their layout is uniform: a central core connects two wings of apartment. In the core are two elevator shafts. Frequently the elevators do not operate because of overuse or abuse. The Rescue Squad is constantly called to high rises to free trapped residents. Many residents have to use the stairs because the elevators are "down."

In the midst of a cold snap which lasted a long three weeks, we had to endure temperatures below zero with a wind chill of 30 to 40 below zero. The winds constantly blew, and ice and snow did not melt, it just piled up and stayed.

Andy, a middle-aged black man living on the seventh floor, bundled up and went out to his favorite night spot. It was a little bar six blocks away that had go-go dancers. He thought they would "warm" his spirit.

The medic units in the Fire Department, had picked up several people and treated them for hypothermia (over-exposure to cold with dangerous loss of body heat). On the earlier shift, we had had three cases of hypothermia. We preferred staying in the warm station, and found it difficult to understand why people went out unnecessarily in this kind of weather.

It was now, early morning. Andy helped close the bar. It was 2:15 a.m.; he tried to kiss some of the girls as they left but they would have no part of it. Andy reeked of alcohol. He used to joke about filling up on anti-freeze to keep him from freezing.

The bartender escorted him out the front door, where he shivered and pulled his collar up. Tucking his head down in the wet, falling snow, he took his first step toward home. It took him about 25-30 minutes to reach the apartment complex.

When he arrived in the open lobby, he brushed the snow off his coat. Chills pierced him like darts. He couldn't get warm. The strong gusts sneaked around the open corners and walls and created a wind tunnel. He felt so cold. He maneuvered over to the elevators and pushed the button.

After what seemed an eternity, and the elevator did not arrive, he began the trek down the long hallway and up the stairwell that hugged each side of the building. He reached the third floor but couldn't go anymore. He walked down the third floor hallway back to the elevators.

The central core is a fenced open lobby area on each floor where the elevators stop to pick up and discharge passengers. Winds blow constantly through the area and in this cold snap a person could not wait long before retreating to the stairs. That is, a person who was not drunk.

He waited and waited but the elevator did not come. A waiting couple finally took the steps. Andy was left alone. Slowly, he slid down the wall and sat next to the shaft. He pulled his knees up to his chest and cradled himself as he shivered uncontrollably. By morning, Andy was dead.

We got the call about 6:30 a.m. along with Truck 13. Both units arrived at the same time. From the third floor, a police officer waved through the fencing. We quickly found out that the elevators weren't working. We advanced up the endless row of steps. The officer waited for us and when we got close, they signaled that this was a DOA.

I approached the huddled body sitting up against the wall. The man looked comfortable. The firefighters stood back as I began to survey the patient. As soon as I touched the body, I knew he was dead. Andy's body was as hard as rock. When I say hard, I mean hard. It seemed that if he had been knocked over, his frozen body would have shattered into a million pieces.

I searched the body as best as I could for any sign of foul play but found none. The only eerie thing was Andy's still-open eyes. But they were colorless, two solid orbs of white.

Fred Ehrlich and I shared several calls one busy Sunday morning. One thing about Fred, he loved to tell the men about a run he had.

In between calls, while we were in the firehouse kitchen, Fred ruffled the feathers of at least five people. Even as we left the kitchen area when we received a call, firefighters jokingly urged him to "Go on. Get out of here! Get another one. Get!" They knew this would irk him because he hated to ride in the ambulance.

The call came in for a possible DOA at an apartment in the old Albion Hotel.

Fred was a good driver. With professional ease, we arrived at the hotel.

As we were getting out, a foot patrolman came out of the main entrance and moseyed on over to us in a matter-of-fact way, while twisting his nightstick. "I'm really sorry to bother you guys like this but I had no choice. This guy's dead. I just have to have someone pronounce him dead."

He became abjectly apologetic. We told him not to worry, it was our job, just like it was his to call us.

The Albion was old, dark and dreary; the hallways narrow. It was difficult to walk two abreast. We walked down a long hallway and turned left to the first room on the left.

The officer went in first, then myself and finally Fred. I carried the clipboard and Fred toted the med kit. The room was small, which surprised me. From the outside, the hotel appeared grand with large rooms. The shades had been drawn, on the other side of the room was our patient.

He was an elderly, black man about 55 to 60 years old. The man had apparently been watching television before he died. But he didn't look normal. It didn't feel right. Even Fred looked puzzled. Then he smiled and said to the cop, "Looks like a normal death to me!" "No, Fred," I responded. "No one dies standing like that."

Why do I say that? The bed was on our left, the television on a dresser on our right . He looked as if he had died en route from the bed to the dresser, in a position of still life, no pun intended. His left arm was reaching out as if he were going to change a channel, his head leaning forward. His right arm was cocked toward the rear as if in a walking stance. His entire body leaned forward. The only thing that stopped him from falling was the support of his left hand on the television set and his right leg against the bed. It was as if he were on a camera and the film stopped.

One reason he hadn't fallen was because he was as hard as a rock. Rigor mortis had set in. We looked at the cop. "I told you he was dead. It looks like natural causes to me!" Natural! It was anything but natural. Someone probably found him and placed him standing up in this position.

The officer said he would handle the call and would contact the medical examiner. He asked us to give him the pink copy of our report and we could be on our way.

Suicide. The word sends shivers down the spine. I have been told that everyone thinks about suicide at least once in their lives. The call I will describe was a suicide, or so said the police on the scene. You be the judge. Don't be biased by my opinion.

Wayne and I took a call for a gunshot victim on West Pratt Street in West Baltimore. It was late afternoon as we flipped the switcher transforming us from a regular vehicle to an emergency ambulance. We plowed through the traffic on Lombard Street and eventually turned left on Monroe. At Pratt we again turned left and were immediately greeted by four police cruisers.

At the scene Wayne met the officers as I secured the medic unit, and picked up the med kit before joining Wayne and the police. They escorted us into the house, near the end of a long row of similar homes.

We followed the police down a long hallway to a basement door. The officers went down first and we followed. They turned right at the bottom of the stairs and moved toward the front of the building.

The basement was very cluttered with trash and debris. We had to dodge cobwebs that adorned the wood-beamed ceiling. There, at the front of the basement resting against the wall, was our patient, a middle-aged black man. He was well-dressed and looked well taken care of. I stepped over the man's legs and maneuvered around the police officers to reach the body. I put my fingers on his carotid artery on his neck to feel for a pulse. The coldness of his skin told me it was unnecessary.

As Wayne and I scanned the body, we found a large hole in the back of the man's head. We saw dried blood in his mouth, which led to the hole in the head. There were no other wounds that we could find. Dried blood splattered on the wall behind his head. We stood back and studied the rifle that laid across the man's lap. The victim's arms and hands were resting on top of the rifle. Wayne and I looked at each other. "How could he shoot himself in the mouth and then lay the rifle on his lap?" Wayne asked me. "I'll be darned if I know." I answered, perplexed.

"Well, he's dead for sure," I told the cops. "But do you guys really think he committed suicide? Look at his hands and arms." The police officer answered, "Looks like suicide to me!" The others nodded in agreement. Wayne finished for us, "Well you guys are the pros. Here's our ticket." He handed them the ambulance report and we left the building. Once outside, we looked at each other. "Wayne," I began, "how could he kill himself?" Wayne assured me that answering that question was police work.

13 The Big One

Firefighters in every city and town wonder, when "The Big One" will hit. Where will it strike? How much of the city will it devour, how many civilians and firefighters will it claim as human sacrifices? When certain calls come through, your gut says, "This is going to be big, real big. This is THE ONE!" You feel a mixture of fear, dread and excitement. No firefighter looks forward to this, but when it happens, *every* firefighter wants to be in on the alarm and play his part.

In its heyday, Camden Yards was a hub of activity. Shops, storehouses, warehouses, and markets filled several square blocks. The wood and brick buildings had been put to good use, but now they were out-of-date. The timbers were dry and old. One by one, the buildings were vacated and let run down. They were an arsonist's dream.

I had been in the department only a year when arsonists began to torch city buildings. In fact, on most night shifts, we would answer at least one two-alarm fire, if not more. One by one, the old buildings began to die. Some were repeatedly set by fire starters. They became charred beyond recognition, their history burned in ashes.

Some of the smaller fires were probably caused by kids. But, some of these smaller blazes got out of hand, too.

One winter evening, just after midnight, the firefighters were resting in their bunks. In the USF&G Insurance Company building near the harbor, Carl Gentry, a computer operator, had been busy at work. His tired eyes cried out for a rest. He took off his glasses and soothingly rubbed his eyes with his hands. As he did so, he walked across the room leaving his machine running. Carl reached for the coffee pot to pour a cup of coffee and gazed out the window. Something caught his eye.

He looked again, startled. Across the rooftops and the buildings of lower downtown, he saw a fire. He called the Fire Department. "I want to report a fire in the vicinity of Hanover and Camden Streets! It looks like a building," he chattered excitedly. "OK, sir. Units are being dispatched right away. Can I have your name and phone number for verification?" the dispatcher requested. Carl complied.

"Engine 15, Truck 2 respond to Hanover and Camden Streets. Report of a building fire." The engine and truck carried their men to the vicinity of the address. The chill of the winter night awoke the sleepy men. When they arrived, the men searched the area thoroughly, but found nothing. Was this another false alarm? The officer of the truck called in, "Truck 2, we're on location. Don't see nothin'. How'd you receive this call?" "The call came in from the USF&G Building. One of their workers said there is a fire in a building nearby." the dispatcher answered in a perplexed manner. "Well, we don't see anything around here," the lieutenant continued. Again the dispatcher answered, "I'm on the phone with the man right now. He said you can't miss it. Just keep looking up. You've got to see it." "We'll look around once more," he concluded.

Instead of walking, the men mounted their chariots and rode around the block. As they turned the corner, they continued to scan upward. Suddenly, and with a vicious force, superheated gases blew out the upper story windows of an old Victorian building. Yellow and orange flames licked at the sky. The startled eyes of the eight firefighters revealed the seriousness of what they saw. "We've found it, communications. We have heavy fire in a building at Hanover and Camden Streets. Strike out a third alarm."

They immediately went to their positions for attack. The "red enemy" was engaging in heavy warfare. Reinforcements were on the way. Engine 15 grabbed a fireplug on the corner and began setting up 2-1/2-inch and 3-inch hoselines. Truck 2 set up its ladder pipe assembly. Master streams would have to put out a fire of this magnitude. The enemy climbed upward from floor to floor while crushing sounds of dying floors cried from within.

Help soon arrived. Pumpers hooked up to hydrants. Companies took hose lines from them and set up their battle lines on opposite sidewalks. Ladder companies joined Truck 2 as aerial ladders moved skyward with their powerful nozzles ready to spew thousands of gallons of water onto the ravaging foe. The five-story building was rapidly hollowed out as timbers crashed, too weak to hold up the heavy floors.

Buildings on either side became affected. The radiated heat was beginning to sear their unpointed bricks. The battalion and deputy chiefs agreed that hose companies should set up streams spraying the exposed structures. Once in a while, shattering glass could be heard exploding from windows that could no longer contain the heat. The deputy chief moved the fire up to six alarms.

The fire was changing in appearance. From the street, it looked like a red, orange, yellow and white tornado. Its swirling gases sucking in fresh oxygen from outside crested its own wind, a wind that created havoc. Embers fell on nearby rooftops. Companies would be needed to wet down hot spots. The deputy called for eight alarms.

The half-block square building was dying a rapid death. There was nothing to save it. The job of the department was to contain the fire. We watched the fire die. It sought to destroy more, but we had beaten it.

Two and a half hours later, it was called under control. Four firefighters had been taken to the department infirmary for minor injuries.

I arrived at the Firehouse about 6:00 a.m. the next morning. My car radio talked about the terrible downtown fire the night before, and about four firefighters who had been treated and released. The only casualty had been the building. The radio announcer suggested alternate routes for morning commuters. It must have been a good one, I thought to myself.

As I walked into the station, I noticed that the firehouse was empty, except for the incoming shift. In fact, most of the city houses were empty. Baltimore and Anne Arundel Counties had come in to help our depleted forces. The men in the station talked excitedly about the "big one" and I felt myself wishing that I had been there.

Our lieutenant came into the kitchen as we drank coffee and ate breakfast, "I want everyone to be ready to leave by 7:00 a.m. We'll be relieving on the fireground." We packed up our gear and got in the reserve chief's car and rode the few blocks to the scene of devastation.

It was awesome. A large section of the building still stood. Firefighters from the night shift surrounded the huge structure. Hose streams sprayed the many hot spots that refused to be put out. Hot steam and smoke continued to escape into the atmosphere, creating a haunting image. The many flashing red lights made a person feel as if he were in a discotheque.

When we arrived, we could not get closer than one block, because of the many vehicles in the area. We gathered up our turnout gear and walked into the battlefield to look for the night shift of Engine 23.

We found them almost directly in front of the hollow building. The apparatus sat exhausted next to a fireplug. The men of Engine 23 had taken a 3-inch hoseline from the engine and moved across the street onto the fragments. There they sprayed water on the building as huge cranes were tearing it down. Every once in a while we could hear what sounded like small explosions coming from the heart of the fire. We were told it was gas pockets in the debris. Sounded good!

The night shift was consumed with fatigue. They sat on the hose and aimed the nozzle at the falling bricks. Ever so glad to see us, they jumped up and handed the hose to us. The two officers exchanged information and the night crew left.

Now it was our turn. Our lieutenant told us to climb up into the debris and move in about 15 feet into the once-proud building. We alternated the stream left to right to try to get maximum saturation on the large pile of rubble. After a while even a 3-inch hoseline feels heavy. So, we too, sat on it with the nozzle pouring its coolant upon the heated debris. Scattered across the field we could hear the pockets of exploding gas.

Engine 59's crew was the other crew helping to wet down. We both were well into the former structure. The cranes were doing a formidable job tearing down the last few walls. We were careful not to get in too close while our hoselines poured in gallons upon gallons of water.

People wonder what it's like to be in an earthquake. The crew of Engine 23 and Engine 59 have a pretty good idea. Let me explain. As we hosed down the rubble, the gas explosions intensified. All of a sudden, without any warning, the ground beneath us began to shake. When I say shake, I mean *shake*. It was hard to stand up. "Let's get out of here!" the lieutenant screamed. Both crews began running while other nearby firefighters watched in astonishment. The nozzle men tried to save the nozzle and hose when the officer yelled, "Drop that line. Get out of here!" Not hesitating, we did exactly what we were told. As we went sailing over the wall of debris, a loud, crashing noise consumed the background. We rolled down the rubble to the safety of the sidewalk. Firefighters came running to make sure we were all right. One by one, we got up and brushed ourselves off. Naturally curious to find out what happened, we walked up the mound and looked at our former positions. Our hoselines were covered with debris. The first floor of the building had collapsed into the basement. That was the rumbling and crashing noise we had heard. If we had not moved as fast as we did, we would have all been buried alive.

Two more companies moved to the sidewalk where we had been and now safely spread a cool blanket over the rubble. Eventually we retrieved as much hose as we could but the nozzles and a few sections were lost, casualties of war.

A chilling incident happened in the winter of 1989. A call came in for a dwelling fire in Locust Point, near Fort McHenry. It was 2:30 in the morning when the units were dispatched. The fire was in a dwelling in a long row of houses on Hull Street. When the first engine company turned the corner from their station, the officer filled the airways in his excited transmission, "Engine 17, we have *heavy fire* showing. Make this a working fire!" Heavy fire is an expression we use to indicate a lot of fire being visible. A *working fire* is one that will require all companies to stay and fight it.

Luckily, no one was at home when this fire started. Flames jumped out the windows 20 feet into the cold winter air. After waiting for water to be placed in their hoselines, the firefighters advanced. The battalion chief arrived and sized-up the situation. He realized the potential for spread and danger to nearby homes and quickly called for a second alarm.

Rescue 1 was called, being dispatched on all second alarms or greater in the city. Firefighter Acting Lieutenant Bob Wagner was in charge. We listened to the radio communications as we responded. It was a hot fire but units were keeping it in check.

As we arrived on the scene, Bob ran to the chief to find out if he had special orders for us. The chief advised us to split up. Bob and Charlie Huber went to the roof with a saw and axe. They would help open the roof. Doug Wagerman and I were to check extension to the two houses on the left of the fire building. Bob and Charlie ascended the aerial ladder and began their work. Even through the battle of the fire one could hear their saws in action.

Doug and I, in full turnout gear and air masks, proceeded to the two dwellings on the left. No smoke or fire was coming from them but we had to check for extension of the fire. We went to the one vacant house next to the fire first. I went up the wooden steps ahead of Doug. We had to check the house even though it was uninhabited.

I opened the metal-framed storm door and tried to turn the knob of the inner wooden door. It was locked. Doug held the outer door open while I took a Halligan tool and slammed it into the door handle area. The door flew open. Smoke came pouring out. I leaned in to try to get a better look but still could not see anything. Doug and I looked at each other. We had to go in.

I took one step in and stopped. I again leaned over, farther in this time, and got the shock of my life. I was standing on the first floor crossbeam. There was no flooring. The entire first floor was gone! Had I taken another step, I would have fallen through to the basement. I signaled to Doug to back up.

First we advised the chief of the condition of the first floor. Next we went into the basement. The amount of trash and debris in the house was unbelievable. We went up to the second floor. Room by room, we advanced through the debris and smoky haze. There was no one there. Then we proceeded out to report to the battalion chief.

Bob called on the portable radio for us to go the roof. Once there, we assisted opening this tar-laden covering. Everyone on the roof assisted in pulling off the sawed and hewn pieces of wood and debris and casting them to a corner of the back yard. After that, we took a "blow" and went to the coffee wagon for drinks and doughnuts. The chief came over and thanked everyone for a good job. He was like that. "You guys can pack up and go home. Thanks again for a good job!"

It was election night, November 4, 1986. Campaign signs were plastered all over Baltimore and throughout Maryland. Red, white and blue posters, banners and handbills blanketed private homes, businesses and billboards. Baltimore had more at stake in this election. Its present Mayor, William Donald Schaefer, was running for Governor of Maryland.

At the Steadman Fire Station, firefighters were getting a little bored with hearing nothing but election results on TV. It was a foregone conclusion that Schaefer had won the gubernatorial election. So, the firefighters started to watch the movie *The Caine Mutiny*. Humphrey Bogart won that election.

Approximately seven blocks away, somewhere between 8:30 and 9:00 p.m., arsonists entered a building on Ramsey Street just north of Washington Boulevard and Poppleton Street. It was a long building, 800 feet by 100 feet and three stories high. They scurried through a section of the building that was not being used. The lethal liquid they carried in the five-gallon cans sloshed around as they proceeded to the top floor.

Once there, they started at one end and moved east, pouring the volatile substance on floors, joists, and exposed frames. Then they moved to the second and first floors, repeating the procedure. Finally, they stood near an outside exit, watching for passers-by or possible witnesses. Seeing no one, the ring-leader struck a match and tossed it into the building.

. . . Aboard the U.S.S. Caine the captain gave his men orders, then counter-manded the orders with new directions. The crew was becoming rebellious. On his next order, the men shouted "NO!" He told them they were under arrest for mutiny. They stood their ground. Outside, the seas were furious, the rain torrential. . . . The drama was abruptly interrupted by an alert tone.

Battalion Chief 5, Donald W. Heinbuch, a veteran of almost 20 years, was on duty. His entire life revolved around the fire department. As a child, raised in East Baltimore, he spent many hours at the station of Engine 24 where he was affectionately known as the "House Cat." When he was nine years old he had decided that he was going to be a firefighter when he grew up. Everyone knew that it was his dream and ambition. When in school, his compositions described firefighting episodes. Later his home was filled with fire memorabilia.

After joining the fire department, he studied training materials, books by distinguished fire chiefs, and subscribed to fire service magazines. He tried to keep abreast of the latest technology. All of his efforts were, he believed, to prepare him for the "Big One" . . . that unusual incident that would demand his best.

The "Old Koppers" company building, a steel manufacturer many years ago, was well known to firefighters. It was located in a building complex known for several "Big Ones." On two previous occasions this building had just escaped becoming involved in fires in adjoining buildings.

Flames raced along floors, walls and beams, forever seeking new pathways. As it raced through the building, thick black smoke spewed out its windows. Residents nearby began to smell something strange. One man went outside to investigate and saw flames licking out of every window on the west side of the building. He ran to his phone and called the fire department.

"Engine 55, 37, 38, 23, Truck 23, 13, Battalion Chief 5 . . . respond for a report of a building fire . . . Washington Boulevard and Poppleton Street, Firebox 53." The dispatcher's voice stopped "the mutiny" in the lounge; firefighters vacated the television area in seconds. Sliding down the poles to their apparatus, each one felt himself getting "pumped up." As they donned their turnout gear, the drivers started their apparatus and turned on revolving lights. The sense of excitement was mounting to a crescendo. As each company was readied, it took off for the incident.

The battle zone was in an area of Baltimore called "Pigtown," so named because long ago pigs were herded through its streets to the slaughterhouses.

Engine 38 left first. As they drove down Lombard Street toward Martin Luther King Jr. Boulevard, the captain saw wisps of smoke over the building tops. When they reached the boulevard, Captain Gerry Schwartz called in excitedly, "Heavy fire and smoke showing!" They weren't even at the scene!

Chief Heinbuch was close behind them. He could see a large plume of smoke and fire from the area of the incident. He knew it was going to be a big fire. He drove toward the west end of the warehouse which extended for almost two city blocks. The entire west end, composed of several buildings joined together, was well-involved in the fire as he approached. He called for the Airflex unit to respond.

As he stopped his car at the curb opposite the fire building, he made his first and most important decision. To some people it may sound nonsensical, but he had to decide whether or not to put on his turnout boots. Normally, he would put them on but he realized he was going to have to do a lot of running. So he decided not to put them on.

Within four minutes of the first alarm, he called for a second alarm and a minute later he called for a third. By 21:30 hours, five alarms had been called in. The sight of the massive fire automatically translated into a need for help . . . and fast. Just before the fifth alarm a special call for two of the massive aerial towers went out. Aerial Towers 128 and 114 were dispatched.

Donald Heinbuch did not immediately realize that the fire was so big it would tax the city's fire department to the limit. Initially, he wanted to mount an aggressive offensive attack. His calls for a second and third alarm were to cut off the fire within the two-block-long warehouse complex. But as seconds passed the conflagration spread into a mass of fire that radiated heat across Poppleton Street on the west and across alleys toward Washington Boulevard on the south.

He abandoned his offensive attack and worked on a defensive strategy. The second and third alarm units were committed to set up a defense on the south side, to protect the dwellings on Washington Boulevard now starting to burn. Only 20 to 25 feet separated some of the homes from the giant inferno. The heat was intense.

Radio chatter was non-stop. Many of the calls were directed to Chief Heinbuch but he was unable to answer most.

The first alarm engine companies dropped parallel lines from their hydrants after seeing the size of the fire. Companies coming in later hooked up to their pumpers and were provided with instant water supplies.

On the north side, a gate prevented companies from getting into the yard. Truck Company 23 forcibly entered and set up ladder pipe operations. On the west side, things were going badly. Explosions added to the chaos as the entire west end began to collapse. Heinbuch could hardly keep track of giving orders to the arriving units but "recording this information and passing it on to my superiors was a task that had to be done to preserve some semblance of command." At the height of the blaze he realized that if they failed to hold their defenses, they would lose many buildings. "We pulled out all stops to hold the fire."

The civilian population in the immediate area was in a state of panic. People were running helter-skelter to get away from the fire. Many ran back into their homes to grab valuables. Police were on the scene to maintain order and prevent looting. One by one, the rowhouses began to emit smoke as the raging inferno spread.

On the west end of Poppleton Street, a man abandoned his pickup truck. The heat engulfed his truck in a ball of flames, further extending the potential for disaster to the homes on that street. Electric wires fell and arced on the streets, causing more hazards to passers-by.

Many of the firefighters were impressed with the fire's brightness. Chief Heinbuch remembered that it was as bright as daylight, and even seemed to blind some of the firemen who looked at it directly.

Pumpers that had mounted deck guns placed them in service, showering homes with a refreshing coolness. In fact, Engine 37 on Calender Street had to evacuate their position because of the intensity of the heat nearby. The real danger was to the homes on Washington Boulevard and west on Poppleton Street.

Companies were now being used to wet down the nearby homes. The southwesterly wind spread the fire farther. Ladder pipes from truck companies sprayed the two blocks of homes and commercial businesses. Nevertheless, a few dwellings caught fire.

Heinbuch now set up a command post at Washington and Martin Luther King Jr. Boulevards. It was a good site because its width gave needed access to companies for receiving orders.

Between 21:37 and 21:47 hours, the fire progressed to eight alarms. Chief of the Department, Peter J. O'Connor, took charge. Then Mayor William Donald Schaefer arrived for an update.

Again on the west side, conditions were deteriorating. Truck Company 2 had to vacate its position because of the intensely radiating heat of the inferno, which burst out its windshield and set the seats on fire. Paint was seared and bubbled. Another automobile burst into flames. Poppleton Street was impossible to use. The companies on the northern exposure were battling the blaze with ladder pipes and deck guns. By this time, the blaze had created its own wind which engulfed the entire building. At this point numerous rowhouses were catching on fire.

Next, the firefighters and their equipment had to be wet down. The fire looked bright white. It grew and ignited houses on Poppleton Street. Arriving personnel sent to strengthen the forces were told to retreat for fear that the west end was going to collapse. Shortly thereafter, the west end fell into Poppleton Street. No one was injured.

From 21:53 to 22:11 hours, four special calls were made. These calls were for more apparatus, although another alarm was not requested. Six more engines and five more truck companies were dispatched. The staging area was being depleted of companies so at 22:16, a ninth alarm was sounded, bringing in four more engines and two more trucks.

Explosions again rocked the west end of the fire building. The warehouse complex slowly began to collapse.

Chief O'Connor now had to make an important decision. He picked up his radio and called communications. He advised them to notify the surrounding jurisdictions that there was a major conflagration in the city and mutual aid was requested. Mutual aid is called for when another jurisdiction sends in replacements for the vacancies created by a major fire. Anne Arundel, Baltimore and Howard Counties sent men and machines to stations throughout Baltimore.

By 23:19 hours, three more special calls were announced bringing four more engines and another truck company. Two of the engines were from the recent mutual aid call from Baltimore County.

Firefighters were finally gaining control of the fire. Reports from the southern and western fronts said that they could contain what they had with existing equipment and men. But on the southwest, near Washington Boulevard and Poppleton Street, another fire was raging. Three buildings were involved, one of them a former engine house that had been closed down in 1952.

On the east side, units had protected a factory from exposure. They stopped the fire at the end of the warehouse and turned their turrets to the north end. This was the last unchecked seat of fire. Huge deluge guns and ladder pipes were pointed at the hotbed. Slowly, it was knocked down. At 00:14, Chief O'Connor placed the fire under control.

Chief Heinbuch recalls that the building's huge steel beams looked like spaghetti. Some beams lay crumbled and bent like flexible toys. The entire complex was destroyed. Overhauling would take days. Scores of homes were damaged as well as vehicles. Over 150 residents were evacuated during the holocaust.

Forty-five engines, 18 truck companies, three aerial towers, one rescue squad and two mutual aid engines were called to put out the fire. The city's forces were taxed to the limit.

When Chief Heinbuch finally became aware of the time, four hours later, he thought that only an hour or two had passed.

For the firefighters, it was a very long night. But it was a job they were paid to do; a job they loved to do.

In the meantime, the *Caine Mutiny* once again become part of history.

And, Chief Donald N. Heinbuch? He too had become part of history, Baltimore's history. Fire Department records cite him as the chief initially in charge of the "Big One" . . . an assignment for which he was well-prepared.

Epilogue

The stories you have just read are true. Most happened to me, but some were told to me by other firefighters.

Though, like all people, the lives of Firefighters, Rescue Technicians, and Paramedics are filled with routine activities, they are every bit as much filled with the pathos of battles lost and the bitter-sweet joys of those only partially won. The heroism these people portray on a daily basis is made greater for their intimate knowledge of fire's destructiveness, but it is the uncompromising nature of their wills which fuels their inner flames. Each call brings something new to test a firefighter's values, strengths, and in many cases, his weaknesses.

We firefighters will continue to do what we do best. We will continue to unselfishly put our lives on the line daily for our fellow human beings. Maybe it is because of the hope that what we do will save a life, prevent some misfortune, or bring comfort to someone in tragedy.

So many of the events involving fire could be avoided by some simple tasks that anyone can do. If you need assistance in having your home or business checked for fire safety, contact your local fire department. They'll be glad to help you.

I hope that the reader of this book has come away with a greater understanding of, and respect for, the men and women who unselfishly put their lives on the line for their fellow human beings. When a siren calls and a fire truck rushes up behind you, please pull to the side of the road — the time you lose may save another's life.

And most of all, as you pass a station where the firefighters seem to be just passing the time, sitting in the sun, don't begrudge them their rest — at any moment they may be called to their last TURNOUT.

About the Author

Bill Hall was born on August 16, 1948, in Baltimore, Maryland, the youngest of six children. He spent much of his childhood thoroughly absorbed with reading books and writing stories.

Within a year after graduating from high school, Bill enlisted in the U.S. Coast Guard for a four-year hitch during the height of the Vietnam conflict. After his tour of duty, he applied for a position as a Baltimore firefighter. It was the work he longed to do.

In 1972, Bill began training at the Fire Academy. He started as a firefighter and soon transferred into the new field of emergency medicine, where he served as an emergency medical technician and paramedic. After eleven years, he returned to the fire service as a member of the rescue squad.

Bill and his wife, Carol, reside in Sykesville, Maryland. They have four daughters. They are actively involved in community service, town politics, and the church.

Bill has responded to over 15,000 emergency calls since his first "turnout" nearly 20 years ago.